AN ARISTOCRACY

OF EVERYONE

BOOKS BY BENJAMIN R. BARBER

The Conquest of Politics, 1988

Strong Democracy, 1984

Marriage Voices (A Novel), 1981

Liberating Feminism, 1975

The Death of Communal Liberty, 1974

Superman and Common Men, 1971

COLLABORATIONS

The Struggle for Democracy
with Patrick Watson, 1989

The Artist and Political Vision
edited with M. McGrath, 1982

Totalitarianism in Perspective
with C. J. Friedrich and M. Curtis, 1969

AN ARISTOCRACY
OF EVERYONE

THE POLITICS OF
EDUCATION
AND
THE FUTURE OF
AMERICA

Benjamin R. Barber

BALLANTINE BOOKS · NEW YORK

All rights reserved under International
and Pan-American Copyright Conventions. Published
in the United States by Ballantine Books, a division of Random
House, Inc., New York, and simultaneously in Canada by
Random House of Canada Limited, Toronto.

Grateful acknowledgment is made to the following
for permission to reprint previously published material:
Harper's Magazine: "The Philosopher
Despot" by Benjamin Barber. Copyright © 1987
by *Harper's Magazine*. All rights reserved. Reprinted from
the January 1988 issue by special permission.
The New York Times: Excerpt from
"What Do 47-Year-Olds Know?" by Benjamin Barber.
Copyright © 1987 by The New York Times Company.
Reprinted by permission.

Library of Congress Cataloging-in-Publication Data
Barber, Benjamin.
An aristocracy of everyone / Benjamin Barber.
p. cm.
ISBN 0-345-37040-6
1. Education—United States—Aims and objectives.
2. Educational change—United States. I. Title.
LA217.2.B37 1992
370'.973—dc20   92-53157
                                                      CIP

Design by Holly Johnson

Manufactured in the United States of America

First Edition: October 1992
10 9 8 7 6 5 4 3 2 1

This book is dedicated to America's teachers

ACKNOWLEDGMENTS

Unlike most books, this one owes its existence mainly to the intervention of others. Joëlle Delbourgo at Ballantine put the idea in my head of giving systematic expression to my thoughts on civic education, then waited patiently while I did just that. Her enthusiasm for the project sustained me at every phase of the writing. Ashton Applewhite offered a critical editorial eye, and when I was prudent enough to let her, enhanced the clarity of my arguments. My research assistant, Christine Kelly, not only provided intensive and ongoing collaboration on footnotes, bibliography, and research, but acted in the early stages of the project as a foil and a prod for my thinking. I am especially indebted to my colleagues at Rutgers University with whom I worked in many different ways on the citizen education and community service program: David Burns, Bryan Barnett, Sharon Grant Henry, Richard Battistoni, Linda Zerilli, Claudia Gittelman, Roland Anglin, Michael Schaefer, Mary Hartman, Viola van Jones, James Reed, Rod Hartmann, Lionel Tiger, Frances Lawrence, Grace Losso, Jon van Til, James Dunn, Richard Nurse, Wendy

Gunther, Anna Huggup, and Ron Nieberding. I am also grateful to the many students who contributed to our efforts.

I have dedicated this book to America's teachers, but there is one who played a special role in its genesis. Edward Bloustein, the late president of Rutgers University, offered me the opportunity to build a center around the culture and politics of democracy, initiated the Rutgers community service project, engaged me in it at a very early stage, and supported it with all of his considerable energy and talent until his untimely death. His spirit animates my arguments, as his devotion to education energizes my convictions.

CONTENTS

AN ARISTOCRACY

OF EVERYONE

PROLOGUE

Around the world the cry "Democracy!" has shattered tyranny's silence and caused the most stubborn of dictators to lose their confidence in the politics of fear. Walls are coming down and iron curtains are being drawn for the last time. The Statue of Liberty is an icon for young men and women who have never known freedom in lands that have never been democratic. Even in these hard and cynical times, America remains for many abroad what Lincoln called the "last best hope." But is it still that for Americans? Can it be? That is our paradox.

Millions of immigrants vote annually with their feet to come to a land where nearly half of us don't bother to vote at all. A paragon of democracy abroad, America often seems to be ruled by apathy and privatism at home. People die around the world in the struggle to acquire freedoms we sometimes don't seem to notice we have. They struggle to establish free political parties while we abandon ours in the search for candidates untainted by party or politics.

Because we regard ourselves as born free, we take our liberty for granted. We assume that our freedom can be enjoyed without responsibility and that, like some great perpetual motion machine, our democracy can run forever without the fuel of civic activity by engaged citizens. The most sympathetic overseas critic America has known, Alexis de Tocqueville, once issued a warning to all would-be democrats: There is nothing so arduous as the apprenticeship of liberty. Are we Americans willing to be journeymen citizens? Are there institutions where we can learn liberty? Can our schools be nurseries of citizenship?

There is endless talk today about education, but between the hysteria and the cynicism there seems to be little room for civic learning, hardly any for democracy. Yet the fundamental task of education in a democracy is the apprenticeship of liberty— learning to be free. While we root our fragile freedom in the myth that we are born free, we are in truth born dependent. For we are born fragile, born needy, born ignorant, born unformed, born weak, born foolish, born unimaginative—born in chains. To cast them off as angels might is our unrealizable fantasy. The best we can do is rationalize or legitimize them. Our dependency is both physical—we need each other and cannot survive alone— and psychological; our identity is forged through a dialectical relationship with others. We are inescapably embedded in families, tribes, and communities. As a consequence, we must *learn* to be free. That is to say, we must be taught liberty. We are born small, defenseless, unthinking children. We must be taught to be thinking, competent, legal persons and citizens. We are born belonging to others; we have to learn how to sculpt our individuality from common clay.

The literacy required to live in civil society, the competence to participate in democratic communities, the ability to think critically and act deliberately in a pluralistic world, the empathy that permits us to hear and thus accommodate others, all involve skills that must be acquired. Excellence is the product of teaching and is liberty's measure. There is no excellence without freedom. From Plato to Mill, philosophers have understood that only the free and self-sufficient can be virtuous. For them, so few were virtuous because so few were free. They understood virtue as the excellence (they called it *areté*) of cognitive, affective, and associational practices: living well and living justly in the human world.

Human association depends on imagination: the capacity to see in others beings like ourselves. It is thus through imagination that we render others sufficiently like ourselves for them to become subjects of tolerance and respect, sometimes even affection. Democracy is not a natural form of association; it is an extraordinary and rare contrivance of cultivated imagination. Empower the merely ignorant and endow the uneducated with a right to make collective decisions and what results is not democracy but, at best, mob rule: the government of private prejudice and the tyranny of opinion—all those perversions that liberty's enemies like to pretend (and its friends fear) constitute democracy. For true democracy to flourish, however, there must be citizens. Citizens are women and men educated for excellence—by which term I mean the knowledge and competence to govern in common their own lives. The democratic faith is rooted in the belief that all humans are capable of such excellence and have not just the right but the capacity to become citizens. Democratic education mediates the ancient quarrel between the rule of opinion and the rule of excellence by informing opinion and, through universal education in excellence, creating an aristocracy of everyone.

Is this phrase no more than a provocative oxymoron? An impossible contradiction, as advocates of classical aristocracy may say? To certain critics of democracy, the *aristoi* must be more than merely excellent or virtuous, for to them the superiority of some depends on the inferiority of the rest. What can it mean to excel in a world where everyone is regarded as possessing a potential for the best? In their eyes, excellence cannot be entirely self-referential but, like vanity, must exist in terms of the relative merit of others. Without the *hoi polloi*, that mindless rabble who go under the name *plebes* or *demes*, the *aristoi* cannot conceive of their own superior worth. Who wants virtues anyone can have?

It is not enough for me to win, goes the old half-serious jest, others must lose.

The democratic educator seeks a different sort of excellence, an inherent virtue that does not depend on comparative standing. To grade on a curve is a popular strategy in highly competitive, elite institutions where some must fail for others to succeed; but in classrooms devoted to cultivating the intrinsic excellence of each student, there may be more A's than C's (or more D's than B's). Democracy insists on leveling—that is the price of equality—but it aims always at leveling up, never at leveling down.

When democratic citizenship insists on leveling, then: it demands that slaves be emancipated not that masters be enslaved; that suffrage be granted to the dispossessed not taken from the powerful; that I win the exercise of my rights not that you lose the exercise of yours. Aristocrats condemn democracy because they believe it subjects the wise to the rule of the foolish; but the aim of democratic education is in fact to subject the foolish to wisdom in order that they may both govern themselves *and* govern wisely. Jefferson knew something about the aristocratic distrust of popular sovereignty. If you deem ordinary people insufficiently discrete to govern, he advised, don't take away their power, educate their discretion. Perhaps this is how he managed to be an aristocratic Southern gentleman farmer *and* the founding generation's most persuasive democrat. It is certainly why he considered his founding of the University of Virginia to be among the most decisive political acts of his career on behalf of democracy; for, if his tombstone is to be believed, along with his authorship of the Declaration of Independence and the Virginia Bill of Rights, he prized his dedication to education more highly than his two terms in the presidency.

Lincoln, too, tempered realism with hope, believing always that even the darkest human natures were counseled by "better angels" with whom a teacher or statesman or preacher (he was all three) might yet collaborate in making small men larger. He knew that freedom was not natural to men and women. He also learned in the course of the Civil War that unless all possessed it, none could securely enjoy it and that the teaching of liberty was the greatest political challenge of all.

If, as Rousseau sometimes seemed to think, we were really born free and only subsequently made dependent by adverse conditions, teaching would be little more than a matter of preservation. "Build a wall round your child's soul," he implored in *Émile*. If, as Plato argued in *The Meno*, we were born with traces of an ancient knowledge, then teaching would be a question of recovery. Plumb the soul's memory for clues to deeply ingrained knowledge, then restore to consciousness memory's secrets. But born dependent, we require an education in liberty. Born selfish, we must be taught mutuality. Born hungry, we need to learn moderation. Born distinctive and differentiated, we have to acquire tolerance, civility, and mutual respect. Born in a variety of shapes and sizes and colors, we are anything but peers and our equality is a precious acquisition: something to be slowly, often painfully, learned in spite of the evidence of our senses.

Rousseau wanted to persuade us that equality was natural, and there is little harm in regarding it as a disposition of all humans if that helps us think of it as deeply rooted and thus reinforces our commitment to it. But for all practical purposes, equality is not the condition of learning and experience but is produced by them. If education must create both liberty and equality, it becomes the foundation of all individual growth and of all collective civilization. Nothing is more important. The great country, the great society, the great community is, first of all, the well-educated country, the learned society, the community of excellence. This nation knows it, proclaims it, even rhapsodizes about it. Then it busies itself with other matters. It talks pedagogy but spends its resources elsewhere. It denigrates teachers as unprofessional but refuses them professional wages. Compare the starting salaries of lawyers, doctors, engineers, and teachers, and it becomes obvious why it is the schools that are in crisis.[1] In his final Harvard commencement address before retiring in 1991,

President Derek Bok could only sigh at the "eerie indifference" that hangs over a land perpetually in crisis over its bankrupt educational establishment which seems to produce only poverty, crime, and illiteracy among its young people.

CRISIS—AND AGAIN, CRISIS

It seems histrionic, even alarmist, once again to proclaim a crisis in education, for crisis has been the norm for decades. Over twenty years ago, Vintage Books published a two-volume *University Crisis Reader* chockful of materials on the then-current controversy in the liberal university.[2]

The tocsin was first sounded when the Soviets sent *Sputnik* aloft at the end of the Eisenhower era, seeming to threaten this country's technological leadership. When toward the end of the sixties all authority, pedagogical as well as political, seemed in jeopardy, there was again a "crisis." When educational scores began to tumble and reading ability to deteriorate in the seventies, there was another "crisis." In the early eighties, when the National Commission on Excellence discovered a growing illiteracy that put the future of the nation "at risk," crisis loomed anew.[3] When, during President Reagan's second term, Secretary of Education William Bennett and philosopher Allan Bloom brought to the notice of the American public the disintegration of the traditional canon and the erosion of academic standards at every level of the educational establishment and blamed liberals and pedagogical progressives, there was a still more profound "crisis." And today, as the nation grows less and less competitive with its economic rivals in Europe and Asia; as its corporations are forced increasingly to institute their own programs to develop a marginally literate work force;[4] as more young black men are ending up in jail than in college and a whole generation of inner-city youth is being ravaged by a tripartite plague of drugs, gangs, and AIDS; as more than 20 percent of the nation's children (45 percent of black children) are growing up in poverty and more than 30 percent are dropping out of school before receiving a high school diploma; as a million teenage girls are having babies before they graduate and 2.5 million adolescents are contracting sexually transmitted diseases; as media-manufactured hysteria over "political correctness" and compulsory multiculturalism turns every pedagogical debate into a terminal ideological struggle, a yet more desperate "crisis" arises.

But crisis by definition cannot be chronic. On tenth hearing, the alarm bells inspire despair rather than action. Tired out by our repeated crises, we roll over in bed. A long sleep becomes more and more like death, and a radical awakening is called for. At risk are not only our children, but our future; not only our schools, but our democratic institutions.

Most of the books published on the newest episode of our chronic educational crisis have preferred to sunder democracy and education. In their conservative, antidemocratic thrust, Allan Bloom's *The Closing of the American Mind*, Roger Kimball's *Tenured Radicals*, John Silber's *Straight Shooting*, Charles J. Sykes's *Profscam*, and Dinesh D'Souza's *Illiberal Education* all associate educational crisis with progressivism, radical professors, and a concern for equality (among students, cultures, and pedagogical paradigms).[5] The premise of this book is that education and democracy are inextricably linked and that in a free society the link is severed only at our peril. Education must be both public and democratic if we wish to preserve our democracy's public spaces. Thus, my argument is less an argument for education than a cry for democracy; less a plea for the rehabilitation of the classroom than an appeal for the restoration of the community; less a defense of the present than a challenge for the future; less a call for reform from within our schools than a manifesto for a revolution in how we understand them. We need in education a transformation as far-reaching as the one that has seized Eastern Europe and what was once the Soviet Union, as radical as the abrupt ending of the cold war, as profound as the metamorphosis of

America's vanquished enemies in World War II into its most dependable allies and most formidable rivals.

Yet, astonishingly, in the great American polity dedicated to the future, to prosperity, to tolerance, and to democracy, education is the orphan of the Enlightenment—much wailed over, little nourished, the subject of endless editorials but of pitifully small-minded spending and painfully constricted ideological debate. In 1991, Minnesota's teacher of the year, Cathy Nelson, was laid off (for the fourth time). Although she had thirteen years of service to Fridley High School, others had more. In this same year, the Richmond, California, Unified School District, praised for its innovative approaches by the Bush administration, went bankrupt for lack of funding.[6] Dollars alone won't buy education, any more than dollars alone provide national defense. But just as dollars will buy the tanks, planes, and military training requisite for defense, so dollars can buy the facilities, teacher-to-student ratios, equipment, and quality instruction requisite for education—if they are put in the right place.[7] Dollars at least move us a step beyond talk, but in fiscally tight times, the cheapness of talk is precisely its virtue.

So there is rhetoric aplenty but no revolution. In this "Decade of the Child," America's infant mortality and school drop-out rates look positively third world. In New Haven, Connecticut, home of Yale University, the infant mortality rate is the highest in the nation. The Europeans still send their children to school 240 days a year; with only a few brave exceptions, we remain satisfied with 180.[8] There is talk of reform, but little change: For all the experimentation of the eighties, according to the Carnegie Foundation Report Card on School Reform, teachers themselves remain "dispirited, confronted with working conditions that have left them more responsible, but less empowered." Even more frustrating than "loss of status, bureaucratic pressures, negative public image, and the lack of recognition and rewards," teachers tell of a devastating decline in morale. "During this period of unprecedented activity on behalf of education," concludes the report, "49% of teachers say morale has gone down, less than one-fourth say it has gotten better."[9] One can find a spirited classroom with a relatively independent teacher, but it's often in a neighborhood so poor as to have little effect. One can discover empowered parents, but in Chicago, school districts are so implicated in politics that parental corruption is inevitable. Yes, there is an innovative district in California with real successes to report, but one which has been allowed to go bankrupt. There are model classrooms in New York City, but in schools rife with drugs and crime and stripped of teaching resources.[10]

Teachers remain among the least respected and least remunerated of American professionals. Every year, I ask an introductory political science class of three to four hundred students how many plan to make a career in primary or secondary education. In the past five years, I have never counted more than five hands. When asked how many plan to go to law or business school, over half the hands routinely go up. Teach for America, a brave new organization devoted to bringing graduates of some of the nation's most elite colleges and universities into some of its most wretched classrooms, has had to assure candidates that they need not necessarily commit themselves to a career in education. The group's first year of operation saw a large minority of its teachers leave their posts. Why? Because these and other young people find themselves in classrooms where they enjoy neither the authority to pursue their own pedagogical strategies nor the respect of their own students, let alone their country.

Conservative critics continue to blame radical teachers and their (consequently) incorrigible pupils, as if in an otherwise literate, civilized society a bunch of lazy young anarchists and their unprincipled wards had somehow gotten loose inside the schoolyard and were wreaking havoc on an unsuspecting and undeserving nation. To such critics, there is something oxymoronic about the very idea of democratic education. Democracy implies a lowering of standards to suit the masses, a lowest common denominator appropriate to ignorant majorities; education implies a raising of standards and a pedagogy for the best and brightest. For them, democracy means substituting rap for Bach and subway graffiti for Rembrandt, whereas education means reminding people of the culture of excellence to which they ought to be aspiring. That may be why at least some of these conservative critics have expressed a reluctant (or not so reluctant) willingness to toss democracy overboard in an attempt to rescue a ship they call excellence, by which they mean not civic competence but high culture and the canon. One simple way to improve educational standards defined this way is to educate only "the best." You cannot fail if you exclude those most likely to fail.

In a recent book, John E. Chubb and Terry M. Moe reconfirmed earlier research showing that students' abilities, along with the social and economic status of their parents and peers, are decisive in determining how effectively schools educate their charges.[11] The "best schools" and the "best colleges" are best, not because they offer the "best education," but because in large part they draw the best students—best prepared and best equipped, and possessing the best social and educational backgrounds. Like the good theater director who knows that his most important task is to hire fine actors who require little direction to shine, the conservative knows that the good educator is the one who seeks out fine students who require little effort to shine. But the object of public schools is not to credential the educated but to educate the uncredentialed; that is, to change and transform pupils, not merely to exploit their strengths. The challenge in a democracy is to transform every child into an apt pupil, and give every pupil the chance to become an autonomous, thinking person and a deliberative, self-governing citizen: that is to say, to achieve excellence.

Advocates of democratic education too often rise to elitist criticism by insisting that, if the choice is between educating some well and everyone badly, let's hold our breath and educate everyone badly. They often seem as anxious to jettison excellence (or just plain competence) in the name of educational equality as elitists are to jettison equality (or just plain fairness) in the name of educational excellence. Many public school teachers and administrators are exhausted and burned out. For them, excellence is as remote as suburban schools, where every student has a computer and 90 percent of the class goes to college.

This book admits no dichotomy between democracy and excellence, for the true democratic premise encompasses excellence: the acquired virtues and skills necessary to living freely, living democratically, and living well. It assumes that every human being, given half a chance, is capable of the self-government that is his or her natural right, and thus capable of acquiring the judgment, foresight, and knowledge that self-government demands. Not everyone can master string physics or string quartets, but everyone can master the conduct of his or her own life. Everyone can become a free and self-governing adult. Everyone can have a stab at happiness.

Education need not begin with equally adept students, because education is itself the equalizer. Equality is achieved not by handicapping the swiftest, but by assuring the less advantaged a comparable opportunity. "Comparable" here does not mean identical. Math whizzes may get high school calculus, while the less mathematically inclined get special tutoring. Who knows, the math whizzes may even be invited to become the math washouts' tutors. Schooling is what allows math washouts to appreciate the contributions of math whizzes—and may one day help persuade them to allocate tax revenues for basic scientific research, which math illiterates would reject. Schooling allows those born poor to compete with those born rich; allows immigrants to feel as American as the self-proclaimed daughters and sons of the American Revolution; allows African-Americans, whose ancestors were brought here in bondage, to fight for the substance (rather than just the legal forms) of their freedom.

The fundamental assumption of democratic life is not that we are all automatically capable of living both freely and responsibly, but that we are all potentially susceptible to education for freedom and responsibility. Democracy is less the enabler of education than education is the enabler of democracy. Americans need to reexamine the relationship between their schools and their political institutions, between the classroom and civil society, between education and democracy. There was a time when the relationship was taken for granted. Public, private, and religious schools in America's earlier days expressed a common commitment to education as a concomitant of democracy. Historically, the meaning of *public* education was precisely education into what it meant to belong to a public: education in the *res publica*—in commonality, in community, in the common constitution that made plurality and difference possible.

So many modern reforms, radical as well as conservative, seem to have lost sight of the public meaning of public education. Multicultural curricula achieve a needed broadening of perspectives and permit many Americans who have felt excluded to achieve a sense of group worth, yet this often is achieved at the cost of what groups share with one another. Voucher schemes enhance parental choice and increase competition among different kinds of schools, yet they thwart common schooling and subordinate education's public ends to private market choices. In the search for choice, for difference, for pluralism, for participation—all worthy aims in a society too often limited in choices, insensitive to difference, and attached to a bogus unity rooted in one dominant group's hegemony—the fundamental linkage between schooling and community and between education and democracy is simply lost.

Learning begins at birth, and much of it takes place at home or in the marketplace, in the streets or in front of the television. Yet what happens in these venues is largely a private matter. While society can cajole and hint and guide and suggest, the greater part of what transpires in the minds and hearts of the young is beyond it. This makes formal schooling, however inadequate, our sole *public* resource: the only place where, as a collective, self-conscious public pursuing common goods, we try to shape our children to live in a democratic world. Can we afford to privatize the only public institutions we possess? Must we choose between excellence and equality?

I do not think so. In the tradition of Jefferson and Dewey, I believe it is possible to understand all public education as liberal education—teaching liberty—and thus to understand liberal education as democratic education. Education in vocationalism, pre-professional training, what were once called the "servile arts" (*artes serviles*), may be private. But public education is general, common, and thus in the original sense "liberal." This means that public education is education for citizenship. In aristocratic nations, in elitist regimes, in technocratic societies, it may appear as a luxury. In such places, education is the private apprenticeship in the professions, the credentialing of elites, and perhaps the scholarly training of a few for lives of solitary intellect. But in democracies, education is the indispensable concomitant of citizenship. Where women and men would acquire the skills of freedom, it is a necessity.

The autonomy and the dignity no less than the rights and freedoms of all Americans depend on the survival of democracy: not just democratic government, but a democratic civil society and a democratic civic culture. There is only one road to democracy: education. And in a democracy, there is only one essential task for the educator: teaching liberty.

CHAPTER 1

TEACHING TEMPORALITY

What does it mean for a people to be free? Liberty is a deeply contested idea. Some understand it as a liberation from time, some believe that it requires a historical context. In this chapter, I want to reflect on liberty in time's context; to confront identity as a product of history and set democracy within "our" story (whoever "we" turn out to be).

Does this mean permitting the past to burden the present and hobble the future? Quite the opposite: Liberty can be taken seriously only within the framework of temporality. Not, however, simply as a matter of schooling. Men and women have always gone to school to learn the civic arts of liberty. But the schoolhouse has often been a marketplace or a battlefield, a church or a theater: wherever events unfold and stories are told that help people define themselves. Tribesmen listen to a shaman telling a story of the mystery of their birth as a people. Expectant mothers gather with their mothers and their mothers' mothers, whose stories tie them to generations of women they cannot know. Men marginalized by the powerful conceive a story of roots that gives them the strength to rebel. Even in the highly formal West, with its rational bureaucracies and written languages, storytelling plays a crucial role in the founding of civilization.

Consider ancient Greece. Several times a year, the citizens of Athens gathered together on their hillside amphitheaters to watch dramatic reenactments of stories about the founding of cities and the life and death of the legendary Greek clans: the House of Thebes, the House of Troy, the House of Atreus. These poignant cautionary tales resonated powerfully for a people seeking to understand their origins and destiny in what they proudly regarded as a free and just city. In the epic *Oresteia*, they relived the story of Agamemnon's sacrifice of his daughter Iphigenia for reasons of state (demanded by the gods in return for a breeze that would allow the Argovian fleet to sail against Troy), of Clytemnestra's betrayal and murder of her husband Agamemnon to avenge her daughter's martyrdom, and of her children's reluctant immersion in the sea of vengeance that engulfed the unhappy family. This vivid tale was not simply a family drama, it was a parable. Through it was revealed how Athenian justice came to be uprooted from its antecedents in rustic popular religion and "earth vengeance" (associated with women) and, with the Furies (women!) domesticated and established as household gods, reestablished as a new cosmopolitan fairness (the impartial heavenly fairness of Pallas Athena, which became associated with male justice). It is Athena who ultimately forgives Orestes his matricide, saves him from the Furies' rage, and thereby brings the new justice to Athens—at least in Aeschylus' telling.[1]

The epic stories were not pointedly Athenian, but each taught Greek parables from which a viewer could draw an Athenian lesson. In the Theban trilogy—the story of Laius, his son Oedipus, and Oedipus' daughter Antigone—the people of Athens beheld another parable, this one depicting the folly of believing identity could ever be severed from blood origins. Wishing to elude his roots and the dire prophecies that attended his birth (You shall murder your father! Betroth your mother!), Oedipus all the while rushed toward them. Creon, Antigone's uncle and king, wished to put patriotism above kinship, but in ignoring the claims of blood he lost both kinsmen and kingdom. History was no esoteric diversion for the Greeks; it was prudence's teacher and wisdom's most precious resource.

Priests at the Temple of Apollo in Delphi had always recommended two forms of virtuous conduct: "Know thyself!" and "In all things, be moderate!" These same lessons—self-knowledge as the foundation of truth and moderation as the imperative of good government—were equally palpable in the dramatic legends borrowed from Homer's oral traditions by the poetic craftsmen of the fifth century B.C. The Greeks were pleased to rehearse and explore their history over and over again (the plots of ancient tragedy in their many variations were known to all, and the point of going to the theater was hardly to discover how things turned out) in order to establish their identity and fortify their civic virtue. Drama afforded an immersion in temporality. One generation engaged in a kind of time travel, visiting their forebears in order to steal a glimpse into the future, patterning their destinies on the template of the past.

We have come a ways since Aeschylus and Sophocles wrote their dramatic trilogies for the poetry competitions of the early Athenian republic. Some would even claim that we can measure our progress precisely by the distance we have put between ourselves and tribal peoples imprisoned in their clannish histories and mythic stories. They would see in our capacity to define our identities individually, unburdened by time, the very essence of our modernity. As Cronos once devoured his children, we have devoured Cronos, emancipating ourselves from his stern punctualities. At our postmodern best (or worst), we believe ourselves to be free: as free in general as we are free in particular when we leave our towns and homes to escape from family, from clan, from tribe, from caste, from class, and from religion. And from gender as well: for even gender can now be understood as a product of arbitrary socialization and thus potentially subject to choice—a pliable product of an acculturation process we control, up to and including the radical option of "sex reassignment" by surgical means.

Technology spells liberation from the constraints of conventional history and conventional identity. Bizarre forms of parental surrogacy promise offspring to postmenopausal women and encourage infertile couples to borrow other women's wombs. The power of abstraction lets us conceive ourselves as thinking wills that invent identity. The future is a blank tablet on which we can write stories we make up. Storytelling becomes a matter of prophecy, while memory, once identity's best source, is traded in for the unchecked imagination. For in the new postmodern critique, memory is a repository only of selected (and selective) images that are left behind by the prejudices of the powerful.

Just a hundred years ago, struggling in exile to cross the threshold of liberty's new age, Henrik Ibsen still found himself locked in combat with the ghosts of ancestors. Hedda Gabler and, in *A Doll's House*, Nora Helmer were prisoners of gender, confined by histories they were allowed neither to write nor to overcome. Oswald Alving, the uncomprehending victim of *Ghosts*, lies dying for the sexual sins of a father from whom the new age should have set him free. All of Ibsen's compromised heroes yearned for open space but lived behind time's enclosing walls. Less than a century ago, history still had the feel of the inescapable.

No more. When we think about liberty today it is often only as liberation, which we construe as a willful obliviousness to the past. This willfulness is reflected in modern educational curricula that shunt history off to a cul-de-sac to be traversed only by the curious or those in need of diversion. The future is treated less as an exercise in continuity than as an experiment in innovation. Is this really what is required by civic liberty? Does living in a democratic world entail living unencumbered by time?

Actually, we are not really so much less embedded in time than our antique progenitors, as the current controversies over multiculturalism and American identity make evident. We think of ourselves as offspring of the Enlightenment, and we do like to mimic the impertinent Voltaire, construing the past as so many crimes, follies, and errors, a dark legacy of superstition that a free people must forget or even annihilate. Yet in our studied forgetfulness, we are prisoners of our heritage, casting ourselves as injured children of an imagined history—whether it is the history of Enlightenment, liberation, and progress, or, as skeptics will argue, of the rationalization of oppression and injustice by Enlightenment, liberation, and progress. Whether the stories are true or not is of little consequence, for, as we shall see, stories and myths overlap with and condition reality. In a peculiar sense, the reality and the myth converge.

Every people in their self-conception give proof to the proposition that there is still no identity, no community, above all, no liberty, without a journey through time. There is always an encounter with origins, if only in the name of their denial. America's history of liberty imagines a founding in which the American story of emancipation (as we would it were) can be grounded. In such popular traditional school texts as Henry W. Bragdon and Samuel McCutchen's *History of a Free People*, Henry F. Graff's *The Free and the Brave*, and Gertrude Hartman's *America: Land of Freedom*, we celebrate our liberty by writing our history.[2] And so it turns out that imagination has not really displaced memory after all, for it is memory that is driving imagination. As we make war on history, we reinforce its hold over us. To imagine even the most novel futures is to deconstruct and then reconstruct the past. Even the past turns out to be the product of an act of imagination.

Thus all useful education begins with and circles back to historical understanding. Since time gives knowledge a narrative structure, self-knowledge means storytelling. And when the self-knowledge is collective, the storytelling is shared.

Education is systematic storytelling. No wonder there is such tumult surrounding the attempt to identify the right stories! As storytelling, education discloses temporal connections and compels an encounter between unreflected present, reconstructed past, and contrived future. History is not some specialized subject in technical education, it *is* liberal education: it is an account in the narrative mode of our being as a people, as a "public." "Defined and understood, the "I" entails a "We," and "We" is always a story whose end points back to beginnings and whose outcome is conditioned (though not necessarily limited) by history.

Living as moderns under circumstances the successful among us associate with liberation, it is easy to forget that even liberation is implicated in a story. To be progeny of the Enlightenment, to live in an America which, in Henry Steele Commager's phrase, is reason's empire, has consequences, if only the consequence of feeling relatively immune to causes. For even where it entails the denial of history, meaning, and fixed significance (the deconstructionist version), the story anchors us in the past. Postmodernism, with its deconstructing strategies, is tethered to the meanings it challenges. What exactly is the "modern" to which it stands as "post"? And to which "ancient" does "modern" itself refer? The anarchist mood is always conditioned by the rational orderliness against which it rebels. All relativisms are not equal; each is branded by the specific mode of certainty it negates.

Education is historical because it is historicizing; it sets aspirations in a context that conditions and limits identity, not to diminish possibility but to make it realistic. In times when we sometimes seem to treat possibilities as limitless, acknowledging boundaries can be the first step toward meaningful change. In so doing, we acknowledge historical identity—even if our object is to modify or overcome it. History may be a storehouse of knowledge or a warehouse of prudence, but more than this it is the birthing room of our common character. We know ourselves by understanding our temporality, our embeddedness in time, our connection to roots—even roots from which we have knowingly severed ourselves. Deracination too has roots. It is a sorry biologist who thinks that because they float on the wind, spores have no genealogy.

It is in this context that the debates about the appropriate place of formal history and the proper role of our cultural "canon" and of multiculturalism in popular education (issues that will be fully explored in subsequent chapters) belong. The canon is simply (or not so simply) a distilled version of the past, our story reconstructed as a coherent and authoritative body of ideas authored by the forebears of our culture. It contains our virtues and vices alike. It reflects how power has been traditionally distributed, but also how the distribution of power has been challenged. It is always a contentious and controversial story or set of stories, and consequently it always changes radically over time. Some novice proponents of new curricula proceed as if, until this moment, there has been only one account of American identity—WASP or white or male—hegemonic and monolithic. In truth, the American story has been contested from the beginning.

In *America Revised*, Frances Fitzgerald offers an astonishing picture of changing fashions, evolving ideologies, and plastic self-images in her account of American history textbooks.[3] Long before Hispanics and Asian-Americans began to vie with Native Americans and African-Americans for a suitable place and space in the American story, similar arguments were being waged between English and Dutch, Puritans and freethinkers, Protestants and Catholics, farmers and manufacturers, owners and workers, slaveholders and abolitionists, federalists and antifederalists, "natives" (last year's arrivals) and immigrants (this year's), urban dwellers and rustics, unitarians and pluralists, progressives and conservatives, and countless other combative factions. Each posed the same hard questions: What does it mean to be an American? Which America are we talking about? Whose history, whose story is it? To whom does that historical, nearly mythic "We the People" really refer? Does the Constitution belong to the elite who wrote it in order to disguise their hegemony in a veil of universalist rhetoric? Or does it, should it, can it belong to those whose victimization the rhetoric had rationalized? These debates are as old as America itself. Schoolbooks teach each generation a story, but it is never the same story.

Who are we really? WASP nation? Melting pot or pluralist paragon? Are we a refuge for the persecuted of the old world, as the Statue of Liberty promises? A new republic preserving and extending the best of Athens and Rome, as embodied in an Atlantic republican tradition? Is the nation to be understood as a consensual arena of absorption and assimilation or as a multicultural tapestry? Rainbow or mosaic? Worriers about the power of "the canon" must be asked, "which canon?" In the late nineteenth century in elite British schools like Eton, there were roughly two dozen classics masters for every teacher of math and science. Which canon, then, were Bertrand Russell and Winston Churchill taught? The American Founders read Thucydides, Plutarch, Epictetus, and Livy; was their canon ours?[4] We shall enter these debates more thoroughly in Chapters 3, 4, and 5. Yet it is already clear that if we take textbooks to be condensations of the canon, there appear to be nearly as many canons as there are textbooks.

Like our culture and values, our story distilled as a canon has been an uneasy amalgam of fixity and change, of unity and diversity, of authority and freedom. If the story of our past is made too rigid, we are impaled on it; but if it is too pliant, it fails to define us. The nostalgic classicists who want to fix the canon once and for all would bury us in our past. Their canon sits on the present like a fallen mountain. On the other hand, those who want to abolish the canon in the name of emancipating identity from the bonds of ethnicity or gender or some other historical "power paradigm" actually risk obliterating common identity, and with it, communal liberty. For us to abjure all stories or to consign their composition to arbitrary invention (thus arbitrary power) is to uproot memory and live in the world as arbitrarily self-created beings. It is to think that to be free it is enough for us to be without a past.

As the story we are telling here perhaps shows, this is to misconceive the nature of human liberty as well as to misunderstand history. Ours is a tradition that likes to think of freedom as the absence of all constraint. To Americans steeped in distrust of government, to be free is often equated with solitude, with privacy, and with rights. Following our English forefathers, we think of freedom as being unmeddled with, being left alone (*laissez-faire*) above all by government (which we imagine is always on our backs) to do as we please. Nor do we have to be of English or even of European ancestry to see in America a land where women and men are left alone to pursue their private destinies—and more significantly, their own private fortunes; for liberty here has often meant the right to acquire property without limit or restraint. For most Americans, then, it has been easy to think of freedom in theory as freedom *from* somebody or something and to conclude that that is all there is to freedom. In the political domain, we have paid less attention to what we are free for than to what we have emancipated ourselves from.

Yet in the setting of human development and civil society, freedom is closely connected with community, with common possibility, and with self-realization in contexts that are inevitably social. Although its rhetoric may be negative, liberty has in practice had a more positive resonance. Although we may use the imagery of laissez-faire as the key to our liberty, most people simply do not conceive of liberty in practice as being tied up with solitude, anarchy, and endless choice. People feel free concretely not simply when they have choices, but when their choices feel meaningful; not when there is chaos and disorder in which anything is possible, but when what is possible is a set of life choices ordered by ethical or religious values they have chosen for themselves; not when they are left alone, but when they participate in the free communities that permit them to define common lives autonomously and establish common identities freely. There is more freedom in choosing to embrace one's religion of birth than in being told by the state you can believe anything you please, more freedom in choosing to give up cigarettes as part of a life plan than in choosing which brand to smoke.

Metaphysically, freedom may appear as abstract indeterminism: My actions are not caused by anything external to me, and hence, because undetermined, are free. No one has a gun to my head; no manacles shackle my hands. When we think politically, many Americans implicitly buy into this metaphysic. If I can do anything I want, choose as I please, be who I wish to be, I am free. Yet psychologically and politically, freedom is relational and depends on a nexus of social linkages, and when it comes to the rest of our behavior, we assume richer meanings for freedom. My actions are chosen by me in response to a communal world of values and life plans that I share with others, and in whose determination I may ideally participate. Truly to be free, my choices must truly be mine—must accord with the "me" with which I associate my core identity. I must make them in keeping with rational life plans. They cannot be triggered by invisible external or covert influences; they must make manifest a will that is unfettered yet rationally informed by life plans. When liberty is contextualized as a feature of identity and history, it no longer appears as synonymous with deracination. It stands in relation to roots as the Prodigal Son stands to his parents: defined not by his departure from home, but by his voluntary decision to return. This richer understanding of liberty ties emancipation to time and endows history with powers of transformation.

Liberation, then, requires more than disposing of the past. The salient goal for people in bondage has always been freedom through history rather than freedom from or against history. Some Jacobins, it is true, made war on history as well as the regime history produced, but theirs was the least successful moment in the French Revolution. Rather than disowning it, successful revolutionaries generally assay to join history—particularly where history can be construed as progressive and where liberty is its goal. This understanding makes history an integral feature of liberal

education (education about liberty!). Far from being some authoritative recounting of "The American Story," it is an ongoing
argument about what our story might be, about who "We" are.

From this standpoint, it is easier to comprehend the spectacle
of school texts which from generation to generation tell different,
even contradictory stories. "We" are the British race, made anew
in America. "We" are Puritans and Protestants struggling against
a tide of foreigners who, like those we fled in the Europe we left
behind, are Catholic, corrupt, and unassimilable. "We" are a
melting pot, absorbing wave after wave of newcomers from alien
cultures and assimilating them into the American way. "We" are
a pluralist nation of immigrants, a rich tapestry of multicultural
difference that does not melt down but contains and encompasses
many worlds. "We" are a mosaic in which the common pattern
is constituted by separate pieces whose distinctiveness is essential
to the design. "We" are the great American majority, the propertyless, the enslaved and oppressed, women, nonwhites, farmers,
and workers, more abused than liberated by America, more betrayed than succored by its supposedly democratic constitution.
Which story is ours? It depends on who "We" are. Who are we?
It depends on which story—which stories—we claim as our own.

There has been no single historical canon, but an evolving
argument. And if the canon turns us into "Us," we in turn transform the canon into "The Canon": It creates Us as we create It.
As we are heterogenous, our story in time necessarily becomes
plural, plural in that each generation rewrites it, plural in that it
must confront the reality of pluralism in the makeup of the nation. The more inclusive the story, the more pluralistic its plot.
As we aspire to be free, our story will necessarily have to recount
servitude no less than emancipation, the forces against which freedom has struggled as well as the ideals in which name the struggle
unfolded, those left out as well as those included (who may be
the story's original scribes but are now besieged defenders of an
old story line few accept). Freedom, historically grounded, points
to the unfreedom it has overcome. Freedom uprooted from the

history of its struggle becomes vaporous sentimentality—the hypocrisy of the powerful trying to legitimize their dominion.

THE CANON AS A STORY

Since canons are how we fix the past, whether we define them rigidly or loosely, unitary or plural, closed or open, will define the relationship between past and present and thus help establish how we understand our liberty. The canon is various within our own culture and over time, but more obviously it varies across cultures as well. Because each society has its own history, there can be no universal story, although there may be universal moments in each particular story. Inasmuch as it is ours, our story naturally strives to unify experience, seeking common denominators and the language of universal discourse. *We* are part of the human family; our story is the human story. At the same time, the story is hemmed in by difference, by the plural and the particular. Every story has a parochial specificity: *we* are unique, special; this is *our* story alone—my story or your story. To insist that our story is The Story is more likely to impose a particular history on everyone than it is to disclose a truly universal tale. However, when we recognize the plurality of stories, we can begin to focus on what they share without permitting any one story to become paradigmatic. Since the cultures they capture are forever in flux, canons cannot be canonical. Fixed canons are always distortions. What we need are loose canons that are as protean as the people who invent them.

The canon must always be understood as an argument. We cannot be completely other than it makes us, but we have considerable power to make it what we choose. If the American story—in the traditional mode—is told so as to include no Native Americans, or is told in a way that casts them as vanquished primitives, our current identity will be less than plural and encompassing. It may even become an emblem of exclusion that defines us by those who are powerful among us. In their early incarnation before the Civil War, our textbooks at least sometimes offered a rich and respectful account of Indians as a distinct and edifying culture. There was a sense of a story shared. After the Civil War, with the opening of the West and the redefinition of Indians as obstacles to the "progress" that was the moving frontier, they were shoved out of the American story and cast as half-civilized savages, cruel and brutal, an obstacle standing in history's way. Our story contracted and lost some of its capacity to encompass.

On the other hand, if in reaction to this blindered orthodoxy the American story is conceived merely as the story of imperial aggression and genocide, and—in the fashion of some forms of radical revisionism—is recounted as a story whose *sole* aim is exclusion, our current identity loses the possibility of idealism and justice. A too-prettified past looks hypocritical and inspires cynicism rather than idealism, particularly among those it leaves out. In distorting their history it robs them of a future. That may be why so many young Americans of color disdain the traditional monumentalized account of an America wrapped in July Fourth bunting: such a nation clearly does not belong to them, any more than the four presidents who stare out boldly from Mount Rushmore at the Dakota plains belong to the Lakota Sioux whose sacred mountain was seized for Black Hills gold booty by greedy white men.

Yet a vilified past also robs history's offcasts of hope, and, in making them victims, takes away the possibility of change and reform. Washington, Jefferson, Lincoln, and Theodore Roosevelt were notably insensitive to America's natives, but they can also be cast as mostly beneficent models of a heritage of freedom that has made equality, justice, and hence a sensitivity to the impact of American history on Native Americans a genuine political issue.

We cannot do without a canon, but neither can we do without a permanent argument about what it is and to whom it belongs. To abjure it wholly, and with it, the past, is to lose our identity; but to abjure our power over the past, to surrender to a canon we do not periodically remake, is to lose our freedom. The roots that hold us to the ground also connect us to one another. We are hearty fruit trees rather than onions or potatoes: though well rooted, our essence lies above ground, turning freely in liberty's clean breeze.

THE PAST AS FUTURE

The story we tell about ourselves defines not just us but our possibilities. Liberal education, I have argued, is historically grounded, by which I mean grounded in time. That suggests history cannot stand alone in the educational curriculum. To portray an American story is necessarily to look forward as well as backward. To be an American is to have an inkling of what an American can be, should become, will turn into.

In a country accustomed to living in the present and gazing out at past and future as if they were foreign lands, this is not easily undertaken. Time is a river, a continuum, but in educational curricula, history is often frozen. The present comes to feel like a static enclave equally distant from past and future; and the future, which is a mere millisecond away, can appear as remote and unconnected to a given now as the petrified past. The future begins only when the present ends; but from a certain viewpoint, the present never ends. Thus the future never begins. Consciousness of time is always mired in paradox and deception—countless discrete nows run together like so many film stills to produce a moving picture. This is why, though in truth it incarnates our vital temporality, the present so often cuts us off from both past and future.

Our current conditions, our modern technologies, exaggerate these familiar temporal paradoxes. We live under circumstances that have hastened the atrophy of history and facilitated indifference toward (or perhaps fear of) the future. The atomic age and the twentieth-century history of dictatorial and totalitarian societies (now apparently under challenge, but not necessarily coming to an end) have infected us with a sense of our mortality that makes the future look more nightmarish than utopian. In this spirit, our modern prophetic fictions have been dysutopias that, from *1984* to *On the Beach* and from *2001* to *The Handmaid's Tale*, see in our future a horrific fantasy of nature, science, and man run amok. Whereas a few centuries ago, technology promised deliverance, today's fictions make it the source of our destruction (the *Terminator* movies, for example). If government and science often combine in our nightmare to forge an alliance of oppression, nature seen through the dismal mirror of ecological disruptions promises only to punish the human race for its hubristic tampering with a fragile earth.

Television has played a special role in our alienation from the temporal continuum. In its ubiquitousness, it is everywhere and ever ready to convey instantaneously the new and the now. Before a single newspaper could print news of the outbreak of hostilities in the Gulf War, CNN viewers were literally in Baghdad witnessing the initial aerial bombardment. We have seen Judge Clarence Thomas damned and redeemed, seen the *Challenger* blow away our cosmic dreams, seen John Kennedy's apparent assassin, Lee Harvey Oswald, himself assassinated "live" on television. Today lawsuits are being filed to bring state-sponsored homocide to the small screen in the form of televised executions. Legislatures, juries, and politicians conduct present business for TV audiences, while birthing mothers and grieving fathers answer the question "How do you feel?" as they participate "live" (that is, on television) in the birth or death of their children.

By definition, yesterday's news is no news at all, while tomorrow's news, which can be imagined but hardly televised, cannot be worth thinking about. Television shines a brilliant spotlight on a present already privileged by our senses, leaving both memory and imagination in shadows. Where books pull readers out of the present, television thrusts them comfortably down into it, as into an overstuffed TV lounge chair. Some of the latest technologies call for more active spectators, but, ironically, the technology associated with what is called "time shifting" permits us to make past and future "present" at the touch of a button without necessarily even being conscious of a shift in time. "Tomorrow's" program can be captured and frozen while we vacation and then, when tomorrow has vanished into last week's yesterdays, can be conjured up in our "present." Time is not so much shifted as carved up digitally and rendered permanently available to us in our secure presents. Computer-generated information banks give us the same instant accessibility to data usually associated with a discrete time frame and accessible only by dint of extended research, again creating the illusion of a ubiquitous here and now reaching out to swallow up all the theres and thens that define past and future. We no longer travel in time propelled by imagination; we drag past and future into our own time, where they can be imbibed without time's assistance. Television is an insistent present's self-consciously self-regarding eye, fixed stupefyingly on itself.

The result is an obdurate present-mindedness perilous to the continuity of a free society. Societies can push out into the future only by extending their past; but when they are taught to disdain their past, they become resistant to innovation. Free societies can cultivate an imagined future only by using a remembered past to will that future into being. In the absence of will, freedom easily expires. I will argue below with Allan Bloom and other conservative critics about what the young ought to be reading, about *which* taught past best supports a democratic future. But, in truth, such internecine educational debates are of little moment in a world where the young cannot and do not read at all; where sound bites and the rapid intercutting of images favored first by MTV, then advertisers, and now politicians and their scriptwriters take the place of linear storytelling altogether. Temporality and the linear do not retain much intellectual viability in a postmodern climate where time must be "demystified, deconstructed, and digitalized."

As a powerfully present-minded medium, television does badly with ideas and documentary history. It eschews education, insisting (accurately) that its virtues are those of powerful imagery: sentimental affect, entertainment, and titillation. Its connection to democracy has become so remote that citizens are required to pay fortunes to buy civic time (political ads) on "airwaves" once thought quaintly to be "public." As I shall try to argue in Chapter 6, television is the true "great American educator," and little that the schools attempt to do or undo can compete with it. Indeed, television is infiltrating the classroom, its capacity to mesmerize and pacify now being turned to the purposes of a certain kind of pedagogy. What the young learn about values, goals, money, history, and time from the omnipresent tube will not be unlearned by a few earnest teachers hectoring them.

An awareness of time—memory and anticipation—is one crucial mark of being human. To live only in the present is to live as impulsive animals, with memories extending backward only days or occasionally weeks, and wants and needs extending forward by minutes or sometimes hours. Most of the large issues faced by government are issues meaningful only in the context of extended temporal horizons. Ecology and environmentalism are temporally situated concepts that compel thinking about extended periods, decades if not centuries. The half-life of radioactive materials demands that the horizon be pushed out to nearly 20,000 years. On any given day, there will be no compelling environmental crisis, nor can there be. The very idea of a crisis entails changes over time. Only the terminal crisis defies time, ending all the days and bringing time itself to a halt.

Cancer, AIDS, and other modern forms of pestilence are diseases embedded in time whose causes are too far removed from consequences to be fully grasped in so present-minded a culture. AIDS is a kind of punishment, not for an obliviousness to sexual

33

morality, but for an obliviousness to time. We refuse to recognize the implications of present behavior for future states of being. To terminate a pregnancy, at least for some women able to understand the options, is no longer to defy community morals, but it may be to defy time. I am not responsible for my acts as they reappear in the future in forms I did not intend at the moment I enacted them.

AIDS and abortion are complex and provocative issues. My object in raising them is to suggest that many such complex issues are actually related to our conception of time and require a school curriculum focused on temporality, memory, and responsibility. Obliviousness to time almost always reappears as social irresponsibility. Irresponsibility frequently reflects a denial of continuity, a refusal to see in our former selves beings for whom we have a responsibility. Promise keeping, which undergirds the social contract and all the subsidiary contracts it invokes, holds civilization together and sets crucial parameters for responsibility.

Responsibility is simply incoherent if we do not recognize the earlier selves for whom we are supposed to answer. "Sorry to be breaking my word," says time's orphan, "but the me who promised you *that* isn't really *me* anymore." Marriage vows are abandoned by the bushel on the basis of such logic. The "me" generation is actually a "me-now" generation that therapeutically disavows responsibility for all the "me-thens" from which it has issued. Extracted from the continuum of time, rights become emblems of me-now demands severed from the me-then responsibilities that give them meaning and legitimacy. This is ultimately deadly to democracy. The liberty that is my "right" has significance only in the setting of my civic responsibility, which, through participation and civic engagement, gives life and sustenance to democracy.

Americans are reluctant inhabitants of the past, but many believe they are strongly oriented to the future. Regarding themselves—as Americans—as preternaturally progressive, as inventors of the science of futurology from the moment they first took

over a continent conceived as "the land of the future," they saw
themselves as vested in the future. Abjuring the past comes easily
to people whose journey to America is often a journey out of
and against some parochial, confining history. American immigrants pride themselves on their dogged optimism. As apt students of the future, they may well congratulate themselves as
progressive authors of liberty (understood as limitlessness)—the
future as boundless possibility.

Yet our American presentness belies this conceit and it crip-
ples us as inhabitants of time. Weak on the past, we are less secure
in the future than we might think. The impairment of memory
diminishes imagination. Teaching the future turns out to be part
of a continuum defined by the ability to teach the past. Our
incapacity to think imaginatively or constructively or responsibly
about the future—whether in economics, environment, social security, family planning, energy management, nuclear prolifera-
tion, crime, or, above all, education—has its origins at least in
part in our historical obliviousness, our incomplete sense of ourselves in time.

Think of how we identify ourselves in social settings: con-
sumers, clients, preference holders, patients, voters, choosers, and
interest advancers. In every case, we conceive ourselves as raw
bundles of autonomous needs, wants, and desires largely unmediated by reason or goals or values or social context, largely
unencumbered by relationships, responsibilities, or extended
communities, largely unmediated by reason or goals or values or
social context, largely severed from temporality. Needs and wants
are here and now, whereas values, relationships, and responsibilities link the here and now to the past and future. Unencumbered
spatially by others, we are liberated from time's constraints as
well. The consumer, the wanter, and the needer are constructions
of the self unencumbered by particular history or background.
The time-blind client has her own current needs and engages in
relationships of bargaining only to satisfy them. Rationality for
her is little more than a prudential instrument of calculation ("If

I want my needs satisfied, I may have to stroke his ego"). The time-embedded patriot, on the other hand, cannot flourish unless her community flourishes as well, and to see that this happens she must engage a historically embedded community over time. The time-immune voter faces only a choice of which candidate better meets his unmediated interests; the time-acknowledging citizen is part of a large complex of social relationships in which public goods, civic duties, and historical communities must figure.

The time-oblivious patient seeking therapy can immerse himself in the deep and solitary pool of his present self; the time-conscious spouse or parent must navigate waters crowded with other human vessels and must face outward. I am suggesting, then, that there is a kinship between our radical individualism that ties us to grasping, naked selves and our static, unhistoricized vision of time. Ripped from time, atomized individuals are without strings, without givens, without parents, without responsibilities—literally outside of time. Unencumbered, they are removed from time's continuum. Unconnected, they lose their place in history.

The past and the future are also linked in our attitudes toward risk, in our relationship to hope and despair. Pessimism is the lesson of a too-hard past applied to a fearsome future; it makes time an enemy and constructs a future that is as hopeless as the past has been unfruitful. Conservatives permeated by pessimism will thus see change as inherently hostile. Optimism, on the other hand, may appear as the product of a past overthrown or overcome or a past simply forgotten, where hope is born of the possibility of emancipation from the temporal; or of too little respect for limits; or of the belief that boundaries can be transgressed and surpassed.

Yet neither hope nor despair necessarily reflects real knowledge. Indeed, they tend to reflect ignorance of both past and future. No one who visits history's slaughterbench can be unmitigatedly optimistic: Its story of error, catastrophe, and death are written into the record in blood. The fragility of ideas, the mortality of men, the hypocrisy of liberty's stories, the failures of emancipation are among its chief lessons. Yet no one acquainted with the story of history can be unmitigatedly pessimistic either: evolution, progress, even liberation, all do occur in error's spite, and in mortality's grim face. They are themselves, no less than slaughter and death, products of history. We are less free than we would wish, less free than we would be if we could abolish the past; but we are freer than our fears allow us to think, more free than we would be if history were not the story of liberty as well as of oppression, the story of life as well as of death. To teach temporality is to teach these lessons, for the future is tied to the past by time's ribbon.

The first step toward teaching the future is thus teaching the past well. Our conception of tomorrow is rooted in our conception of yesterday, and there is no better teacher of the meaning of time, time gone, time still to come, than history itself. Nonetheless, the future is not simply the past, and though we need in our schools to disclose the intimacy between them, teaching the future is not the same thing as teaching the past. This is clear from the role of the canon—one of history's primary instruments, but of less use for teaching the future. Time relies on both memory and imagination, but each has its own pedagogy. Yet an idea such as that of immortality suggests how close the two are, for the illusion of immortality arises out of a deficiency of both memory and imagination. It is the illusion of presentness; as I am defined only by my present, absent memory of birth, absent imagination of death, I feel immortal. Presentness offers a simple syllogism: I am alive today. Today is forever. Therefore, I am forever! Only when memory and imagination allow me to project myself into the great cycles of time do I acquire a starting point and an ending point. Only then can I grasp the story of my life, the story of my death. My private mortality moves me, then, to consider the larger communities and generational associations in which I am embedded and which alone afford my identity some insulation from death.

THE GREEKS AGAIN: OLD STORIES, NEW STORIES

It was to secure their place in history, acknowledge their communal lot, and thus confront death that the Athenians gathered periodically in their amphitheaters to witness the great mythic tales described at the opening of this chapter. These tales carried cautionary lessons and taught the meaning of community, responsibility, and civic virtue. They enabled the Greeks to teach liberty's complex meanings to the entire citizenry. Freedom, it could be easily seen, was as much a matter of men acknowledging themselves as encumbered by community as it was of loosening community's bonds.

As in all traditional societies, birth and death were tied together by the cycle of life. Where an American might say in the manner of Ayn Rand's great egoist, Howard Roark, in *The Fountainhead*, "I came here to say that I do not recognize anyone's right to one minute of my life. Nor to any part of my energy. Nor to an achievement of mine . . . I come here to say that I am a man who does not exist for others," an Athenian would say, "My life is also part of the life of my community; my energy and achievements are its energy and achievement. I am a citizen who exists for others and even as a man, I exist also by their deeds, their history, their grace." Freedom for him will consist in recognizing embeddedness and obligation and utilizing them as strengths. To teach liberty in Athens was necessarily to teach responsibility, to teach civic virtue, to teach membership in the demos and service to the polis. In those more classically communitarian times, the odd concept of an individual was rendered by the word "idiot," suggesting a fool too ignorant to see that man—being neither animal nor god—cannot live alone. Only exiles from the polis and exiles of the spirit (philosophers) were individuals, the former reluctantly, the latter futilely. Liberty belonged to communities, not individuals, and to teach its lessons was to teach the history of community. Vested in individuals, freedom could only sunder being from time, obscuring its relationship to promises and responsibilities (the past) and to purposes and ends (the future).

To be sure, Athens is a distant star in our modern firmament. With its slave-based economy, its disdain for women as citizens, and its warrior ways, it is a poor model for democrats. Yet in its appreciation of temporality and in its insistence on the rootedness of liberty in community and community in a common history, it modeled the great stories of the Judaic and African civilizations from which it drew sustenance, and it can still instruct us. Its lesson for modern societies like America that affect to be free is that to teach liberty is, first of all, to teach time: both past and future. To teach time is not simply to teach conventional history or some high school version of pop futurology. It is to transmit a sense of our story as a people—the narrative of our struggle to become a people. It is to investigate the course of liberty as aspiration and the course of liberty as a historically realized (or historically unrealized) actuality. To teach liberty is thus to teach imagination. It is to teach creativity, to teach responsibility, to teach autonomy, and to teach embeddedness. Its vessel is not so much curriculum as an approach to curriculum: one that is interdisciplinary, civic-minded, and critical; one never too far removed from the story, too often lost in a present-minded culture, of what it means to be an American. It is to that story, often forgotten and radically contested when remembered, that we now shift our focus.

CHAPTER 2

TO BE AN AMERICAN

Living in time, every people has a history. To teach liberty effectively, Americans must be taught theirs. But every history is contested. No one people is likely to elicit the consent of every member to a particular version of its history, and in nations encompassing more than a single homogenous people dissensus may run deeper. To understand who the "American People" is (to understand if there *is* an American People), the American peoples have tried to understand themselves within the confines of a singular narrative, a story whose terms define their identity, even if that narrative tells a story of diversity.

The American story has perhaps never been quite so controversial as it is today, but it has always been more controversial than elites might have wished. The multicultural perspective is new in name only. The Puritans who settled Massachusetts and conceived of this land as a second Eden beckoning those wronged by Christian Europe had to contend with dissenters who objected to the new Protestant orthodoxy. Under Roger Williams, some of them fled Massachusetts and founded Rhode Island, creating an alternative and more secular model of America. The James-town settlers contended with the native peoples to whom the land was ancient and who were constant reminders that the Americas were a "discovery" only for Europeans. The English, regarded by critics today as a historically hegemonic elite, were everywhere confronted with Dutch, Spanish, and French competitors with their own views on hegemony. Nor were those wealthy traders and merchants who came to the new-world in the spirit of exploration, adventure, investment, and empire likely to see themselves—merely because they were all "English"—as the kin of impressed sailors, religious fanatics, and exiled prisoners who came because they had to. And of course, by the time the great New Republic was founded, nearly a half million slaves had been dragged from Africa into a new-world bondage, the story of which could not easily be incorporated into any respectable version of America's self-imagined history. Consequently, they were read out of the story Americans had fashioned about themselves. But they lurked on the periphery, casting shadows on liberty's brave rhetoric and pricking the conscience of the men who affected to speak it.

In other words, as any careful reader of American history cannot help but notice, America has always been a tale of peoples trying to be a People, a tale of diversity and plurality in search of unity. Cleavages between Protestant and Catholic, plowman and proletarian, banker and borrower, Christian and free thinker, Englishman and Dutchman, farmer and rancher, proprietor and tenant, Spaniard and Frenchman, new immigrant and old immigrant, freeman and slave, rustic and cosmopolitan, German and Scandinavian, frontiersman and city dweller, and, of course, woman and man have irked and divided Americans from the start, making unity a civic imperative as well as an elusive challenge.

The purist view of a WASP nation was never more than the peremptory hope of one part of America's immigrant population. It survives today, ironically, primarily as a target of cynical crit-

ics. The waves in which immigrants swept onto American shores
and inundated the young republic before and again after the Civil
War, before and again after the two world wars, threw off a
constant spray of conflicting metaphors: Melting pot or crazy
quilt? One integral nation or multicultural tapestry? Newfound
land or Indian nation? Land of slavery or home of the free?
America's diversity—geographical, demographic, ethnic, and economic—was always distinct from the much less striking forms of
pluralism found in the European nations from which many em-
igrated. The Founders spoke warily of an "extended" and "compound" republic that seemed immune to the conventional laws
of political development with which the more homogenous histories of Europe's traditional principalities and republics had been
captured. A continental nation, half industrial, half agricultural,
one part free, the other hospitable to slavery, peopled by what
was even in prerevolutionary times a remarkably heterogenous
immigrant population sharing the land uneasily with natives who
could be romanticized or vilified but not easily ignored—this was
a nation that, if it were to hold together, would require some
bold storytelling indeed.

Now, as then, diversity remains America's most prominent
virtue and its most unsettling problem. It is a source of American
pride even as it complicates and muddles the meaning of what it
is to be an American. *E pluribus unum* is our brave boast, but we
are neither very united nor very comfortable with our diversity.
Alexis de Tocqueville had warned that nations conceived in liberty might have a particularly troublesome time maintaining integral unity of the kind that came naturally to despotic traditional
regimes. He knew that religion, a great bond in conventional
societies, could not necessarily be counted on in modern ones
rooted in political will and constitutional artifice, and under pres-
sure from secularism and diversity. He could only hope that
America might maintain its religious bonds (though they too were
plural) to hold together a nation that, conceived in liberty, could

easily end in anarchy. Hence, for America the problem was one of finding a surrogate for religion—a secular bond, what Rousseau and the Jacobins (each in a different fashion) had conceived of as a civil religion. This faith would be a religion only in its healing, integrating powers. The natural foundations of religion were gone, and a civil surrogate could promise only artificial customs, conventions, and mores—secular holidays in place of saints' days, for example—to bind together people divided by passions and interests. To hold a country together in the face of multiplying differences and a liberty of individuals so extensive that solidarity and unity seemed permanently at risk was no easy task.

In a historical shorthand for what had actually taken place, the great seal of the United States carried the proud boast already cited: *E pluribus unum*. From a diverse, confederated group of peoples would spring a powerful union. But the logic of American politics has in fact run in the other direction: it was the *unum* wrought from diversity that made a continued *pluribus* possible. That unity ultimately took the form of the civil religion that republicans like Rousseau and Tocqueville dreamed of—what Sanford Levinson, following Justice Hugo Black, has aptly called "constitutional faith"[1] and what Jurgen Habermas, in search of a German equivalent, has dubbed "constitutional patriotism." Divided by private faith, by race and gender, by class and ethnic origins, by geography and economics, Americans have no faith in common other than a faith in the commons, no shared faith but their public faith. And that faith is civic: a fidelity to the Constitution in its most generic sense. Yet it took a bloody civil war, America's true revolution, to impress upon all Americans the virtue of their fragile constitutional faith.

The Roman term for constitution, *res publica*, or "public things" (principles, laws, order), is a translation from the Greek *politeia*, which stood not simply for the ordinances and sumptuary laws by which public life was ordered but for the underlying principles governing all common life. A constitution is more than a set of written formulas for governing; it is literally what constitutes a society—that which ties together a collection of private persons and sectarian groups into a society. America's constitutional faith is thus a faith in how society is ordered—by its written constitution to be sure, but also by other founding documents, such as the Declaration of Independence and the Bill of Rights, by seminal presidential inaugural and farewell addresses, by Lincoln at Gettysburg and Kennedy in Berlin, by the Emancipation Proclamation and the Civil Rights Act of 1965. And, more consistently than anything else, by those decisions rendered by a changing Supreme Court, which has defined over time the evolving meaning(s) of a constitution that refuses to stand still. The constitutional faith of Americans is a public faith in a public order: an order that, quite precisely by separating public from private, makes possible the diversity and private freedoms Americans most cherish.

Yet even within the civic church of constitutional faith there are significant confessional differences that impair union, above all over the question of how democratic the order really is. Critics of democracy never tire of saying, "This is a republic, not a democracy!" and the degree to which the American story can be told as a tale of emancipation and democracy is the most disputed feature of a highly problematic history, as we shall see presently.

How, then, might the American story be told so as to encompass its endless variety yet yield a definition of what it means to be an American compatible with constitutional faith and a democratic civic religion? How ought history to be taught in the public schools responsible for the education of democratic citizens but increasingly peopled by young, predominantly nonwhite Americans who have considerable grounds for cynicism about the historical record of American democracy?[2] Hispanic- and Asian-Americans have been less skeptical, but African-Americans, the nation's oldest immigrant group and the only one that came wholly against its will, are least persuaded that "our" story can ever be "their" story. The abyss that can open up between interpretations was recently underscored in the reactions to the American story by the only two African-Americans to have sat on the Supreme Court. For Justice Thurgood Marshall, who had argued school integration before the Supreme Court in 1954, in *Brown* v. *Board of Education*, long before President Johnson appointed him to it, there is little to be proud of in the Founders or their handiwork. Upon his retirement in 1991, he said again, as he had said so often before, that for him there could be no question of constitutional faith for black Americans until well after the Civil War, and then only with a strong dose of skepticism. His replacement, Associate Justice Clarence Thomas, declared upon his nomination to Marshall's seat that "only in America" could such an astonishing thing happen to the grandson of a sharecropper. When the battle over the American story is at its most intense, those often seem the choices: America as a monument to constitutional hypocrisy and to the struggle against (but not the victory over) hypocritical elites, and America as a bold land of endless opportunity for all.

INVENTING OURSELVES

As we have noted, there is no group that does not have its own private version of the American story. Is there a public version upon which some modicum of concord is possible? Most standard tellings of the story share two characteristics. First, each discloses a purportedly special story: an exceptional tale, unique to us. Whether the story is of slavery or liberty, it is treated as unparalleled in human history. Second, in almost every version standard accounts offer a story about liberty—about liberty's achievements, and thus of progress and the victory of aspiration over history, or about liberty's hypocrisies and failures, and thus of hegemony and the victory of history over aspiration. Either way, it is a unique story whose chief player is liberty and whose chief antagonist is the past, history itself. This much even neoconservative zealots of the canon and multicultural skeptics have in common.

From the outset, then, to be an American was also to be enmeshed in a unique story of freedom, to be free (or to be enslaved) in a novel sense, more existential than political or legal. Even in colonial times, the new world meant starting over again, meant freedom from rigid and heavily freighted traditional cultures. Deracination was the universal experience for the subordinate as well as the superior. After the men in Philadelphia had designed a new constitution for the newly independent nation, liberty took on an explicitly political aspect. To be an American was not to acquire a new race or a new religion or a new culture; it was to possess a new set of political ideals, ideals that, even in the less than egalitarian early beginnings, were comparatively democratic. Or it was to be a victim of those ideals' hypocritical failure.

The feisty English emigrant Frances Wright, herself unable to vote, nonetheless could write back in the 1820s:

> What is it to be an American? Is it to have drawn the first breath in Maine, in Pennsylvania, in Florida, or in Missoura? Pshaw! Hence with such paltry, pettifogging . . . calculations of nativities! *They* are Americans who, having complied with the constitutional regulations of the United States . . . wed the principles of America's declaration to their hearts and render the duties of American citizens practically in their lives.[3]

Rank and privilege were prohibited and the sovereignty of the people (initially circumscribed fairly narrowly) was guaranteed. America represented a new kind of nation and proffered to Americans a new kind of identity rooted in principle. To Ralph Waldo Emerson, America offered "new lands, new men, new thoughts." President Theodore Roosevelt was only echoing the language of Emerson, and before him of *Federalist No. 1*, when he insisted that America was a "question of principle, of idealism, of character, not a matter of birthplace, of creed, or line of descent." More recently, Justice Felix Frankfurter defined naturalization as a process by which one must "shed old loyalties and take on the loyalty of American citizenship," citizenship itself being a kind of a "fellowship which binds people together by devotion to certain feelings and ideas and ideals summarized as a requirement that they be attached to the principles of the constitution."[4] This self-consciously idealized portrait of a unifying constitution is reaffirmed regularly. Just a few years ago, Jack Beatty, then writing for *The New Republic*, reminded July 4th readers that "ours is a patriotism not of blood and soil but of values, and those values are liberal and humane."[5] Still more recently, President George Bush celebrated American victory in the Gulf War by declaring that we had "regained confidence in America's special decency, courage, compassion and devotion to principle."[6]

To invent an identity rooted in principled liberty takes a certain hubris, but the Americans never lacked in hubris. To realize in practice the principles in whose name they claimed an identity took more, however. Their hubris was reinforced by their self-conception as a special people capable of realizing a special destiny. The American story was promoted as exceptional, not simply in the sense that every people has its own distinctive story, but in the sense that among stories conforming to general historical laws, the American tale was without peer. America's uniqueness consisted of a self-imposed exemption from history and from time. As Louis Hartz tried to show in his still-powerful account of the American story,[7] liberal America has been able to see itself as a nation that evaded feudalism, and thus eluded the weighty baggage of the postfeudal European legacy. The nation was to be conceived as an exercise in novelty. Even those ill-starred Africans taken into slavery and sold into new-world bondage were sundered from their roots and compelled to live out destinies not their own. Ripped from time and place, they too lived new lives in which their distance from liberty became their defining attribute. A few years before the Philadelphia Convention, the American farmer Crèvecoeur was writing about the American as "a new man."

To become a new man was to forget the old. Americans became skilled forgetters, deriving their new identities from imagination through a laborious exercise in studied obliviousness. What melts (if anything melts) in the storied American melting pot is memory. With sea passage to the new world came the promise that pasts could be forgotten—displaced by new stories newly tailored to fresh needs and desires, in a world that started each day anew.

Nonetheless, the new country without a history still had to tell a story, if only the story of a flight from time. Only Native Americans had a traditional story to tell about a land they had belonged to for eons, and that was certainly not the story the immigrants wished to tell. For the newcomers—the invaders who needed to legitimize whatever injustices were occasioned by their intrusion into their new world by reference to the injustices done them in the old—a story had to be wrung from art. In naming his study of popular sovereignty in America *Inventing the People*,[8] Edmund S. Morgan was only rehearsing an argument we can find in Alexander Hamilton's language (in *Federalist No. 1*), where Hamilton reminds critics of the new constitution that it had been given to the Americans, alone among peoples, "to decide whether societies of men are really capable or not of establishing good government from reflection and choice, or whether they are forever destined to depend for their political constitution on accident and force." A few founders alluded to the Indian federations as if Americans might actually learn something from those they had displaced, but for the most part the natives were made to vanish—first as history, then as facts—in order to maintain the fiction of a "blank tablet" on which a fresh history and a novel constitution could be inscribed.

This is not to say that we are entirely without origins in the tribal and national and confessional identities of Europe associ-

ated with "blood and soil." We work at but do not always succeed in our obliviousness. Michael Walzer is only one among
many who argue that our "national" culture is finally plural and
that Americans are necessarily going to remain hyphenated for
the foreseeable future.[9]

In his book *Under God*, Garry Wills makes a similar argument when he tries to demonstrate that religion plays a far deeper
role in society today than is recognized by the secular establishment on the two cosmopolitan coasts. "No ignorance is more
securely lodged than the ignorance of the learned," he quips, in
challenging the intellectual communitarians and civic republicans
who talk about citizenship as the crucial moment in American
identity.[10] While the United States might then appear ideally to
itself as an exemplar of the pure assimilationist nation, where
citizenship in a principled polity is the chief form of identity, we
cannot afford to trust appearances uncritically.

As it happens, the story of America has to account for a
compound identity that mixes melting pot assimilationist imagery organized around a patriotism of the constitutional ideal
with both a monocultural identity rooted in Anglo-Saxon Protestantism and a multicultural identity that is pluralistic and contradictory—not necessarily divisive, but much less unitary than
the ideal Americanism conveyed by citizenship. To be an American is to be just a little bit schizophrenic, as the intrusive hyphen
that defines so many Americans' pre-American roots makes evident.

George Bush is a reminder of the dominant culture's staying
power. Those who pretend this durable elite is no more than one
among many equal partners in citizenship may believe they are
describing America, but they have clearly never lived in it. Who
actually belongs to the mythic WASP elite is something else again:
as a model of a certain America, many aspire to it and so change
their names and cast off their immigrant's costumes and rid themselves of accents. Even today, there is far less interest in multiculturalism among the most recent immigrants from places like

Central America and Vietnam than from minorities with a long-standing presence in America. Traditional immigrants were even known to have manufactured WASP identities out of whole cloth. Remember Mr. Dooley's gibe about how "a WASP is a German what's forgot who was his parents."

Yet the WASP image, if our dominant paradigm, is hardly our only model. America is also a crazy quilt of Indians, Jews, Irish, blacks, Hispanics, Germans, Asians, and countless other peoples, each of which, to some degree, has retained or even rein-vented important features of some original immigrant identity that is clung to in the face of the alienating abstractions of the new theoretical "American" identity. Thus, even as they assume an abstract national identity for purposes of education, employ-ment, and civic participation in the new country, hyphenated Americans continue at least once a year to unfurl into the all-American breeze the flags of their mother cultures in parades that honor the parent (Greece or Italy or Ireland) rather than the child (America). Today, as multiculturalism plays a growing role in educational curricula and in the self-consciousness of Americans, many see behind the idealized identity of the American solely a dominant cultural paradigm (WASP, male, Anglo, Eurocentric). From the perspective of some feminists, even women can be sev-ered from their American identity by their embeddedness in gen-der differences. By Michael Walzer's definition, to be an American, if it means anything at all, is to recognize and tolerate this pluralism of roots and identities. Yet, ironically, it is pre-cisely this tolerance for diversity and openness to difference that constitutes the common ground of American citizenship.

No one would be fooled by the story of multiculturalism into thinking of the United States as a nation of distinct tribes and peoples—a Nigeria or a Switzerland. No one expects the United States to follow the disunited ex–Soviet Union and the disinte-grated Yugoslav federation into anarchy. Among hyphenated Americans, the "American" suffix has rendered the "Japanese-" or "German-" or "Jewish-" prefix fairly innocuous. Indeed, the prefix is often more the subject of a nostalgic quest than an emblem of a firm sociological identity. Walzer seems to suggest that there is a certain equity between the terms on either side of the hyphen, but this seems to me to be a considerable exaggeration. So innocuous for the most part is the prefix, in fact, that those in need of a symbol of distinctiveness have often had to rummage around in the library of neologisms to find labels that do their rhetorical aims justice. In just a few decades, Americans of color have moved from "colored" (a pejorative designation by whites) to "Negro" to "black" to "Afro-American" to "African-American" and back to "colored" again (as in "people of color") in search of a satisfactory linguistic home for their distinctive American identity. The prefix suggests a wish or an ideal rather than a fact.

The use of hyphenated forms for American identity has never raised questions of civic loyalty (as they have in France, for example, a nation with equally open access to citizenship but far less tolerance for group pluralism)—except perhaps among bigots and certain kinds of nativists wishing to impute the motives of immigrant groups they fear or detest, or during wartime when a particular prefix may coincide with the name of an enemy nation and thus stigmatize rather than Americanize its bearer (as the label Japanese-American did in 1941 and as Arab-American sometimes does today.)[11] Indeed, the American experience with naming has in the main involved a rather crude Americanization, often the result of an Ellis Island immigration official's impatience with an unpronounceable surname. But it was equally often because a Sammy Goldishinski, pursuing fame and fortune in the all-American make-believe of a place like Hollywood (America raised to the nth power), rebaptized himself Sam Goldwyn (borrowing the "wyn" from an all-American New Yorker) and lived happily and prosperously—like "a real American"—ever after.[12]

What citizenship cannot do to homogenize immigrants has often been done by America's pervasive commercial culture. If to be American is not quite captured by subscription to the liberal's political principle, it seems well encompassed by Holly-wood, Madison Avenue, Television City, and Disneyland, where the images that define America throughout the world are invented and distributed by men and women like Sam Goldwyn, themselves often first-generation immigrants. It is true that projections from demographic statistics suggest that sometime after the middle of the next century America will cease to be a nation whose majority is white (the public school population in many states is already predominately nonwhite). But will these Americans of color be any less homogenously American than the Irish and Italians and Poles are today? Not if Americans continue to vote, shop, go to the movies, and watch television together (see Chapter 6).

Yet this prognosis depends a great deal on what happens in education. Recent debates about multiculturalism (see Chapter 4) and English as a primary school language suggest how controversial hyphenation can be when more than names or parades are at stake. Proponents of America as a democratic ideal and as a commercial republic generally insist that English must be its Esperanto; multiculturalists argue that to preserve a genuinely plural America requires bilingual educational programs. The consequences of this debate for an American future are anything but hypothetical. If teaching in public schools entails teaching liberty, then there is little question that it is the common public culture that must be taught. But which first? Can secondary languages be stations on the road to self-confidence for immigrants that eventually permit the most effective mastery of the language of the public realm—English?

These questions will be reviewed in detail in the following chapter. Here it is sufficient to note that even in our controversial times, most Americans, including as many new as old immigrants, like the story that portrays their nation as an aggregation of peoples who have been thoroughly assimilated. After all, it is the magnetism of that story which drew them to America in the first place. The new integral identity, although it leaves some space for the calibration of distinct identities and the celebration of roots, is more about the future that immigrants face in common than about a past from which many are in flight. Once here and subjected to the usual disappointments of a too-eagerly awaited new life, immigrants may change their minds, but on their way in most envision their journey as a way out of confined destinies. To them America is an escape hatch from the past. Ask any recent emigrant (green card or no) from Vietnam or Hungary or Syria or Mexico. Difference divides, principle unites. Thus, principle rather than culture has been crucial to American identity from the earliest times.

Thomas Jefferson wrote nearly two centuries ago, "Let this be the distinctive mark of an American, that in cases of commotion he enlists under no man's banner, but repairs to the standard of the law."[13] Where there is no commotion, there is ample room for roots. Where there is competition, turbulence, and commotion, common principle has to be the standard—if there is ever to be tranquility and freedom.

THE STORIES WE TELL

Let us narrow our focus. There are many Americans and many stories, but one has been dominant. To be sure, it is preeminent in part because of the dominion of those who tell the story, but it has a broad appeal. It is the story of America as a self-invented nation forging unity from abstractions that has fired the minds of poets and metaphor makers: America the beautiful, they have chanted; America, newfound land and City on the Hill and Second Eden; America, land of the new beginning, promised land, chosen land, sweet land of liberty, and land of the free; tabula rasa and virgin continent; America exempt from time; America outside history.

Most striking in all this idyllic self-imagery is the insistence on innocence. In her 1847 history textbook, the indomitable

Emma Willard wrote: "In comparison with these old and wily nations [of Europe], the character of America is that of youth simplicity, of maiden purity."[14] In 1991, President George Bush, celebrating the military victory over Iraq, used remarkably similar language in addressing a joint session of Congress: "Americans are a caring people. We are a good people, a generous people. Let us always be caring and good and generous in all we do." From Herman Melville's Benito Cereno to Henry James's Daisy Miller, America in the world has been limned as the sad tale of innocents abroad. No heart of darkness in America's light (and white) American soul. Or is there? How did America manage to conceive so pristine and precious a story about itself in light of what unsentimental observers might describe as a typical Western imperial power born in slavery and delivered by war? How could innocence establish a global empire, an American century, four hundred years of racial oppression?

In the extraordinary rhetoric of America's self-identification can be found a story of liberty's promise and liberty's failure. To achieve in reality the aspirations of the melting pot, and of innocence reclaimed, Americans had to share in several prior stories: the story of America as a child of Europe, a land born from the European Enlightenment with its faith in the inventiveness of men. As we have seen, this was the story of America as an orphan, as an exception from all the laws that normally constrained political development. The exceptionalist story rested in part on the Calvinist (and Jewish) idea of an Elect, a Chosen People with a special destiny. Yet we have also noticed it was the Enlightenment notion of a tabula rasa that was truly to exempt Americans from Europe's grim historical laws. It was to the "empty spaces" of the new world that John Locke pointed when, in his *Second Treatise on Civil Government*, he recommended to those dissatisfied with the social contract the *loci vacuii* across the seas. Enlightenment was born in Europe as idea, but it found a permanent home—the Americans boasted—in the uncontaminated innocence of the new world.[15]

If the story of the Chosen People had ancient roots in Judeo-Christian culture, the old aristocratic vision of a Chosen People was nevertheless transformed in the American setting into a new democratic story of a Choosing People: men and women capable of denying themselves the blood consolation of an exclusive ascriptive community in favor of membership in an inclusive voluntary community rooted in choice and law. The voluntarism of this new form of association was what permitted Americans to conceive of themselves as operating beyond the circle of constraints that otherwise had governed the growth and decay of republican societies from ancient times.

Guided by these two stories, America became, in Hegel's words, "the land of the future," contrived in free minds, inscribed as a novel constitution on the blank tablet of a country without a history, and imprinted finally on the empty land itself by a people who dared to choose its own destiny.

The first generation ashore in the new world still defined itself as rebelling against the old tribes of Europe—secular and religious—and thus needed to bar rank and privilege by law. But the second, already at home in America, was quite literally born into an equality that appeared natural (as long as it was male and white and propertied). For this generation, America was less a nation invented in reaction to Europe's history of persecution and intolerance than an artful instrument for the circumvention of history altogether. As Louis Hartz suggested, those Americans who enjoyed the free standing of citizenship were not born equal in a merely hypothetical sense, as a legitimizing device of their rebellion; they were born equal concretely and actually as a consequence, they believed, of American exceptionalism. "Can a people born equal," Hartz queried, "ever understand peoples elsewhere that have to become so? Can it even understand itself?"[16]

The story we tell about ourselves as an exceptional nation exempt from history (from the lessons of other peoples' stories) is a perfect representation of what it means for a nation to have a defining story as well as of why defining stories need to be contested. For the exceptionalist story is not merely a retrospective ideology foisted on the past by arrogant moderns or a product of nineteenth-century imperialist revisionism reading its own ambitions back onto the past. Exceptionalism was a concomitant of the American founding—indeed, one of the principles by which rebellion was justified. As Conor Cruise O'Brien reminds us in his splendid essay *Godland*, John Cotton preached exceptionalism to a contingent of Pilgrims embarking for America from Boston, Lincolnshire, more than a hundred years before the Revolution. Using as his text a prophetic passage from Samuel, Cotton proclaimed: "Moreover, I will appoint a place for my people Israel, and will plant them, that they may dwell in a place of their own, and move no more; neither shall the children of wickedness afflict them anymore."[17] Roger Williams, who, as noted earlier, had fled the Puritan Commonwealth of Massachusetts in search of a society where state and church might be kept apart, spoke disparagingly of "Godland" as early as 1644, but the notion of a special destiny for the new country persisted.

By the eighteenth century, new Americans like J. Hector St. John Crèvecoeur had attached themselves to the full-blown myth of exceptionalism, fortified both by religion and (ironically) by the Enlightenment philosophy that had been developed to challenge religion. In his celebrated *Letters from an American Farmer*, published shortly before the Constitutional Convention, Crèvecoeur announced a "new man" and portrayed Europe's emigrants as poor folk escaping to "the great American asylum," where "everything tended to regenerate them: new laws, a new mode of living, a new social system: here they are become men: in Europe they were as so many useless plants . . . [here] they have taken root and flourished."[18] Crèvecoeur asked, "By what power hath this surprising metamorphosis been performed?" True to Jefferson, he answered, "By that of the laws."

A few years later, Tom Paine deployed a similar rhetoric, insisting that "the case and circumstances of America present themselves as in the beginning of the world . . . we are brought at once to the point of seeing government begin, as if we had lived in the beginning of time."[19] Indeed, far from being a later accretion, exceptionalism would seem to have been America's conventional self-characterization from the outset, while challenges to it, such as those of the multiculturalists or (earlier) the Progressives, must count as revisionist.[20] The original story has been embellished, challenged, and then punctured as a windbag's overblown hypocrisy. Yet it is a story that, in the very telling, has helped create the nation the story envisions.

Founding stories are never strictly historical in the sense that professional historians might wish. Yet history is always a story, a tale with prescriptive and moral implications. The story of American exceptionalism was more than just wishful thinking. It was a rhetoric meant to provide a constitutional framework that would permit the new nation to elude the classical dilemmas of traditional European political theory.

James Madison, for example, believed that Europe's republican theories geared to small polities and homogenous peoples could offer little to men who wished to create a constitution for a republic of continental extent. His eye on novel conditions, he set about looking for novel solutions. The constitutional devices of representation, federalism, the separation of powers, judicial review, and constitutionally embedded rights were intended to meet the challenge by giving to the abstractions of the Enlightenment an institutional form: power checked by power to avoid the contentiousness all too familiar to Europe's quarrelsome little republics; federalism, to assure a vertical balancing of powers between central government, the states, and municipalities no less efficacious than the horizontal separation of powers that divided executive and legislative branches into contending, offsetting bodies; an independent judiciary to ensure the rights of states and peoples; and a representative system to insulate the government from the passions and interests of fractious individuals and sects—passions and interests that would be passed through a "filter" of the "best men."

Together, these institutions were intended to guarantee that the identity of the new American citizen would rest on the autonomy of the political domain and its sovereignty over a pluralist culture (which could only divide Americans, placing a strain on their capacity for tolerance). The plural conception of culture could flourish in the private sector without creating a dominant, uniform national culture oppressive to historical differences in immigrant groups.[21] Once it was disestablished, religion could flourish and serve as a kind of social glue without becoming an authoritative enforcer of public belief that might stifle diversity, freeze liberty, and undermine tolerance. A political framework was proffered for the ongoing integration of immigrants and other outsiders (as well as those insiders left on the outside by the evolution of inegalitarian social relations and economic slavery). Thus, outsiders in America were able to campaign for citizenship and legal status through rather than against the American system—something that more than anything else spared America a revolutionary history of instability and made the American story more than a paean to hypocrisy.

America's patriotism was rooted in ideas, not blood; in law, not kinship; in voluntary citizenship, not given roots; in constitutional faith, not religious orthodoxy. The story of what it meant to be an American started with a claim about rights—"All men are created equal," we proclaimed—and ended with the demand for citizenship: we are *all* men—those without property, those who were here before the Europeans came, those who were brought here as slaves, those who bore and nurtured children. Thus, we all have the right to be citizens.

WHOSE STORY IS IT, ANYWAY?

This story, although we have punctuated it with queries and cautions that point to our theme, is for the most part the conventional story: the dominant version as it has been advanced by mainstream historians and constituencies (mostly powerful and successful winners in the American sweepstakes). It takes the claim to innocence at face value and turns it into an integrating virtue. It is not just a tale told by the victors, for it still seduces millions of immigrants every year and is intended to offer a plural nation some modicum of unity. Still, to a wide-awake world the tale rings a little hollow. It is simply too good to be true. To Americans for whom the story is but a dream, it may even seem a subterfuge and a lie: a sleight of hand by which America distances itself from those "European" stories of oppression and injustice based on class and religion, which in truth remain America's story as well—at home and, in the conduct of foreign policy, abroad as well.

We are exceptional, the skeptic may argue, only in our capacity for self-delusion. If it depicts a people born in innocence, raised in liberty, and united in equality, whose story is it, anyway? Can it be said to be the story of Africans brought here as slaves? Of women disenfranchised for all but the last seventy-five years? Of all the immigrants who came in search of a dream and woke up to an American reality as laced with bigotry, intolerance, and economic exploitation as anything they had known in the old country, but sugared over in the new country with a sickly sweet layer of civic homilies?

Behind the particular doubts Americans may have about their story are two forms of skepticism about historical mythmaking. These play an important role in America but are not finally decisive, for in the end they lead back to and, paradoxically, reinforce the particular story of liberty that so rankles those who feel less than free. There are questions to be raised about the metaphor of exceptionalism that undergirds much of our self-valorizing mythmaking and about the socioeconomic naivete of a perspective so focused on universal rights and political struggle that it fails to notice or even helps conceal real social and economic inequality. These challenges to the American story raise important issues of inclusion and exclusion that go to the heart of the question: Whose story is it, anyway?

It is understandable that critics of American exceptionalism and the story of Enlightenment on which it is based should be wary of a national identity so wedded to what are quite nearly mythic abstract ideas. Americans, they properly point out, typify peoples who affect to be a nation when in fact they are several nations held together by the domination of cultural elites. The language of natural rights and legal personhood that pretends to unify America only conceals the endless inequalities that differentiate Americans by birth and station in life. If it is self-evident that in America all men are born equal, that is only because in America there are a great many bipeds who are not, in the rhetoric of American mythology, men. Women, for example, or Native Americans or black slaves (though in many of the states, free blacks did qualify for local citizenship, and women, though they could not vote, were seen as citizens with respect to rights).[22]

The felicitous story of a nation of new men devising new institutions by which the past might be overcome once and for all works only because it leaves so many out—excluding them quite explicitly precisely at that point where they have demanded entry. One cannot even argue that the American story has evolved in a linear manner toward greater freedom. The Indians, we have noted, were more respected before than after the Civil War; and quotas enacted in the 1920s based on immigrant populations already established in the United States discriminated against Southern and Eastern Europeans. (The quotas were repealed only in 1965.) Some statistics suggest that the condition of Americans of color has worsened in the last twenty years. In his shattering account of American race nonrelations, *Two Nations: Black and White, Separate, Hostile, Unequal*, Andrew Hacker offers devastating evidence for his claim that black Americans have never become full citizens, and that conditions today remain appalling.

Is this a story of liberty evolving from less than liberal origins? Or of liberty lost?

Underlying the particular suspicion of American exceptionalist language is a still more generic skepticism about political language in general: the dubious legitimacy of rationalizing the stubborn power realities of human relations. As Thrasymachus once rebuked Socrates (who was trying to conjure an ideal image of justice) by reminding him that justice was no more than a rationalization of the interests of the strongest, so the skeptic rebukes American storytellers, reminding them that the politics of inclusion is no more than a rationalization on the part of white male property holders wishing to give a universalist aura to their own exclusionary interests. *Their* story is not the story of slavery, of the annihilation of the Indian tribes, or of the exclusion of women from political suffrage (up until women wrested it from them after a century of struggle). Stories conceal what the scrutiny of interests reveals. Names are not to be trusted, and words always mystify and obfuscate. Such are the suspicions of many Americans—some, economists, Marxists, or sociologists of class; others, poststructuralists and deconstructionists; still others, simply battered survivors of a tale in which they cannot locate themselves.

Such charges are eye-opening and important. These critics' substantive argument is more closely questioned in the next chapter. In this historicized form, however, the changes are not very discriminating. After all, there is no national identity that is not a construction of storytelling; all stories are made of words. There is no definition of nationality that is not rooted to some degree in a story with "mythic" overtones, for a myth in this sense is a story raised to a higher degree of legitimacy by a people's need to define itself. Every nation has its stories and its myths: the myth of blood, if not of principle ("the principle of blood"); the myth of tribe, if not of right; the myth of common history, if not of common law. All efforts at defining human beings in common depend on what the French historian Ernest Renan called "common misconceptions"—shared inventions by which common memory is created and preserved.

Social communities are per force socially constructed; and while some constructions prove more lasting than others, while some cement our social relations more firmly than others (as Tocqueville taught us, fraternity seems more effectively affective than legal equality, and kinship is more binding than the state of nature), all are alike constructions or notions. It is not that some are words and others things, some names, others objects; it is only that some words are more socially efficacious than others, some notions more politically viable than others, some ideas more likely to kindle consent or even fidelity than others. Which is the better source of political legitimacy: King Tantalus (Argos)? The father Cadmus (Thebes)? The wolf-raised twins Romulus and Remus (Rome)? The archer William Tell (the Swiss Confederation)? The semi-fictional Aeneas (again, Rome)? The god Wotan (Aryan Germany)? Or the Founders Jefferson and Madison? The political potency of such figures lies in their symbolic power as personifications of a founding act, rather than in how closely they can be made to accord with historical fact. We are united into communities by a common belief whose link to history will always be contentious and contended. Washington's historicity may make Wotan look wholly fictional, but his role in legitimating our historical conception of ourselves is not so different than Wotan's in legitimating the "idea" of the German people.

History and storytelling are not exactly the same thing, but history is the story we choose to believe in, and our beliefs help shape what we understand as history. There are important independent standards for validating historical knowledge, but history is always necessarily more than independently validated historical knowledge. Its meanings and entailments are subject to its uses and abuses and cannot be altogether separated from them. Here is an example.

A standard American history textbook tells students that the first slaves were shipped to America in 1619, the year before the *Mayflower* arrived.[23] Multicultural skeptics from the Council of Interracial Books for Children are provoked to reply that "free Africans, as well as slaves, were in the Americas before 1619" and go on to argue that there was a "slave rebellion" as early as 1526.[24] Their source is a work by Herbert Aptheker who, like other historians (but with a vengeance), had his own political agenda.[25] What constitutes a "slave rebellion"? Did Spanish settlers in what was to become the Carolinas really "return to Haiti" on account of the rebellion? What weight should such an incident have in the story of American slavery? None of these questions can be answered in purely "objective" terms, because each of the crucial terms—slave, settler, rebellion—receives its (contested) meaning from the narratives of which it is a part. The words and the events for which these terms stand comprise the story, but the story gives meaning to the words. Quantifying data cannot qualify the critical terms. "Between 1663 and 1665 more than 100 slave revolts took place on land. At sea there were 55 revolts" reports a popular text, with a precision more suspect than reassuring.[26]

For all its controversy, the American story seems to rely on a narrative with a rather more empiricist flavor than, say, the German story. But law, although odorless, is no less of a metaphor for social relations than blood. Blood, it happens, congeals into a better social glue than law. Law, it happens, is potentially a more inclusive principle than blood. Skeptics can fault American storytellers as historians, but only inasmuch as they fault the very idea of history (which, of course, they often do). American storytellers are not *more* engaged in the rationalization of interests through mythmaking than the storytellers of any other nation.

There is a particular and more telling objection behind the skeptic's generic caution, however: that the American story is too radically *political*, making it seem more inclusive than it really is. Insufficiently attuned to culture and economy, it tells a tale blind to what (and who) is left out. The practice is simply far more exclusive than the legalisms of a strictly political telling of the story allow. This objection suggests that the reality of a dominant culture and the inescapability of class, conflict, and war on the European model have shadowed America from the start and have finally caught up to the country, bending it under the weight of historical laws it imagined it had eluded. If to be an Indian or a black or a woman is in some significant sense not to be an "American" as defined by the American story, what can it possibly mean to be an American? If wealth and class continue to divide Americans and the oppressions of race, religion, and gender are at best whitewashed by the rationalizing niceties of the Constitution, how different from Europe is America?

In the present section, we have witnessed how Americans have paraded themselves as hearty innocents in the face of a perverse overseas world of sin. In "Benito Cereno," Herman Melville tells the tragic tale of the American sea captain Amasa Delano, "whose generosity and piety" render him completely "incapable of sounding such wickedness" as is represented by a slave revolt occurring under his very nose on a Spanish vessel he has boarded.[27] American foreign policy even at its most imperialistic has affected a kind of virgin moralism: We went down to Mexico for the good of democracy, President Wilson was pleased to announce, in the first of scores of whitewashes that were to paint over America's twentieth-century imperial ambitions. Even conservatives have tried to cast Americans as righteous victims of a squalid European nihilism from which they must be protected (see Chapter 5). If the truth is that we are more like than distinct from our European cousins from whom we try so hard to distance ourselves, then what does it mean to call America an exception? A conception of nationality that ignores the persistent primacy of culture and economics in the real evolution of American society would seem to conceal rather than reveal the ways of power and thus to mask the real face of the nation.

This is in part the charge leveled by Progressive historians like Vernon Parrington and Charles Beard, social critics who see class conflict rather than political consensus as the dominant reality of American life. The story they tell identifies the nation with the very European conflicts of interest and class from which exceptionalists have assiduously worked to distinguish it. Myths like the melting pot and the chosen people paper over harsh realities of servitude, exclusion from citizenship, and exploitation. Once perceived, these realities reveal America as a typical exemplar of an all too familiar history of domination and subordination, of inclusion for the privileged and exclusion for the rest. America's special character melts away.

Yet to portray America in exceptionalist imagery is not to insist on its immunity to contradiction or to the corruptions of its actual historical practice. It is only to say that in helping to disguise class biases, the story of an exceptionalist nation identified by its common ideals rather than its plural origins may have also helped it overcome them, at least in part. By boasting of their country's openness, Americans were hard-pressed to keep it as closed as some might have wished. To be sure, the language of universal citizenship as the common denominator of Americanism, especially as conveyed in the rhetoric of the Constitution, is contradicted everywhere and in every American epoch by prejudice, discrimination, exclusion, inequality, and economic exploitation. Yet the use of a radically nonexclusionary language anchored in universalist rhetoric—men are born equal, we the people, equality of rights—helped many groups originally excluded from the social compact preserve their hope and thus enabled them to mobilize political institutions that in time helped them win genuine suffrage. Perhaps it goes too far to say that a people who stole their land from the natives, farmed it with slaves, and built great cities on the equity of wage labor were either blessed or chosen. Few African-Americans or Native Americans or unenfranchised women can have felt chosen for anything other than bondage in a country that cast them as perpetual losers in a cruel lottery organized by their enemies. Abraham Lincoln, no stranger to the moral insufficiencies of the American dream, knew better: in the midst of a bloody fratricide he spoke not of a chosen people, but of an "almost chosen people."

The language of politics has nonetheless offered Americans an open road, and not a few in servitude have, by following it, found their way to freedom. How? Through the very rhetoric of rights that disguised and rationalized their earliest bondage. Rights language embedded in a responsive legal framework turned out to be a powerful reinforcer of America's founding stories, as well as a weapon with which to strike down the hypocrites who deployed those stories only in order to shore up their privileges.

RIGHTS AS A LANGUAGE OF INCLUSION

There has been in America a simple but powerful relationship between rights and democracy, and this relationship has been the key to making good on the promise of the story of America as a land of the free. Rights rebuke both progressives and skeptics by working to make real the equality critics say they occlude; for, the story recounts, rights are claims that free beings make on one another, and they entail and give rise to—indeed, they enjoin and demand—the equality of those who claim them. Democracy is the politics of equality. Without democracy, rights are empty words, dependent for their realization on the goodwill of despots. Absent the democratic ethos in America, rights could not have achieved their victory. Absent rights, democracy might never have become a part of the story. It is rights that promote and promise emancipation, suffrage, and enpowerment. The American Constitution was not a notably democratic instrument; its object was as much to protect government from impetuous majorities as to institutionalize popular rule. But the rights with which individuals were to be protected from both majorities and government also turned out to be vouchers redeemable for suffrage and thus passports to equality.

Even James Madison recognized that rights without supporting political institutions were so many "parchment barriers" to tyranny (one reason for his early opposition to a separate Bill of Rights). Late in his life, like so many Americans who had once feared the people as a rabble, he had come to take a less harsh view of democracy. On the question of the enfranchising of the propertyless, he came to acknowledge that

> under every view of the subject, it seems indispensable that the Mass of Citizens should not be without a voice, in making the laws which they are to obey, in choosing the Magistrates, who are to administer them, and if the only alternative be between an equal and universal right of suffrage for each branch of the government and a containment of the entire right to a part of the citizens, it is better that those having the greater interest at stake, namely that of property and persons both, should be deprived of half their share in government; than that those having the lesser interest, that of personal rights only, should be deprived of the whole.[28]

Madison's use of the language of "an equal and universal right of suffrage" just thirty years after a founding consecrated (as the Progressives are quick to point out) to limiting both popular suffrage and popular access to government seems startling, but the American story was framed in rights language and this language permitted no other evolution. If popular government and laws understood as self-prescribed limitations on private behavior are the real guarantors of liberty, if natural rights are secure only when political rights are guaranteed by popular government, then the right to suffrage turns out to be the keystone of all other rights. This relationship between suffrage and the securing of all other rights was increasingly recognized in the real democratic politics of the early nineteenth century. It was eventually written explicitly into the Constitution with the Thirteenth, Fourteenth, and Fifteenth amendments. As Judith Shklar has written, American citizenship was marked above all by equality of rights. Hence, although this equality existed "in the accepted presence of its [slavery's] absolute denial, . . . the excluded were members of a professedly democratic society that was actively and purposefully false to its own vaunted principles by refusing to accept these people or to recognize their right to be voters and free laborers."[29]

Because the American story was rooted in principle rather than blood and expressed itself in common rights rather than common identity, it was by its very nature always potentially an increasingly progressive and democratic story. The language that boasted of "We the People" in time pressured those who employed it to make "we" into a category that truly encompassed all the people. There are some stories that, in the very telling, push to make themselves true. The story of America as a nation conceived in rights was just such a tale. By understanding who they were in terms of rights, the Americans committed themselves to equality. After all, to say "I have a right" is to posit that I am the equal of others and at the same time to recognize the equality of the persons to whom, on whom, against whom the claim is made. No master ever said to a slave, "Give me my rights!" for rights can be acknowledged only by equals. Likewise, the slave who proclaims, "I have the right to be free," says in the same breath, "I am your equal," and hence, "You are my equal." In a certain sense, to speak of equal rights is redundant: rights are equalizers. Equality is expressed in the idea of rights. Individuals may use rights to insulate themselves from others, to wall in their privacy, but their rights claims depend entirely on the proposition that as claimants they are the equal of all others, that no one as a person living in a free and democratic society is privileged because of who he happens to be by virtue of race, gender, or religion.

More than anything else, this is why the story Americans told and tell about themselves has been liberating in its thrust—if never fully or satisfactorily so. A constitution rooted in rights cannot systematically exclude whole classes of persons from citizenship without becoming inherently incoherent and thus unstable. As early as 1783, the Massachusetts Supreme Court had ruled that slavery was inconsistent with the state's constitution, and this inconsistency with principle became a permanent burr in the side of the new constitutional body politic.

How in the long run could the American story as the tale of an exceptional nation comprised of persons without conventional histories be other than a democratic story? Even where government was antidemocratic in its institutional provisions, it inclined politically toward democratization and tended over time toward greater inclusiveness. Its failure to live up to its principles fully and its inability to wash the marks of slavery from its history left Americans to live into our own day with a legacy of "pain, guilt, fear, and hatred."[30] As hypocrisy is the tribute vice pays to virtue, so guilt and inconsistency are the compliment continued discrimination pays to democratic ideals. Few nations have had histories more racist than America's; even fewer have so resolutely held those histories up to critical self-scrutiny in the name of the standards history violates.

As we have seen, and as the Progressive historians have often repeated, America was at its founding not a notoriously democratic country. There was considerable suspicion of democracy, even bristling hostility against it; for democracy was feared as the rule of a propertyless rabble that would bring private prejudice and impassioned interests into the judicious deliberations of government. Many of the Constitution's devices were aimed at insulating the people from power and interposing filters between their rank prejudices and the careful deliberations of the governors—the best of men chosen from their peers by electoral colleges.

These provisions notwithstanding, in the course of the first half of the nineteenth century, America generally followed the story line of its principled rights and liberties rather than the antidemocratic suspicions of its Founders. That the Constitution included provisions implicitly recognizing slavery (the three-fifths compromise, or the twenty-year license for continuing the slave trade, for example) was a shameful comment on the Founders and called into question their supposedly liberal motives; nonetheless, such provisions sat poorly on the Constitution's rights-lined stomach and were in time regurgitated. This resulted not simply from pressures brought to bear from the outside, but also from the inherently universalizing character of America's founding story, written in the expansive language of rights. Rights talk pushed against artificial boundaries of every kind and made inequalities increasingly indigestible.

What "rights" meant to the American story was that the chief American protagonist in our native drama was neither the WASP nor the assimilated immigrant nor the hyphenated American, but the citizen. What Americans shared could be captured neither by origins nor by kinship nor by blood, which produced only an often anarchic and divisive plurality. Rights issued in citizenship and forged a stronger commonality and a firmer identity than the individual histories immigrants were escaping. The right to liberty, the right to self-legislation, the right to be included in a civic polity founded on "popular" (that-means-me!) sovereignty, all pointed toward an idea of the citizen that had an aggressive, liberating character, pushing to extend to the very periphery of the universal.

Today as we continue to tell America's story as a tale about rights that create citizenship and citizens who possess rights, we approach the very edge of our species' boundary. Still we push onward, outward, the story issuing in new aspirations to still greater inclusiveness, so that finally we can speak of "economic rights" or "animal rights" or "fetal rights" and still seem to be extending rather than perverting our story. What struggle from our own epoch has not been fortified by the language of rights? From the lunch counters of Montgomery to the all-male clubs of New York to the straight streets of middle America, black Americans battling for civil rights, women demanding equal rights, and gays calling for equal standing before the law have waged their civic wars with rights talk. While critics deconstruct such talk, exposing its hypocrisies, today's new immigrants from Vietnam and Cuba, Mexico and Korea, Nigeria and Lebanon can be found successfully employing it, insisting on their rights under the law and working to become citizens so that they can achieve the "standing" which, as Judith Shklar shows, is crucial to the status of the American citizen.

What is perhaps most notable about the American story in this telling is how it has worked at every crucial crossroads in our history, not only to secure the propertied and the powerful (as, skeptics remind us, old stories and well-established canons always do), but also to capture the aspirations of the excluded and to extend the boundaries of power and property.

The disenfranchised knew this as well as the enfranchised, though the enfranchised knew it well enough to be embarrassed by the slavery they condoned and the exclusions they practiced. As a consequence, successful popular movements aimed at the emancipation of slaves, the enfranchisement of women, the recognition of Native Americans, the inclusion of immigrants, as well as the empowerment of the poor, the working class, and others cast aside by the American market, have all had in common a devotion to the language of rights. Indeed, the single most important strategic decision faced by those who have felt left out of the American way of life has been whether to accept or reject the exceptionalist story; to buy into or spurn the rhetoric of rights; to try to possess the American founding, understood as the Declaration of Independence, the Constitution, and the Bill of Rights, as a story that belongs to us all; or to unmask and discard the founding as the hypocritical and deceitful strategy of the powerful seeking to legitimize their tyranny.

Movements that have made war on the Constitution, holding that its rights promise no salvation to the powerless, have on the whole failed, although (as the next chapter shows) there are good reasons for a measure of skepticism. But in denying themselves the consolation of the story, in seeing themselves as excluded from it, such movements abjure its liberating power. The fragility of the stories we tell ourselves is here clearly revealed: to disbelieve our story is to falsify it. By the same token, to believe it is thus to help render it "true." Movements that have insisted that the founding can and must make good on the promise implicit in its universalizing rights rhetoric have succeeded fairly often, although by no means always.

The bold women at Seneca Falls in 1846 mimicked the Founders' language as well as the rhetoric of great English rights jurists like Blackstone in their own militant rights claims—"We hold these truths to be self-evident," they asserted, "that all men *and women* are created equal"—providing a clear example of holding rights language up to the test of its own entailments and using it to make good on promises its originators may have had no intention of keeping.[31] And although the radical abolitionists at times seemed to declare war on America itself and treat its freedom story as a vast tissue of lies, one of their most fiery leaders tried to make the story of his adversaries *his* own story as well. William Lloyd Garrison, calling it a "Covenant with Death and the Agreement with Hell," burned a copy of the Constitution in Framingham, Massachusetts, on July 4, 1854. Nevertheless, he declared in the *Liberator*, in his "To the Public," and in impassioned speeches throughout the North that he "assented to the 'self-evident truth' maintained in the American Declaration of Independence, 'that all men are created equal, and endowed by their Creator with certain inalienable rights—among which are life, liberty and the pursuit of happiness.' " On this foundation, he concluded, he would "strenuously contend for the immediate enfranchisement of our slave population."[32]

The American story was large and encompassing. It had Walt Whitman's broad reach, its embrace containing the North and the South, the East and the West. Better to fight one's way into its arms than forever to remain outside them.

Some might say that radicals in America were embracing part of the story in order to discredit the rest; that they were trying to drive a wedge between the liberating story of the Declaration of Independence and the Revolution and the repressive story of a Constitution written by the propertied elites. Or perhaps they were attempting to offer an alternative story, in which a "First Constitution" of sectarian federalism and slavery betrayed a nation eventually rescued by a "Second Constitution" of post–Civil War Union and individual liberty. That was certainly how later Progressive historians were to tell it. But when John Brown went looking for legitimacy, he found it in the Preamble to the Constitution as well as in the Declaration. When he offered the people of the United States a "Provisional Constitution," he wrote:

Whereas slavery, throughout its entire existence in the United States, is none other than a most barbarous, unprovoked, and unjustifiable war of one portion of its citizens upon another portion . . . in utter disregard and violation of those eternal and self-evident truths set forth in our Declaration of Independence. [T]herefore we, citizens of the United States, and the oppressed people (deprived of Rights by Justice Taney) . . . do ordain and establish for ourselves the following Provisional Constitution and ordinances, the better to protect our person, property, lives and liberties, and to govern our action.[33]

If the story of America is told as a story of expanding citizenship, then the Civil War and Reconstruction amendments ending slavery and involuntary servitude and guaranteeing universal male suffrage, due process, and the equal protection of the laws to all citizens of the United States were not a reversal of America's constitutional history but its culmination. Justice Roger Taney's pro-slavery decision in *Dred Scott* was, by the same token, the last gasp of those trying to stem the flood tide on which rights were sweeping through history. Taney's problem was how to combat the rights story, whose thrust was emancipatory. He had to show that "We the People," synonymous with "citizens," could somehow be construed to exclude the Negro race. His decision tortuously avoids the entailments of the idea of citizenship and instead turns on the "historical fact" that Negroes "were at that time considered as a subordinate and inferior class of beings." The eighty-year-old Taney takes care to avoid a careful examination of how such crucial terms as "person," "citizen," and "right" worked in the American story. For it was precisely to gainsay this story that he was rather desperately trying to construct a new story of his own—one in which America is comprised of different classes of beings, not all of whom are human and capable of citizenship.[34]

Taney's was a tough assignment. Even at the time of the founding there had been powerful opposition to slavery as an embarrassment to the language of the Declaration and the Constitution's Preamble. John Adams and John Jay were vigorously eloquent in their opposition to it (although not at the Convention), and there were many statesmen who sympathized with George Mason's refusal to sign the Constitution because its twenty-year extension of the slave trade was "disgraceful to mankind."

James Madison had acknowledged the "moral equality of blacks" and in *The Federalist No. 54* had allowed that they did "partake" of qualities belonging to persons as well as to property and were thus protected in "life and limb, against the violence of all others." The slave, Madison said, "is no less evidently regarded by the law as a member of the society, not as part of irrational creation; as a moral person, not as a mere article of property."[35]

To be sure, Madison had also supported the thesis that slaves were property, and when Missouri applied for admission to the Union, he had reconfirmed that view. But rights were seeping into the American mainstream, and Madison was to change his tune; in 1825 he wrote that "the magnitude of this evil among us is so deeply felt, and so universally acknowledged, that no merit could be greater than that of devising a satisfactory remedy for it."[36] Slavery simply did not fit the evolving American story of a nation knit together by common citizenship, a polity in which all could participate and through participation overcome their differences.

WHOSE STORY IS IT, ANYWAY? REPRISE

The concept of the American nation as self-constituted is anything but unproblematic. The story is anything but finished. Just review the history of the South after Reconstruction when the resurgent Democratic party, the Ku Klux Klan, and Jim Crow laws undid many of the gains of the war and the radical Republican Reconstruction; the sad history of restrictive immigration from 1924 to 1965 that gave legislative force to nativist sentiments left over from certain marginal Protestant strands of nineteenth-century Know-Nothingism; and the continuing inability of women and Americans of color to achieve in practice the social and economic standing promised to them in theory by citizenship. Together, these strands of the unfinished tale create a picture of democratic victories far from won. Yet "The New Order of Things" promised by the Great Seal of the United States still offers hope of a community held together by bonds free of the taint of blood and the repressive hierarchy of kinship. For all its contradictions, to many Americans it looks more promising than other forms of national identity.

The twentieth century has exposed how frail the alliance forged by liberals and nationalists after the French Revolution really is, how vulnerable liberty can be to nationalist ardor, how buoyant nationalism feels when undergirded by irrationalism and xenophobia. The Italian nationalist leader Garibaldi and the revolutionary prophets of German nationalism from Johann Fichte and Johann Herder on tried to make an impassioned patriotism the driving engine of cold reason—to give to Enlightenment the impetus of *Gemeinschaft*. The history of Italy and Germany in subsequent times can only disenchant those who believed in the alliance. Resurgent Islam today has pushed aside its own Enlightenment and declared war not just on modernity's obvious vices, such as commerce and materialism, but also on modernity's supposed virtues—freedom, pluralism, and tolerance. In the past year alone we have witnessed once again in Eastern Europe and the ex–Soviet Union how factiousness and ethnic tribalism can decompose artificially held together states when rationalizing ideologies such as communism and common principles such as republicanism are annihilated—just look at "Yugoslavia."

Given this tragic history, moderns will be forgiven for continuing to treat the American hybrid—its multiple hypocrisies notwithstanding—as a last best hope for humankind; for the aspiration to create a nation rooted in the autonomy of politics, in the sovereignty of reason, in the universality of citizenship, and in the capacity of women and men to transform themselves through community life appears to be a rare and precious alternative to state religion and blood nationalim. As Tocqueville was persuaded, religion may be "simply another form of hope." To him, unbelief was always "an accident, and faith ... the only permanent state of mankind." But it is hope rather than religion that we cannot do without, and in the absence of religion, the ideal of a self-constituted nation still offers hope. Its power is found not in its democratic achievements, modest, incomplete, often defective, but in its aspirations. As the extraordinary writer George Steiner has often reminded us with the eloquence of his despair, we dare not live in a dangerous world without skepticism, without a shuddering regard for the intractability of our condition. But it is also true, and it is the lesson taught by America, that we cannot live in the world without hope and its fragile promise of a modest political deliverance from perpetual fear and injustice. If the American story is to mean more than rationalization, if it is to be a tool in teaching liberty, it can mean only this: To be an American is not to have secured equality and justice, but only—with the help of a story of unprecedented aspiration—still to hope and to struggle for them.

CHAPTER 3

LOOSE CANONS

To do battle over the American story is one way of recovering a usable past for Americans seeking to learn the political arts of liberty. The past is present in many other ways too, if not always so visibly. Listening to the media, we might be persuaded that multicultural education, the assault on "objectivity," the debate over political correctness, and the endless peregrinations of critics in search of the truth about truth all converge to introduce an entirely novel set of educational issues into a domain that was previously ruled by complacent consensus.

There is rarely anything new under the sun, however, especially in education. There is only a single perdurable set of educational questions, many of which we have already addressed in confronting what it might mean to be an American. These questions include the relationship of liberty to authority (the place of discipline), the proper balance between traditional canonic knowledge and newer, challenging perspectives, the reconciliation of knowledge as an integrator with the demands of difference and diversity, the possibility of impartiality and objectivity of knowledge in a world where knowers (teachers and scholars) occupy positions of authority and necessarily have subjective interests, and the appropriate place of the school in the larger society it seems both to serve and to challenge (see Chapter 5).

Today's versions of these issues replay debates not just from the sixties, but from the thirties, when Dewey and progressive education advocates initiated a fundamental debate about the role of liberty in learning. Allan Bloom points out that the problems besetting modern universities have their roots in controversies reaching back not just to progressivism, but to Heidegger and Nietzsche, to Reason's Revolution in France in 1789, and to the Enlightenment, whose aims it claimed to embody. Indeed, Bloom is not mistaken in tracing contemporary debates all the way back to the trial of Socrates, when democracy and education first collided in an encounter between elite and mass that has defined the paradoxes faced by public educators ever since. For our purposes here, however, it is primarily the 1960s that are at issue. For Bloom, Roger Kimball, and many other conservative critics, what afflicts our universities in the nineties is a replay of the sixties, grown up, gone to school, and now tenured in the nation's best colleges and universities—which, as a consequence, are now increasingly corrupt.

It was, the critics suggest, the student revolutions of twenty-five years ago that first set the university on its (as seen by the conservatives) calamitous course toward leftist curricula, antiestablishment ideology, and postmodern cynicism about "universal ideals" and "objective truth." This is to put a heavy burden on student "revolutionaries." Still, it is true that while students rarely finish revolutions, they have often started them, lending to rebellion their youth, their education, their optimism, their impertinence, their inexperience, and their foolhardiness. Because the future looms large and the past is but a small space immediately behind them, they have little to lose. They live in a world of artful imagination, free from the onus of reality. "Die Gedanken sind frei!"—Our thoughts are free!—they have gloated in their poetry and their songs. Thoughts are free, but people embedded in practical lives often cannot be. Students, not yet embedded, can define themselves by their thoughts, affording ample room for rebellion.

From the free speech movement at Berkeley to the Columbia occupation, from the free university movement to the Kent State killings, the revolution that was the sixties was above all a student revolution. The civil rights movement, which was born in the fifties and was a source of inspiration for the students of the sixties, was of a different order—not countercultural, but fueled by the churches; not relativistic, but rooted in belief; not "selfish," but motivated by altruism—and certainly was not a creature of students.[1] But by the mid-sixties, the focus was shifting to the them; for the counterculture was a student culture, the war against the war in Vietnam was a student war, the home turf of the rebels was student turf—schools, colleges, universities. The leading organization challenging political and pedagogical authority was run by students devoted to a democratic society (they thought).

As a pamphlet from the era put it, democracy may have been "in the streets," but the streets had names like College Way and University Avenue and were generally filled with students.[2]

Few of the themes that defined the student movement issued in meaningful political change. There were revolutions in civil rights, in poverty policy, in relations between the sexes, and in the struggle to turn Vietnam into a respectable issue for the middle class, all of which had consequences for later decades. But there was little power in flowers and no enduring political legacy for the strictly student segment of the movement, which was unable to rally potential allies in the unions, the racial minorities, and the other constituencies that might have been capable of winning serious victories at the polls.

In the sphere of education, however, the legacy of the students has lasted. In prosecuting the latest crimes of pedagogy gone astray, conservative critics haul out old indictments of sixties' felonies. For example, although *The Closing of the American Mind* capitalizes on the contemporary mood of reaction, it is first of all a book about what happened twenty-five years ago at Cornell, where Allan Bloom, then a young professor of political philosophy, looked on in horror as the real world of race, guns, and power encroached on his intellectual sanctuary. And when William Bennett, as President Reagan's Secretary of Education, shook his fist at Stanford's faculty for (as he conceived it) trashing its own great books curriculum, he was also railing against sixties' cries of "relevance." What Roger Kimball feared was that the revolutionaries of that era had not really vanished but had become teachers, "tenured radicals" whose "object is nothing less than the destruction of the values, methods, and goals of traditional humanistic study."[3]

The generation that challenged the professoriat twenty years ago is today itself the professoriat, or an influential part of it. The long hairs have gone gray and fallen out or been clipped short, but the ideals that once stood them on end continue to infuse sociology lectures on non-Western culture and political science seminars exploring Green politics or revisioned feminist liberation. Marxism has been robbed of its exemplars by the real world failures of collapsed state socialism, but its philosophical advocates remain ardent pedagogues—if not quite the rampaging majority (they are neither a majority nor rampaging!) conjured up by worried neo-cons. Some of the would-be rebels have gone into law or business, where they have been sufficiently constrained by corruptions of a more obvious kind (money and power) to set aside their inconvenient ideals. Others are simply weighted down by the responsibilities of earning a living. Still others struggle to maintain their ideals, but in a predominantly conservative society from which they understandably feel alienated.

Such practical constraints have a lesser effect on those who live and work on the remote periphery where serious American education takes place. Powerless and irrelevant to market America, teachers have had little reason to cultivate conservatism or what passes among conservatives as responsibility. Irresponsibility has always been a duty of the good teacher; that was Socrates' most radical, most truly subversive lesson. For schools to teach only what life teaches—prudence and practicality and limits— would disembowel the future. In the previous chapter, we saw how teaching only utopia and endless possibility eviscerates history and our embeddedness in time; here we need to learn the other half of the lesson: that embeddedness too has its limits and that teaching liberty, to be effective, is necessarily teaching the art of criticism. Education in the first instance is learning history—the story that yields identity; then it must become learning to ask questions—to query identity and its sources, to probe and dissect the story until it can encompass its skeptical challengers.

If education is treated as or reduced to nothing more than giving the right answers—the proper values, the canon, *the* moral Truth—it becomes a kind of indoctrination, what generous social scientists refer to as a form of socialization. It is this model of education as knowing the right answers that leads critics to associate crisis with the vanishing of certainty, and to indict those who question the Big Answers (God, Tradition, Truth, Convention, Morality, Religion) as "corrupters." Messengers like Nietzsche who bring us the bad news about the passing of Absolute Deity are held responsible for the deed and the dead. Teachers who explore with students the hypocrisies of the powerful, who cloak themselves in canonic truth to justify their power, are blamed for undermining the canon. Storytelling becomes myth-making and then dogma, and finally a stale liturgy that does more to embalm than to disclose identity.

Educators know better. It has been the premise of all pedagogy since Socrates that the answer that cannot withstand questioning is not worth much, just as the story that cannot withstand challenge is without value to liberty. Our cognitive discomfort in the face of uncertainty disposes us to impose cloture on criticism and questioning. But the quest for learning that defines the classroom needs to resist "the quest for certainty."[4] The real danger we run today is not the closing of the American mind but the closing of the American mouth. Open mouths, noisy classrooms, impolite questions, impertinent noisiness: these are hallmarks of youthful curiosity and democracy as well. Only when the young are brash, irreverent, and disrespectful of piety (especially when piety is used as a wrapper for power) are the old likely to be honest and tolerant as well as learned and pious. Do we want our students to be True Believers or true questioners? Shall we make piety a home for cognitive arrogance or cognitive humility? For answers alone or also for questions?

It is not that we wish to unsettle truth claims in order to discomfit those who hold them (though there is in the young inevitably some hint of this). It is that the only truth claims we can really have are epistemologically credentialed exclusively by their openness to interrogation. The progress of science rests on doubt not certainty, and the progress of morals must likewise be subject to sharp inquiry. It was the great skeptic and great Christian David Hume who noted that skepticism was the first and crucial step on the road to true belief. To Descartes too, skeptical inquiry had well-grounded convictions as its ultimate aim.

The American story that cannot withstand sharp interrogation is worthless. If we fear that subjecting American ideals to such questioning may undermine them, then these ideals are far too frail. If we believe that querying the legitimacy of some particular appeal to universality (the claim that white male property holders in 1787 embodied "We the People," for example) may erode the very notion of universalism, then we impeach genuine universalism by assuming it cannot be distinguished from its counterfeits. If we think that to expose claims of impartiality to criticism may breed a nihilist relativism, then we end up supporting not impartiality but the hegemony of whichever elite has managed to lay claim to it.

Roger Kimball thinks "politics" has corrupted education. Whose politics? He means radical politics, of course, but in his vocabulary it turns out that the politicizers are those who dare to ask whether the university may not have already been politicized—more subtly, less visibly, to be sure—by the conventional politics of our time. To be apolitical, it is apparently enough for Kimball that one disclaim politics. Anyone professing to see a corrupting political hand at work under the cloak of "impartiality" has not discovered a covert politics but has put it there.

IMPARTIALITY: ROAD TO TRUTH OR CUL-DE-SAC OF HEGEMONY?

From the early nineteenth century, so-called positivists who had founded the new discipline of social science had aspired to a true science of human behavior. It was to be as objective and lawlike as the science of physics. These positivists assumed the essential identity of physical and psychological phenomena and believed that lawlike propositions were as apposite to human beings in motion as to molecules in motion. The "human sciences" lagged behind the natural sciences only because they had gotten under way much later. There was a critical obstacle to the human sciences, however: value. If human social behavior was to be made vulnerable to scientific study, values had to be separated out and isolated, where they could be subjected to objective analysis. Scientists had to rid themselves of values and norms that might identify them with their subjects of study and muddy their impartiality.

By the 1960s, the passion for positivism had come to dominate American social science as practiced in the universities. It was thus that, as with so many other pedagogical controversies, the modern formulation of the question of "impartiality" and "objectivity" in academia first gained currency in that era of excess. Students, by no means all radical, were persuaded that whatever the claims of the "neutral" ivory-tower classroom, its leading positivist positions—value neutrality, impartiality, the separation of facts and values—were spurious. How could anyone believe that universities were wholly neutral venues of abstract learning? How could social scientists separate fact and values when they were themselves necessarily invested in the value outcomes of their supposedly disinterested accounts of political facts? After all, they were engaged in secret research for the Pentagon, they wrote contracts with the U.S. government that proscribed free dissemination of results, they received major funding from corporations interested in profitable research rather than critical education, and they were staffed almost exclusively by white males.

Even in the more pristine colleges, scientists and humanists alike could be shown to possess interests. As sociologists of knowledge such as Thomas Kuhn and Jürgen Habermas had shown, the ideal of scientific or philosophical objectivity simply cannot obtain in its pure form in a world where knowledge is always about (among other things) power, and where truth always reflects (among other things) somebody's interests.[5] If this was true even in the hard sciences, it was true with a vengeance in the social sciences, which explicitly confront questions of value. It certainly seemed that way to students: to isolate knowledge from the status and influence of knowers appeared only to disguise the relationship of cognition to society and hence could end up actually increasing the hold of power over knowledge. The educational authorities that came under attack ended up, not necessarily intentionally, concealing establishment biases under a cloak of neutrality. Claiming objectivity, they heard and saw and spoke no evil; nor for that matter, any good, since value-neutrality proscribed both scorn and praise.

Social scientists deployed a model of inquiry that held the mission of the university to be beyond worldly reproach. That mission called for scientific exploration in a neutral setting of objectivity and impartiality. When protesting students insisted on "revealing" the political commitments in which the supposedly neutral research university was implicated, the university's defenders could only assume the protesters were actually trying to inculcate it with their own. Rather than acknowledging their own biases, these self-righteous defenders attributed all bias to those who raised the issue. Yes, they said, perhaps certain models of society suggested by their paradigms—systems theory, cross-polity survey research, behaviorism, stimulus-response theory, and sociobiology, for example—did produce a picture of government and of human behavior that seemed to legitimize the American status quo; perhaps they left the leading role of white males in it unremarked upon; and perhaps they were averse to political challenge and social change. Yet all of this was no more than an accident, a piece of scientific serendipity. When Gabriel Almond and Sidney Verba published their influential book *Civic Culture* in the mid-1960s, American democracy, measured against a set of "neutral" and "objective" comparative standards, simply turned out to be descriptively superior to the democracy of the other nations in their study.[6] Cynical students might cry "ethnocentrism!" but positivist social scientists were certain that objective science had spoken its neutral verdict.

The students had a point, however. Indeed, as we shall see, it was a point strongly reinforced by conservative critics of positivism, such as Leo Strauss and Herbert Storing. The point was that "objective" social science was sometimes little more than a rationalization of the particular American reality yielded by the complacent fifties. This in turn made plausible the self-congratulatory and static social science paradigms of the sixties. Stability, equilibrium, and passivity were rendered as immutable features of generic social reality. Liberal ruling elites were legitimized as representatives of a universal "We the People." In the late sixties, when these same social scientists bore astonished witness to civil protest, feminist rebellion, racial violence, widespread social unrest, and urban breakdown in their own backyards, their "objective" scientific models could only leave them dumbfounded. The vaunted scientific paragon of American democracy was disintegrating before their eyes, and there was nothing in their science to predict or explain the crisis. It did not take disrespectful students or alienated conservatives to undermine the authority of the social science professoriat in its positivist incarnation: the failure of its paradigms had done that.

Some might say the aggressive political participation and the challenge to authority that came out of the civil rights movement, the peace movement, and the student rebellion actually energized a traditional democracy that had grown passive and complacent. But most social scientists clung to their notion of democracy as the rule of representative elites and regarded the new activism as a threat to both stability and democracy. In a presidential address to the American Political Science Association in the mid-1980s, Professor Samuel Huntington of Harvard University boasted that political science as a discipline has always been on the side of democracy.[7] Along with so many of his colleagues, back in the 1960s and 1970s Huntington was insisting that facts and values had to be sharply segregated and that as a political scientist he could take no position on democracy or its virtues. He nonetheless managed to be critical of participation, persuaded that from the perspective of equilibrium theory, what was called democracy worked best when the public was quiescent.[8] A too-active citizenry, an overmobilized public, and a social movement that insisted on a permanent participatory role in politics could only act to paralyze the political system through a process of what Huntington called "democratic overload."

In the face of such ambivalent and hypocritical testimony, it is understandable how rebellious students might become convinced that conventional political science models of democracy such as Almond's or Huntington's were little more than antidemocratic politics masquerading as neutral social science. Although positivism has long since lost its academic luster, to this day social scientists talk not of democratic politics, but of "elite-mass" politics, and prefer the language of "voters" and "private interests" to the language of "citizens" and "public goods." For them, democratic politics is circumscribed by power, interest, and influence and has little to do with citizenship, civic virtue, and the commonweal. Yet these same scholars continue to assume value neutrality and the objectivity of both social science and the universities where it is practiced.

What rebellious students as well as critics of the university were insisting on in the sixties was that the "objectivity" of the academy and the "impartiality" of the social sciences were sham. The university was no less politically committed than its "politicized" critics, but it was prudently committed, covertly committed, committed to establishment rather than to reformist values and ends. Because they blended in with the backdrop premises of the dominant social order and were not thrown into sharp relief in the manner that challengers' values were, establishment values tended to be invisible. Students had discovered what political theorists on the right as well as the left had been arguing since the early 1950s, when the British historian Alfred Cobban had quipped that "political science" was mainly a device for avoiding politics without achieving science. Neither the university nor the human sciences could possibly be value-neutral, and the pretense that they were would always be hypocrisy of a particularly insidious kind, since it legitimized the established and the powerful while concealing its own connections to power. The university was value-laden. Even the hard sciences were conditioned by "dominant paradigms" and "scientific revolutions" that introduced issues of power into supposedly "neutral inquiry."

For the social disciplines—the human sciences—where the observers were also a part of the landscape being observed, there could be no escaping values, norms, and politics. To be sure, where they were congruent with the larger society, these values and norms were hard to discern. Just as bodies at rest inside a large inertial system which is itself in motion may fancy themselves motionless, so scholars in the mainstream flowing with the epoch's tides could see themselves as at rest: normless, impartial, without an ethical thrust one way or the other, either pro or con. It was necessary to step outside the inertial system, outside the mainstream, to detect the normative movement and political biases of those inside the system. That is just what the students did.

It is also what many conservative critics did. In the sixties they too were complaining about the pretense of scientism and "objectivity" that issued from established social science paradigms, paradigms that conservatives regarded as a highly political version of liberal democracy posing as objective political science. Leo Strauss, the great political philosopher and a mentor and hero to such contemporary conservatives as William Bennett and Allan Bloom, wrote an essay back in 1962 that foreshadowed all the major themes of the leftist sixties' critique of academic positivism and the phony objectivity of centrist political scientists. In it, he said: "The alleged value-free analysis of political phenomena is controlled by an unavowed commitment built into the new political science to [a particular version of] liberal democracy. That version of liberal democracy is not discussed openly and impartially."[9] Of course, back in the sixties, conservatives occupied a different position: a centrist, quasi-liberal establishment was insisting on value neutrality in its argument on behalf of positivistic social science, and conservative critics watching balefully from think tanks on the periphery were alienated and skeptical adversaries of what they regarded as the false neutrality of liberalism and the pretended objectivity of political science.

There have been momentous political changes since then, however, and the students and disciples of Leo Strauss have now become accustomed to occupying powerful positions in the State Department, the National Endowment for the Arts, the National Endowment for the Humanities, and the White House. Allan Bloom's *The Closing of the American Mind* has been a best-seller, and William Kristol (an admirer of Strauss) has been chief of staff for the vice president of the United States, and everyone has been reading Bloom's student, Francis Fukuyama (*The End of History and the Last Man*). Conservatives now stand inside the system and help define it. The cloak of "neutrality" they once exposed as fraudulent is now draped over their own opinions; and while they complain that the academy has been taken over by radicals, they know that most American institutions are in the hands of friends and allies, while the radicals and reformers have been relegated to peripheral think tanks of their own. However, the left, with which they once shared the critique of value neutrality in the university, has had one success: it is now part of the university. It does not run the academy, but it is securely entrenched in it. Thus conservatives now find themselves charging the university with violating a neutrality in which they never believed. They may despise the radical agenda, but they ought to retain a methodological sympathy with the radical willingness to come out from behind the phony neutrality of social science and wage a political fight on behalf of that agenda. In 1962, Strauss concluded the essay cited above by scourging social science for its irrelevance to the real politics of the day. In withering prose, he wrote:

> Only a fool would call the new political science diabolic: it has no attributes peculiar to fallen angels. It is not even Machiavellian, for Machiavelli's teaching was graceful, subtle and colorful. Nor is it Neronian. Nevertheless one may say of it that it fiddles while Rome burns. It is excused by two facts: it does not know that it fiddles, and it does not know that Rome burns.[10]

One need not grasp the full philosophical story to appreciate the ironies of how far the children of Leo Strauss have come. In 1962 they were assailing the bogus neutrality of a centrist liberal academic establishment, calling for relevance, and demanding that political science accept the deeply value-laden character of politics. The left was equally committed to relevance, to a rejection of positivism, and to the need for honest political struggle. Both then and now radicals recognized that Rome was burning. Neither then nor now did they respond by fiddling. This much they shared with their ideological adversaries, and if the adversaries had longer memories they would have to give the devil his due by acknowledging their own kinship with him.

POLITICAL CORRECTNESS

"Political correctness" is a term concocted by conservative critics and media provocateurs to dismiss those who worry about the ways in which speech may reflect power relations. It also serves to divert attention away from the grim racist realities of a society in which minorities are largely powerless, focusing instead on a never-never-land of silly rhetoric in which the powerful white (or male or straight or Christian) majority can pretend it is actually the group in jeopardy. I will be concerned here primarily with speech, and hence will take the critique of P.C. seriously. But upon entering into the world of words, even when they reflect power, it is important to remember how different words are from the elementary and brutal facts of power.

Conservatives fret about the liberties the Yale English Department takes with literature, but they seem not to notice that English departments (like philosophy departments, comparative literature departments, and African-American and Women's Studies departments where the academy's tiny minority of post-modernist, feminist, and nonwhite scholars can mostly be found) are almost always comparatively weak and underfunded as measured, say, by departments of computer science, physics, economics, and business; or that Yale continues to turn out white males (and some females too) who have little trouble adapting to America's elite professions and its familiar cultural biases; or that New Haven has the highest infant mortality rate in the nation and streets on which young black males murder each other regularly, along with an occasional white student at Yale.

Which of these realities is more pertinent to American liberty? Are the excesses of radical Afrocentrism really more dev-

astating to democratic sensibilities than the racist graffiti that continue to decorate collegiate bathrooms? There is a lot of talk
about the new leftist "McCarthyism" manifest in P.C. Who then
are Joe McCarthy's true heirs: the marginalized feminists trying
to "bully" (if that's the word for pushy powerlessness) their way
into a mostly male literary canon and into university faculties in
which tenured women comprise only 5 percent? Or the young
men who persist in raping coeds at a rate that has made many
college and university campuses almost as unsafe as the streets of
America's much-feared inner cities? Metaphors have their political uses: I have heard colleagues decry the "rape of the curriculum" by radical feminists. The metaphor achieves its power,
however, only because the word retains its abhorrent physical
meaning, for women (including thousands of coeds) continue to
be physically violated almost routinely by young men, often fellow students, who still don't seem to grasp what the fuss is about.

One sin does not excuse another, it is perfectly true, and in
a moment I will take up P.C. on its own terms. Yet in a world
of limited resources, limited attention spans, and limited interest
in educational problems of any kind whatsoever, is there not
some virtue in prioritizing the academy's true problems? Heinous
facts speak louder than words, even when politically correct.
Take Olivet College, a small Michigan school founded by the
nineteenth-century abolitionist John Shipard. In the spring of
1992, interracial dating and some minor misunderstandings provoked incidents which quickly turned into racial riots. Two students were hospitalized and all but a handful of Olivet's fifty-five
black students fled the campus, a number vowing never to return.[11] There has been a lot of controversy in the press about
nutty Afrocentric theories postulating sun people and ice people
(see below); will Olivet College's tragedy provoke equal attention?
Have the first amendment rights of its black students been violated?
Will the anti-P.C. watchdog National Association of Scholars
take up their cause? When, one hundred and twenty-five years
after the Civil War and nearly forty years after *Brown* v. *Board*

of Education, America is still (as the title of Andrew Hacker's lugubrious best-seller has it) "two nations, black and white, separate, hostile, unequal," when the white nation continues to put more young men from the black nation in jail than in college and prefers funding labor camps to funding schools for its spiraling population of "delinquents," are we really to take seriously the idea that it is *white* culture and traditional academic freedom that are at risk?

Let us put aside realism for a moment, however, and take the debate about P.C. on its own terms, pretending that the war of words is what really matters. Even here, the anxious critics seem to miss the point. They are content to rest their defense of free speech in the academy on the same wobbly piers that once held up the classical vision of the impartial university and an "objective" social science. Academic free speech is crucial to democratic pedagogy and invites a vigorous defense. But the critique of P.C. is the wrong argument, and can itself have anti-democratic consequences. It casts revisionist radicals who wish to control speech to the advantage of the disempowered as contaminators of neutrality and impartiality. In prescribing one form of speech or proscribing another, the critics argue, ideal liberty inevitably is violated.

There is little doubt that banning certain forms of speech in the name of unprotected progressive political ideals violates principles of academic freedom and liberty of speech. I will suggest below that I think the case for such prohibitions is understandable but weak. However, in grasping the political character of the debate, it is important to notice that P.C. is an invention of the left only in its express and self-consciously acknowledged form. Ideas that are visibly and obviously "politically correct" are simply those that stand out against the background conventions and prejudices built into many university curricula and much of life in and outside the university. Like all insights that have petrified into dogmas, P.C. notions do little to enhance education. But they are not so different from other less obvious dogmas that receive far less attention. The reign of the politically correct began long ago, but in a covert form.

When fraternities, which act as primary residential units for many universities, include and exclude members as they wish, no one labels them champions of the politically correct, but that is, of course, precisely what they are. It is just that the "politics" by which they are made respectable is too mainstream to attract attention. When the story of America is told exclusively as a fairy tale in which liberty is secured in its entirety in 1789 and progress is certain and unwavering thereafter, when colonialism, slavery, and other persecutions are simply read out of history, the alarums on behalf of free speech have too rarely been raised. Dominant stories and conventional paradigms need not be bluntly callow in pressing home their dogmatism: they are the air we breathe. When America unexamined finds its way into the nooks and crannies of liberal arts curricula, few suggest that students are being indoctrinated; but when America hyperexamined makes a small indentation on the heavy boards that bind our standard history books, the hue and cry goes up. When a professor refers over and over again to a collective "we" that is a projection of his own background, race, gender, or when, in alluding to "people," he uses the pronoun "he" in a coeducational class, there is no formal violation of free speech, but there is a shrinking of free discourse, a rhetorical exclusion of women and others from what purports to be a neutral conversation. No one is being formally barred from participation, but some are going to feel alienated to a point where they may spurn it as a foreign conversation that does not belong to them. Although no one is barring them from entry, they will feel excluded from the discourse.

It can hardly be otherwise. Our language is not a neutral medium but the means by which we express our values and interests. It is also the medium through which we try to achieve communication, impartiality, objectivity, even universalism. That is to say, it is the medium in which we attempt to explain our particularism, justify our preferences, ground our values, and en-large (discover common ground for) our interests. As long as we do not confuse the aspiration with the reality, there is no prob-lem. But the actuality is defined by a far richer set of invitations to speech and prohibitions from participation than are given by simple liberal rules of fairness. "Now it is Susie's turn to talk" may seem like fairness, but if Susie has been marginalized by the selective use of pronouns, alienated by aggressive male students permitted to interrupt as a matter of course, and repelled (or perhaps intimidated) by a male teacher who seems to favor (though hardly listen to) the best-looking woman in the room, she may well consider the invitation a threat or a taunt or a joke. She will respond as if the teacher had said, "Let's see if the ugly one can talk."

As with so many other modern pedagogical controversies, the problem here is the lack of balance. Outsiders wanting in are violators of neutrality; insiders protecting their turf are merely waging a struggle on behalf of liberty and objectivity. Finally, I will argue, to silence some kinds of speech to liberate other less vigorous kinds is misguided. The appropriate plea on behalf of the voiceless for an equal voice cannot be *to* silence others; to repress the powerful is not necessarily to empower the weak (which is why revolutions can overthrow tyrants without estab-lishing regimes of liberty). For educators, the choice is never be-tween formal repression and abstract freedom of expression. Every classroom teacher knows that finding a voice for the disem-powered is no easy task. How do you quiet aggressive class talkers (often boys, sometimes not those who are best informed) and create a space for the shy and modest and unself-confident (often girls, sometimes brilliant)? If you shut up the big mouths, you curtail their freedom. But if you let them talk (express themselves "freely") and so let them dominate, you may be curtailing the freedom of the quiet ones. The issue is power. And, once again, neutrality (a "neutral standard," such as "Anyone who raises his hand can speak") can be a screen behind which the powerful have their way. "Let the rich and poor alike be banned from sleeping under bridges" goes the old saw.

If there is genuine neutrality, true equality of speech opportunity where everyone has equal access, then to curtail in the slightest anyone's speech rights is a fundamental violation of the rules of free discourse that define a free society, and even more importantly, a free university. But where is there genuine neutrality in a society riven by differences in power and status? And if apparent neutrality is always belied in the real world by power relations that privilege some speakers before they open their mouths—theirs are the dominant paradigms, they belong to the groups that make the rules, their speech is already part of the background for all speaking, they are privileged by previous education and eloquence—then how can there be genuine equality?

In the absence of a fair playing field, educators may feel impelled to intervene on behalf of the less privileged, to try to handicap the participants accordingly. In my classrooms, I will sometimes ignore the raised hands of "regulars" hoping by enforcing a period of silence to entice less confident speakers into participation. In doing so, I am unquestionably "limiting" the speech of those anxious to talk; they will often complain that I ignore their waving arms and let the class lapse into an extended and embarrassing silence. But I am trying to balance their rights with the rights of others and the pedagogical interests of all. Education requires a genuine dialogue where less popular, less articulate, less self-confident opinions also get heard. This may in turn require my intervention in ways that impeach the integrity of some abstract idea of neutrality.

In short, although it is always fraught with danger, there is in the impulse to constrain who speaks and how much, to constrain what is said and by whom, a pedagogically respectable will to liberation. The aim is to enhance free speech by enlarging its compass and guaranteeing its diversity. Teaching liberty always involves the use of pedagogical authority, and authority always limits immediate freedom in the name of its long-term interests.

A person who cannot or will not see the difference between authority and repression ought not to be teaching, for she will think her only choices are tyranny or anarchy. Whereas the crucial issue actually is whether limits (on speakers or on forms of speech) ultimately constrain or enhance free discourse. It is hard for me to imagine how racial epithets might contribute to a free discourse, although it is not impossible, under rather special conditions, that permitting the angry expression of deeply held prejudices might open the way to more honest debate.

What is amiss with radical critics of conventional academic freedom here is not their wish to equalize speech opportunities or to rectify the kinds of inequalities built into speech situations by traditional power arrangements and historically unjust precedents. Rather, it is their remedies that often are wanting. You do not improve the educational climate for challenging bigotry or respond to those it injures by suspending or expelling violators (assuming no crime has been committed), for they are precisely those most in need of education. When bigotry appears in the classroom, the issues are pedagogical, not legal, and remedies must be instructive rather than punitive. Schools are neither courtrooms nor prisons where the guilty are prosecuted and punished. They are workshops for overcoming prejudice; we would scarcely need them if they enrolled only the tolerant and the just. If the arts of liberty are acquired, we must assume that those who first enter the classroom are without them. Impatient progressive pedagogues would seem to want students to be at the outset what pedagogy must over time make them.

Schoolroom speech is artificial speech whose ultimate goal is moral growth and the development of autonomous, empathetic, critical human beings capable of genuinely free speech in a world of power into which they will eventually be delivered—ready or not. No educator can afford to forget that in John Stuart Mill's great essay *On Liberty*, liberty is treated as a means to the end of moral growth and political liberation, rather than as an end in itself. The frontispiece of his book, taken from the German philosopher William von Humboldt, reads: "The grand leading principle towards which every argument unfolded in these pages directly converges is the absolute and essential importance of human development in its richest diversity." True liberals in John Stuart Mill's sense court freedom because it is married to moral worth, autonomous citizenship, and diversity. They have, quite properly, been convinced by history and experience that free speech is the only climate in which human beings can grow to their full moral maturity—the concomitant of the exercise of freedom—but the pursuit of freedom is for them always constrained by its ultimate aims, which lie beyond liberty and encompass pluralism and moral worth. A true pluralism sometimes calls for a balancing of individual speech interests. Just as the U.S. government may curtail the freedom of broadcasters by prohibiting them from owning print media in the name of encouraging a plurality of voices, teachers may curtail the freedom of some students and some forms of speech in the name of encouraging classroom fairness and a true diversity of opinions.

The professor cited earlier who believes that "he" is a perfectly legitimate universal pronoun that implicitly stands for every he and she in the classroom invites an argument, not a punishment. To remove him from a curriculum committee or vilify him as a gender bigot is as absurd as trying to strip tenure from a famous African-American because he blames the "Jews of Hollywood" for the ills of a racist nation or foolishly impugns the integrity and assails the artistic freedom of a filmmaker trying to retell the life of Malcolm X.[12] Gibberish, even when insidious (some would say, particularly when insidious), needs to be challenged by reasoned argument and common sense rather than quarantined by censure or silenced by censorship—at least as long as the issues pretend to be of concern to pedagogy (something in which neither the defenders nor the critics of political correctness seem very interested).

Teachers will themselves constantly face the question of how to maximize free discourse while maintaining access to it for every student. They will make countless small pedagogical decisions in the day-to-day course of teaching, that, willy-nilly, constrain some and liberate others. A comfortable environment for slow learners in an algebra class is not necessarily fostered by calling on the math whiz in the front row every time he puts up his hand (which is most of the time). Educational strategies addressing these issues ought to be developed out of the political limelight.

After all, many large lecture courses leave no room for discussion by anyone other than the lecturer, and issues of balance never even arise. Is the lecturer a suppressor of free speech? She certainly is. Give her smaller classes and she may be able to liberate her students. Yet even then she surely will want to spend considerable time presenting new material, offering insights, and guiding her students. Careful, cautious teachers worrying only about student "sensitivities" will end up spending more time trying to avoid giving offense than teaching, and are unlikely to be riveting or memorable educators. The issue is not whether someone is offended. With good teaching, as with good art, someone is always offended: the point is precisely to provoke, offend, and spur to critical thinking. If the exchange "That's bullshit, honkie!" followed by "Don't 'honkie' me, nigger!" leads to a spirited and honest debate about the difference between descriptive and derogatory language and puts issues of prejudice on the table, a prudent teacher may permit it, if not promote it, although she'd better be a pretty experienced educator. The bold teacher may even encourage it at a moment that seems either very safe or so unsafe that there is nothing to lose. If it promotes a mini-multicultural race riot (as seems likely) and leads to rage and vitriol only, if it silences speakers—above all, if it silences those the not-so-neutral speech arena already disadvantages—then it needs to be curtailed, not by throwing the abusers out of class, but by exercising the authority of the teacher. Perhaps this can be done by initiating a discussion about why an exchange has been terminated or certain forms of speech temporarily proscribed, or perhaps by simply silencing some or all speakers, without an explanation (using up a small portion of the teacher's legitimacy and stock of goodwill). Perhaps, over time, this can be done by reflecting on the relationship between racial epithets and power: Are French Jews assembled for deportation to Auschwitz who cry "Sales Boches!" (dirty Krauts) at their Nazi tormentors morally equivalent to their persecuting keepers who call them dirty Jews in return? Are "honkie" and "nigger" equivalents in a culture that has known hundreds of years of slavery and racial oppression and where "nigger" was sometimes mere prelude to a lynching? Slanders are freighted with histories and sometimes their "offensiveness" must also be measured by their context and their possible consequences.

As every good teacher knows, there is no hard-and-fast rule. Today's prudent prohibition may become tomorrow's useful provocation; today's rule, tomorrow's exception. A teacher may ban all discussion of race for a month precisely in order to talk about the meaning of the ban the following month. A professor may carry on about how silly and counterproductive ethnic "sensitivity" is in a classroom, until his own ethnicity is offended and he becomes an instant convert to political correctness. Another instructor may insist on "she" as a generic pronoun in place of "he." She may even write "s/he" on the blackboard and ask her students to do the same in an assignment in order to alert slumbering consciousness to the power of the written word. Or she may look for other ways to teach lessons of gender discrimination and rely on "he" as the generic, because using "she" as I am doing in this paragraph seems misleading. Does the instructor really mean "she," the feminine pronoun? Or is her use of "she" a consciousness-raising lesson in generic pronouns? Or is she a stickler for style who simply finds the generic "she" awkward and clumsy?

The homeroom teacher in Riceville, Iowa, who, the day after Martin Luther King, Jr., was murdered, scandalized America in employing "he" with an extraordinary pedagogical experiment, is my model of a teacher concerned with teaching rather than with making political points, correct or otherwise. In a power-fully simple exercise intended to reveal the dynamics of discrim-ination to a third-grade class deeply disturbed by King's death, Jane Elliot divided the group into blue- and brown-eyed, then imposed a series of arbitrary and oppressive rules enforcing the domination of one group over the other.[13] It was risky business, as she recognized it could have gone badly amiss. Elliot made it succeed, however, and was able to confront monocultural rural white kids with a visceral sense of the meaning of prejudice. Could she have initiated her experiment in today's charged atmosphere? Would representatives of the blue-eyed have assailed the brown-eyedism at work in her classroom, which, precisely because it was pretend, was all the more offensive?

There are two crucial points. One is that the relationship between authority and liberty in the classroom should be the subject of pedagogical decisions made by teachers in the class-room, not the consequence of political decisions made by admin-istrators, politicians, or student advocacy groups in the halls outside, interested less in education than in political propriety. Nor is it an arena for legal decisions resting on rights.

"Leave teachers alone!" and "Let teachers teach!" should be the mottoes of those who care about education. We must concern ourselves with teacher training, with common standards, and with adequate mechanisms of oversight and accountability, but other-wise we have to let teachers teach and try as best they can to find ways to further the moral development of their students as poten-tially (but not yet actually) free human beings. We cannot rule out by fiat forms of speech some may find offensive, nor can we ban the use of rules in limiting speech. Free speech will flourish only as it is informed and nourished by the authority of the teacher, and that authority will always set limits to classroom speech.

The second point concerns standards. "Leave teachers alone" is always qualified by the necessity of enforcing common stan-dards for a genuinely public education. "Public" means common standards, if it means anything at all. To the degree public education mandates uniform guidelines on speech in the nation's classrooms, they should be rooted in the principle that any curtailment of speech (including those shadowy restrictions introduced covertly by conventional power arrangements) benefits equality and the moral growth toward freedom of all students. This may be seen as a pedagogical expression of the principle the philosopher John Rawls called justice as fairness. It requires that such inequalities of speech as may be called for by prudence or pedagogy be to the advantage of those whose speech is most disadvantaged at the outset. If there cannot be perfect and genuine equality of speech (there rarely can be), then the inequality should benefit those least equal in their potential for expression. If there cannot be equal access to speech, access should be skewed to benefit those with no access. In practice, this means that if someone is to be given greater opportunity for speech, it should be the modest, the shy, the educationally disadvantaged or disempowered, those for whom the language of the classroom is a second language, those excluded from discourse by lack of access, by uncertainty about speech rules, or by other kinds of alienation from and lack of access to paradigmatic conversation. By the same rule, if someone's speech is to be curtailed in the name of prudent time management or equal opportunity for all, it should be the discourse of the eloquent, the powerful, the advantaged, those whose natural speech skills and opportunities are ample and whose need for specially contrived educational opportunities is minimal.

I have yet to enter a classroom in which women are as aggressively expressive as men. Consequently, I have little difficulty with rules that encourage more speech by women students, even at the cost of ignoring the garrulous males who rarely stop talking. This entails a degree of censorship, but it meets the Rawlsian standard. By the same token, if women became more aggressive than men, I would constrain their speech.

These two rules offer simple and sound ways of responding to the problem of academic balance and neutrality. Balance means equilibrium over time in the larger political and historical context in which the academy finds itself. Neutrality means impartiality with respect to well-established conventional power paradigms, including those embodied in educational institutions themselves, as well as challenges to the paradigms. Both principles are in accord with the experience of the rebels and reformers of the sixties. They saw how hard it was to disguise their own radical challenges to the establishment as "scientific" or value-neutral because these challenges showed up in sharp relief to the general background of established values. They also saw how easy it was for the values of those in power to vanish into the background that produced them, allowing their advocates to assume a counterfeit neutrality. Such values seem neutral only because they are invisible—black cows grazing in a black forest in the middle of the night who moo complacently, "There are no cows anywhere to be seen!"

The missing term in most recent arguments on behalf of neutrality, impartiality, and balance is power. As we noted in our discussion of racial epithets, power skews theoretical neutrality and unbalances apparently symmetrical relationships. There is no symmetry between the homeless vagrant who shuns the rich and the rich pedestrian who shuns the homeless. The repellent slogans "Off the pigs!" and "Kill the niggers!" are equally appalling expressions of hatred and intolerance, but while the antiestablishment rhetoric reflects a desperate escalation by the powerless, the establishment's own resort to polemic is a quite deadly reflection of actual kill ratios in most of the race riots that have occurred in real American cities in real American history, most recently in Los Angeles, where over 80 percent of the casualties were nonwhite. In the classroom, this means that a teacher cannot necessarily treat as equals powerful and embedded systems of thought and radical challenges to them. For example, the story of the American Frontier seen from the Sioux perspective may get a little extra help from the teacher who is satisfied that students are already sufficiently familiar with more conventional perspectives.

This is the fundamental insight of all those on the so-called politically correct and multicultural left who refuse to believe that formal equality and procedural fairness can ever offer them complete substantive equality or actual fairness. They do not want to *be* politically correct, but they *do* want to correct the political imbalance of supposedly neutral curricula. They see curricula shot through with pretended generics and putative universals that turn out to contain the writings of European and Anglo-American men. These men have written extraordinary literature that has often taken them beyond their skins and gender into a domain that belongs to all of us. To escape from particularism is no less the artists' gift than to disclose particularism. Still, they are men and they are white and they belong to a group that has exercised dominion. And when nonwhite or nonmale artists who share their gift but cannot share their power find themselves in competition in universities and at publishers', it is not just a competition of gifts. That is why affirmative action, Rawlsian principles of fairness, and other not quite "neutral" rules have to be invoked. The aim of introducing gender or racial categories into curricular discussions and the aim of challenging formal rules of equality and universalism need not be to fragment and subjectify knowledge or deny the possibility of a true universal in theory. Nor does it have to reduce artists to crass representations of the backgrounds by which they have been constituted. Such reductive strategies, I will argue presently, are as deadly to pedagogical reform as they are to sound pedagogical tradition. The aim, rather, is to show that supposedly objective knowledge is already subjectified and fragmented in covert ways, to disclose how skewed putative universals already are in practice, to expose the threadbare character of strategies of formal equality. Properly used, these challenges can actually help establish a genuine universalism and a truly transcendent culture by exposing those who, by wielding power, counterfeit the genuine article.

A thoughtful teacher under assault from cultural conservatives for teaching women's studies or third world literature might then be forgiven for concluding that behind the concern to protect Western culture from modernity's ravages is a certain sense of cultural anxiety, posing as cultural monism, cultural superiority, even cultural imperialism. Dominant cultural paradigms have always sought the legitimacy of Truth or History or Tradition to protect themselves against fresh voices, even when those voices came from within the tradition. The so-called Western canon is itself a battlefield: alienated challengers and rebellious outsiders like Machiavelli, Rousseau, and Nietzsche banged up against conventional paradigms in their own time with as much noise and discomfort as feminists collide with today's established conventions. The young political theorist David Steiner has aptly described the canon as a dialogue that permits its own renegotiation, and John Evan Seery observed after teaching in the controversial (and now defunct) Stanford great books course that while he started as a skeptic, he soon realized that "the 'Western tradition' consists not of a protracted pack of high-minded cultural elites (or those in effect promoting elitism) but rather encompasses an extraordinary series of cultural subversives, one right after the other, with Socrates and Jesus as the two most famous."[14]

For all the agitation, the canon and its detractors are not so far apart. For one thing, the canon produced its own detractors. For another, its modern critics are not drawn from new immigrants to America (most of whom, assimilation-minded, have little sympathy for multiculturalism) but come from within traditional educated elites, from degree earners at our "best" universities. Unsurprisingly, many of them teach at the very universities they assail and are hired to give legitimacy to the "dominant paradigms" they affect to delegitimize. The competition among a handful of Ivy League schools for the still fewer African-American notables who can legitimize multiculturalism so that these elite institutions can pretend they have somehow slipped the ties that bind them to America's centers of power is almost comical.

There are in turn few critics of the canon who do not recognize their debt to it and who will not acknowledge its continuing importance as a cultural anchor for American education. Above all, those who teach find themselves swimming wearily but also stubbornly between the two ideological currents that constantly threaten to pull them against the rocks on one side or the other of the channel. Education for liberty lends itself neither to fixed canons nor to no canons at all. It flourishes with active students, bold teachers, and loose canons. This was not just a dream of sixties' radicals: it is or ought to be the mature wish of teachers in every era. Even ours.

CHAPTER 4

RADICAL EXCESSES AND POST-MODERNISM

Countercultural radicals who have been critics of conventional canons understand the university and its needs better than do guardians of the cultural tradition. Nonetheless, as I have suggested, although they are hardly likely to boast about it, conservatives share certain elements of the radical critique, having once been allies in the criticism of social science positivism and academic neutrality.[1] Today, though they have resumed their posture as outraged adversaries of educational progressivism, conservatives continue to pose important questions for it.

Unlike established liberals, and like anyone who operates from the periphery (as they once did), conservatives retain a certain sensitivity to issues of power. They rarely pretend it does not exist or that life and thought can be shaped without reference to it. They also tend to understand the ways in which values penetrate and mingle with "empirical" reality, and transform the historian's record into a story and the social theorist's positivist science into an art. Moreover, they can be wise students of community and they know that societies—above all, free societies—

are held together by fragile bonds that need constant nurturing. Democracy depends on a capacity to ask questions and on the faculty for independent thought and action, but democratic communities can be corroded by unending skepticism and undermined by forms of independence that recognize no mutuality. Having given the radical critique of the sixties its due in the previous chapter, in this one I mean to offer a skeptical review of skepticism and to give difference an unpleasantly different perspective on itself.

Traditional orthodoxies have too often been replaced with new counterorthodoxies, no less noxious for being novel, no less inimical to democracy for being offered on behalf of the powerless. Orthodoxy cannot be fought with counterorthodoxy. The challenge is to overcome not to replace dogma, and this requires a critical spirit. I have argued that too many critics of political correctness have drawn a phony picture of neutrality that is oblivious to the realities of power in the modern school and university—particularly when seen from the perspective of the powerless. But pedagogical radicals at times outcaricature their critics and have themselves been oblivious to several of the most insidious modern sophistries, including a species of reductionism that lurks in their own "deconstruction" of traditional academic rationality. They have sometimes aceeded to the temptation to intimidate, to suppress, and to silence not merely the powerful without but the doubtful within. They have been quick to assert as dogma convictions they do not wish to see subjected to critical questioning. And they have all too easily confounded their psychic longing for values with an actual argument on behalf of values.[2]

Powerlessness is a justification for rebellion, but it is not a license for mindlessness. The reality of being without a voice can become part of a good argument, but it is not the same thing as a good argument; it certainly does not exempt the powerless and the voiceless from the obligation to offer good reasons. Indeed, this is precisely why there is both a need and a right to be heard—a right secured only through an education in liberty. This right, however, is not necessarily the same thing as the right to stop others from talking or the right to cease listening. Reason can be a smoke screen for interest, but the argument that it is a smoke screen itself depends on reason—or we are caught up in an endless regression in which each argument exposing the dependency of someone else's argument on arbitrariness and self-interest is in turn shown to be self-interested and arbitrary.

Let us consider the principal sins of the present generation of progressive educators justifiably concerned with the future of democracy—sins more of exaggeration than of attitude. Some of the problem is plain old silliness: the utterly serious and therefore utterly comical insistence on certain campuses that "seminars" be called "ovulars" or the caricatured transformation of Christopher Columbus from a silent movie saint into a silent movie villain, to be known henceforth exclusively as a torturer, plunderer, and proto-imperialist. The instinct of the sympathetic moderate here can only be to cry, "Whoa! Slow down!" In traversing the terra infirma of modern education, I have expressed a cautious solidarity with the progressives who have devoted themselves to institutionalizing in the schools the 1960s' critique of establishment education of the 1990s. Yet by trying to negotiate several sharp curves at too great a velocity, some seem in recent years to have skidded off the tracks. In their understandable haste to arrive at more democratic schools, their grasp on the meaning of democracy has sometimes looked shaky. In their devotion to a public education that can encompass a new and radically heterogenous American public, their feel for the public character of public education has been weakened. Impatience has prompted them to travel at reckless speeds; and so, at what we might fancifully call the curve of critical doubt, they have plunged into a gorge of hyperskepticism, where every argument turns relentlessly on itself and where the demand to ground values reasonably becomes a relativization of all values. At the sharp turn of difference, they have fallen into the ravine of hyperpluralism, where overdifferentiation destroys the possibility of integration and community.

I want to examine here these two perils of the current reform movement. Doubt is a powerful vehicle of learning, but moving at too high a speed can also undermine the process. Diversity is a condition of freedom for all, but when it runs off the rails it can rob the "all" of common identity and ultimately destroy the liberty of individuals.

HYPERSKEPTICISM: PRUDENT DOUBT OR FATAL NIHILISM?

All thoughtful inquiry, and hence all useful education, starts with questioning. All usable knowledge, and thus all practical science, starts with the provisional acceptance of answers. Education is a dialectic in moderation in which probing and accepting, questioning and answering, must achieve a delicate balance. Stories must be told, queried, retold, revised, questioned, and retold still again—much as the American story has been. In periods of rebellion, academic no less than social, when challenging authority means questioning answers, there is an understandable tendency toward skepticism, even cynicism. Michael Wood has characterized Jacques Derrida's approach to method as "a patient and intelligent suspicion,"[3] which is a useful description of one moment in a student's democratic education.

The methodologies deployed by critics of power and convention in the academy do not always find the dialectical center, however, and are subject to distortion by hyperbole. Sometimes they seem to call for all questions and no answers, all doubt and no provisional resting places. This radicalism has many virtues as scholarship, but as pedagogy far fewer. In its postmodern phase, where the merely modern is equated with something vaguely reactionary and post-modernism means a radical battering down of all certainty, this hyperskeptical pedagogy can become self-defeating.

Skepticism is an essential but slippery and thus dangerously problematic teaching tool. It demystifies and decodes; it denies absolutes; it cuts through rationalization and hypocrisy. Yet it is a whirling blade, an obdurate reaper hard to switch off at will. It is not particularly discriminating. It doesn't necessarily understand the difference between rationalization and reason, since its effectiveness depends precisely on conflating them. It can lead to a refusal to judge or to take responsibility or to impose norms on conduct. If, as Derrida has insisted, "the concept of making a charge itself belongs to the structure of phallogocentrism" (the use of reason and language as forms of macho domination), there can be no responsibility, no autonomy, no morals, no freedom.[4] Like a born killer who may be a hero in wartime but, unable to discriminate between war and peace, becomes a homocidal maniac when the war ends for everyone else, radical skepticism lacks a sense of time and place, a sense of elementary propriety.

The questions this poses for pedagogy are drawn in the recondite language of literary postmodernism and deconstruction, but are of the first importance for education. Does the art of criticism doom the object of critical attention to displacement by the self-absorbed critic? In other words, does criticizing books replace reading them? Can the art of questioning be made self-limiting, or do critics always become skeptics? Are skeptics in turn doomed by their negative logic to be relativists? Must relativists melt down into nihilists? Conservatives have worried that this particularly slippery slope cannot be safely traversed at all, and thus have worried about a pedagogy that relies on a too-critical mode of radical questioning. They prefer to think of education as instilling the right values and teaching authoritative bodies of knowledge to compliant students for whom learning is primarily a matter of absorbing information. When these conservatives appeal to the ancients, it is the rationalist Plato to whom they turn, rather than the subversive Socrates.

Yet pedagogical progressives actually confirm the conservatives' fears when they themselves tumble happily down the slope, greasing it as they go with an epistemology that denies the possibility of any stopping place, any objectivity, any rationality, any criterion of reasonableness or universalism whatsoever. Asked to choose between dogma and nihilism, between affirming hegemonic authority and denying all authority, including the authority of reason, of science, and of open debate, what choice does the concerned teacher have but despair? Where she seeks a middling position, she is offered orthodoxy or nihilism. Where she seeks moderation in her students—a respect for rationality but an unwillingness to confound it with or measure it by somebody's power, or eloquence, or status—she is informed that all appeals to rationality are pretense: Bertrand Russell's no less than Joseph Goebbels's, Hannah Arendt's no less than Catherine the Great's, the rationality with which the skeptic skewers conventional reason no less than the rationality the skeptic skewers.

In quite a different context, it has been said that the one thing you cannot do with bayonets is sit on them. Critics of established paradigms have lunged at their adversaries with bayonets, piercing their hypocrisies. But they have been unable to sit on them, let alone build new alternative structures on them. There is little new or surprising in skepticism's consuming appetite. Cynicism has been a tendency of philosophy from the start, and its inclination to move from intelligent suspicion to wholesale paranoia is well documented. In *The Republic* Socrates had to contend with Thrasymachus, who saw behind every claim on behalf of truth or justice a sneaky rationalization of somebody's stealthily concealed interest. Socrates showed that Thrasymachus started with a prudent if furtive suspicion but ended as a moral bankrupt, a sellout to the brute argument of force, unable to defend any notion of virtue or justice. For many of the same reasons, the Sophists of ancient Athens who followed Thrasymachus were understood to be tireless interrogators who could ask, "Yes, but why?" until people with beliefs dropped of exhaustion or surrendered, running out of reasonable "becauses" long before their tormentors ran out of probing "whys."

From their earliest encounters with belief (the claims of subjectivity), knowledge (the claims of intersubjectivity), and truth (the claims of objectivity), pedagogy and scholarship have tried to balance the need to ask questions with the need to offer well-grounded if tentative answers. Since an answer is at least a provisional suspension of questioning, it interrupts the critical process and also suspends the critical element in learning. But unless questioning stops and is at some point provisionally satisfied, there is no knowledge worth the name—neither subjective beliefs, intersubjective values, nor objective truths (however small the t in truth).

The pedagogy of questioning naturally and properly takes the standpoint of suspicion. It looks behind appearances and beneath surfaces, and thus has a penchant for reductionism: turning the immediate into the mediated, turning the observed into the intuited, turning apparent universals into actual particulars, turning putative reasons into sham rationalizations, turning claims to truth into rationalizations of interest—looking always for a concealed reality behind *prima facie* events. A Freudian may thus perceive in a seemingly rational wish a sign of some repressed and irrational fear arising out of a still more deeply seated neurosis. Similarly, a classical Marxist may read into an apparently universal value system the class interests of a group in control of a society's mode of economic production. To reductionists, things are never quite what they seem. Suspicious of truth as an external "empirical" thing or an inherently meaningful text or an uncontested object, they reduce such entities to the conditions (psychological, historical, material) by which they are produced and the interests of those who produce them.

The author of a book, argues Foucault, a reductionist here who sees behind the smoke screen of "reason" a hundred hidden varieties of coercion, is not some vessel of art or creative genius but merely "an ideological product."[5] A book is less a work of literature imbued with truth and beauty or with standards to which human conduct might be made to conform (the old-fashioned view) than a product of its readers or its critics; an emanation of the class, gender, and status of the background that produced the writer or his audience. As David Hume, skeptic and critic of objectivist ethics, said long before deconstruction seized on such arguments, a value is not a symbol for some objective right or eternal good, it is merely a token of someone's preference. To say "It is good" is merely a disguised way of saying "I like it." And whereas (when we allow that objective standards exist) we can presumably assess and argue rationally about human conduct, preferences are purely subjective, and all we can say about them is that at most they exist. The assertion "Cruelty is good" takes a form inviting debate and argument, and may elicit the counterassertion "No, it is evil," which can in turn be debated in historical, moral, and philosophical terms. On the other hand, the descriptive sentence "Cruelty feels good to me" cannot be contested at all other than in terms of its descriptive accuracy ("Does it *really* feel good to you?"). To someone who says "I like being cruel," neither "No, you don't" nor "But cruelty is evil" is an appropriate response. The reductive language of what philosophers call "noncognitivism" makes ethics radically subjective, and it soon vanishes as a subject of moral discourse. Thus, in Jacques Derrida's understanding, the very idea of judging someone else, of "making a charge," becomes incoherent and absurd.[6]

Reducing supposed objective goods to subjective preferences and reducing claims about truth to statements about power and interest are two related forms of a very ancient and very useful but also very risky skepticism. For millennia, both skepticism and reductionism lived as parasites off the host philosophy—which, fortunately, had its own affirmative business to attend to (understanding human conduct in an often unintelligible cosmos). In the last hundred years or so, these two have more or less consumed the philosophical tradition that sustained them. The same thing has happened in literature, as the critic came first to deny the meaning of literature, then to displace it with the activities of the critics. Criticism is now seemingly severed from literature in many universities, leading an independent existence as literary theory in English departments that teach not literature and the art of reading, but theory and the art of criticism. Social scientists and humanists in many other departments, especially those understandably dissatisfied with traditional academe and its spurious appeals to neutrality and universalism, are taking their cue from literary theorists and deploying reductive post-modern critiques against the establishment. This has certain virtues as a tactic but ultimately is poor strategy and bad pedagogy.

Well before literary theory did away with literature, Marxism was disposing of legitimacy in politics and Freudianism was dismissing rationality in behavior in an attempt to obliterate the object in favor of the historically or psychologically embedded subject.[7] Crudely put, Marxism saw in traditional philosophy an instrument for rationalizing the interests of the ruling classes and in radical philosophy as it might become an implement by which the world could be transformed. Up until now, proclaimed the *Eleventh Thesis on Feuerbach*, philosophy has only interpreted the world. The point, however, is to change it. From the standpoint of this historicist form of reductionism, behind every claim to truth lay an economic or material interest; reason was a candy coating on power's bitter pill.

Freudianism (if not necessarily Freud) could be equally reductionist, but looked inward to the *psyche* (Greek for "soul") rather than outward to the material forces of history. It too denied reason any office other than that of rationalizer (and sublimater) of desire and other still deeper psychic drives that lay concealed in the id. More recently, French radical critics such as Foucault and Lacan have combined these reductionisms to expose not reason's abuses, but reason itself as hypocritical: a powerful but hidden coercer. Reason, once celebrated as the torch that illuminated and bequeathed freedom to an otherwise dark and inchoate world, now itself becomes a force of darkness and hegemony. It appears as an instrument of the powerful by which their hegemony over the world is secured through psychic and social manipulation—disguised as liberty. The target of the new criticism is no longer reason's hypocrisies but reason itself. It could once be said that hypocrisy was the tribute vice paid to virtue: by affecting the virtues it despised, vice acknowledged their suasive force. But the radical reductionist, seeing *all* virtue as hypocrisy, no longer retains a standard for virtue and paradoxically is no longer in a position to talk about hypocrisy. Where all reality is counterfeit, the very idea of the counterfeit loses its resonance.[8]

This cursory history of esoteric arguments about the nature of knowledge may seem far removed from the educational controversies of our time. It is offered only as a reminder that such fashionable new forms of radical criticism as deconstruction are but echoes of a very ancient skepticism and a very well entrenched tradition of reductionism. It is for this reason that Allan Bloom pins the blame for the changes in modern education on Heidegger, Nietzsche, Marx, and other maverick critics of reason and reason's canon (see Chapter 5). It is for this same reason that conservatives who esteem the role reason plays in grounding and justifying fundamental values view post-modern skepticism with alarm, and that liberals who care about reform worry that reductive strategies are ill-suited to their purposes. As Edmund Burke once noted, those who destroy everything are certain to remedy some grievance. The annihilation of all values will undoubtedly rid us of hypocritical ones or the ones misused by hypocrites. We can prevent the powerful from using reason to conceal their hegemony by burning the cloak—extirpating reason from political and moral discourse. However, those who come after can hardly complain that they feel naked or that their discourse, absent such terms as reason, legitimacy, and justice, seems incapable of establishing an affirmative pedagogy or a just politics.

Just how crucially such seemingly abstruse issues impact on actual college curricula is unpleasantly evident in this approving portrait of literature and culture in a recent issue of the *Bulletin of the American Association of University Professors*:

> Cultural studies moves away from "history of ideas" to a contested history of struggles for power and authority, to complicated relations between "center" and "margin," between dominant and minority positions. Literature is no longer investigated primarily as the masterworks of individual genius, but as a way of designating specialized practices of reading and writing and cultural production. . . . The renaming of "literature" as "culture" is thus not just a shift in vocabulary. It marks a rethinking of what is experienced as cultural materials . . . [including] media, MTV, popular culture, newspapers, magazines, advertising, textbooks, and advice materials. But the shift also marks the movement away from the study of an "object" to the study of a practice, the practice called "literary study" or "artistic production," the practice of criticism.[9]

How slippery this particular slope has become! What begins as a sound attempt to show that art is produced by real men and women with agendas and interests attached to things like their gender, race, and economic status ends as the nihilistic denial of art as object. What begins as a pedagogically useful questioning of the power implications of truth ends as the cynical subverting of the very possibility of truth. What begins as a prudent unwillingness to accept at face value "objective" knowledge, which is understood to be, at least in part, socially constructed, ends as the absurd insistence that knowledge is exclusively social and can be reduced entirely to the power of those who produce it. What begins as an educationally provocative inquiry into the origins of literature in the practice of literary production ends in the educationally insidious annihilation of literature and its replacement by criticism—the practice, it turns out ever so conveniently, of those asking the questions! Thus does the whirling blade of skepticism's latest reductive manifestations, post-modernism and deconstruction, cut and cut and go on cutting until there is nothing left. Thus does the amiable and pedagogically essential art of criticism somehow pass into carnage.

As epistemology, this is what post-moderns would, in their inimitable jargon, call logocidal—deadly to reason and discourse. As pedagogy it is suicidal, above all to those already deprived of power and voice by the social forms and educational strategies supposedly being deconstructed. It is hard to tell what service a teacher does a ninth grader just learning to read books when she informs him that there is no difference between Emily Dickinson and MTV, both being simply cultural products of interested artisans pushing their particular ideological interests.[10] To make his point about the relativism of cultural values, Houston A. Baker, the current president of the Modern Language Association, tells us there is no more difference between high culture and pop culture than between a hoagie and a pizza. What he means is that there is no more difference between Shakespeare and Virginia Woolf than between Virginia Woolf and a pepperoni slice with extra cheese. This is to say, as John Stuart Mill quipped about Jeremy Bentham's reductionist utilitarianism, that there is no difference between pushpin and poetry.

These are more than theoretical points: Rutgers has offered social science courses not only on film but on MTV, and Duke University teaches Louis L'Amour alongside Shakespeare and George Eliot, not because popular writing deserves a place in the curriculum along with high culture (it does), but in the belief that the distinction between pop and high culture is spurious, an invention of elites trying to maintain their cultural hegemony. Yet without the aspiration to excellence, however contested the end products, "culture" loses its normative and directing power and becomes a cipher; no distinctions can be made between the "culture of pinball machines," "the drug culture," and "skinhead culture," on the one hand, and "Italian Renaissance culture," "the culture of Benin civilization," and "Harlem Renaissance culture," on the other. It is one thing to claim that Eurocentric curricula sometimes are conceived as if culture were an invention and exclusive possession of one particularly powerful colonizing civilization; it is quite another to argue that any collection of social artifacts is a "culture" so that "the culture of gangs," "Nazi culture," and "the culture of wolves" become acceptable usages.

Like all fundamental political and social terms, culture is inherently and necessarily normative. That is why we argue about it, why it is contested. That is what makes multiculturalism worth debating. To annul the power of the word "culture" as a standard of human organization, aesthetic and intellectual evolution, and general excellence does nothing to enhance cultural pluralism or learning in the name of liberty and respect. On the contrary, it creates the impression that there are no standards of excellence whatsoever other than the bogus claims advanced by elites.

The confusion of multiculturalists on this question is evident in their ambivalence over whether to take some significant credit for Western civilization by showing its roots in Egyptian and African sources (thereby paying tribute to its many achievements), as does Martin Bernal in *Black Athena*, or to reject it altogether in favor of a radical "Afrocentric" view that celebrates Africa and subjects Western culture to a not so benign neglect, as scholars like Molefi Asante have done.[11] If Western culture manifests certain virtues, if culture implies standards (however contested) and is more than just a collection of artifacts, then the sources of "Western" civilization are worth fighting over. If not, why bother contest their origins at all?

Sometimes multiculturalists want it both ways, sounding a little like the storied defense attorney who, without taking a breath, managed to argue, "My client is innocent, your honor; he never took the jewels, and besides, he didn't know they belonged to anyone, and anyway they were fake." With the same all-encompassing logic, the Afrocentric multiculturalist at times seems to say, "Western civilization is worthless, dangerous, a colonizing imperium with pretended virtues it never lives up to; and besides, it was originally *OUR* creation, a product of an Egypt we can prove was Black, and anyway Black Africa had a great culture of its own, which we can see reflected in the values of so-called Western civilization *IT* actually produced." Critics have suggested that Afrocentrists are not really multiculturalists at all, but monocultural zealots of a civilization other than Europe's. Perhaps a response in keeping with the moderation offered earlier would be to see Afrocentrism as a stage on the way to a more genuine multiculturalism, itself a stage on the way to appreciating America as a culture defined precisely by its diversity and multiculturalism. This eliminates the harsh attack on Western culture, which is of more use to conservative critics looking to dismiss multiculturalism than to multicultured educators.

Conservatives (who surely have to be congratulating themselves privately on their good fortune in being tossed so splendid a provocation!) have repeatedly expressed their horror over the Stanford march led by the Reverend Jesse Jackson not so long ago in which students protesting traditional curricula chanted, "Hey, hey, ho, ho, Western Culture has got to go!" (although it was the course labeled as such rather than the generic entity they were protesting). As new expressions of anti-Western monocultural intolerance, such slogans are reprehensible. But they are also implicit in the reductionist perspective, which denies "culture" any status other than that of "ideological product." By transforming normative truths subject to rational debate that are embodied in the books, conventions, and institutions that constitute a civilization into an unwholesome product of vested interests, the skeptic undermines not civilization but civility, not rationalization but reason, not dogma but the possibility of consensus and thus community. Along the way, in impugning the inherent authority of the idea of culture, he also manages to impugn the

authority of the non-Western civilizations to which his multiculturalism supposedly pays homage.

Questioning should challenge objectivity but also be capable
of redeeming it. Criticism finds its pedagogical legitimacy in its
powers of redemption: the power to save virtue from hypocrisy,
truth from its counterfeits, reason from rationalization. Anything
else pushes skepticism over the brink and gives to subjectivism
the aspect of narcissism. In philosophy, this narcissism is called
solipsism, a term suggesting a self so absorbed in the mysteries of
its capacity to sense and make sense (or nonsense) of the world
that it ceases to perceive anything but itself. This is a matter of
the eye being distracted from the object to which the finger points
to the finger itself, until the whole world resembles nothing so
much as a finger.

Hyperskepticism is philosophically problematic. But, more
importantly, it is politically and pedagogically disastrous. In destroying all authority, legitimate as well as illegitimate, hyperskepticism leaves room only for brute force. It offers its argument
as if acknowledging that the inexorability of force in human affairs were somehow to contain and control it, but in reality the
acknowledgment acts to legitimize it. Similarly, in denying the
possibility of any legitimate concept of rationality, it invites irrationality to mediate human discourse. We must affirm, says
Derrida, "a world of signs without fault, without truth, and without origin."[12] But in reason's absence—when ideas are only signs
and reason is always construed as a product of interest—interest
becomes reason's only arbiter.

In his splendid deconstruction of the deconstructionists, David Lehman leaves readers asking this provocative question: What
is the connection between the political celebration of power that
is Nazism, and the philosophical demolition of reason that is
deconstructionism?[13] Although they approach from opposite directions, do not both approaches arrive at the irreducibility of
brute force as the ultimate guide for human affairs? Was Paul de

Man's youthful flirtation with the Nazis and his subsequent concealment of that past a contingent indiscretion or an exemplar of the deconstructionist theories of which he later became a champion? Others have put similar questions to Heidegger's radical critique of rationality, which has played a seminal role in postmodernism's development: Was it his dismantling of reason that afforded Heidegger the psychic space to accommodate Nazism—which, at least for a while, he did with zest?[14]

There can be no simple answer to such complex psychopolitical questions, and I certainly do not mean to challenge philosophical reductionism by psychoanalyzing philosophers and thereby replacing one reductive logic with another. Nonetheless, as already suggested, Thrasymachus understood the connection between his brand of reductive questioning and brute power perfectly well: his was the cynicism of the power realist who wanted to convince Socrates' audience that power was all there was. He wished not to legitimize and thus limit power, but to enthrone and sacralize it. This is clearly not the goal of the far more naive advocates of the new hyperskepticism. They are genuine reformers struggling against the dogmas of what they see as a hypocritical establishment. They seek more equality, more justice, better education for all. They want not just to expose the hypocrisies of power, but to tame and equalize it. They want to reclaim true justice from its hypocritical abusers. They chase shadows in the valley of cynicism but trust they are on the path that leads to redemption.

Yet the instruments of revolution they have chosen are more suited to the philosophical terrorist than the pedagogical reformer. Radical skepticism, reductionism, solipsism, nihilism, subjectivism, and cynicism will not help American women gain a stronger voice in the classroom; will not lift Americans of color from the prison of ignorance and despair to which centuries of oppression, broken families, and ghettoized schools have relegated them; will not provide a firm value foundation for the young in equality, citizenship, and justice. How can such reformers think they will empower the voiceless by proving that voice is always a function of power? How can they believe the ignorant will be rescued from illiteracy by showing that literacy is an arbitrary form of cultural imperialism? How do they think the struggle for equality and justice can be waged with an epistemology that denies standing to reasons and normative rational terms such as justice and equality?

The great tradition of philosophy rightly being subjected to stern interrogation, when responding at its best to that interrogation, establishes a middle ground. It holds both True Belief (dogmatism) and unexamined opinion (prejudice) in suspicion, but it knows it must find a provisional resting point for knowledge and conduct somewhere in between these two unacceptable extremes. Somewhere on the prudent road away from orthodoxy and cant it needs to stop, lest it slip down the steep embankment of nihilism. At the bottom of that embankment lie brute force and arbitrary power—the very demons wise critical philosophy is trying to escape in abandoning unquestioned orthodoxy! As always, they stand ready to take the place of deposed reason. The ideal of reason has always been part of the human strategy for climbing down from the clouds of certain Truth to which only gods have access, and at the same time out of the pit of brute force, which is the no-truth of beasts. Reason has found many incarnations: logos, the word, discourse, civility, logic, reason, conversation, even democratic politics (which has talking—*parler*, as in "parliament"—at its core). And reason has been frequently and mightily abused by hypocrites and interest groups in search of rationalizations for their selfishness. Like so many of our most resonant ideas, reason has always been more of an aspiration than a reality, more of a destination than a resting place. As embodied in human thought and conduct, it has often been contaminated by its origins in the pit of those using it. Yet it remains the tool of choice not just for those with interests to defend, but for those with ideals to advance. Indeed, while interest will exploit reason where it can, it is perfectly content to secure its aims with force.

The ideal, however, can be secured only by reason, itself an ideal. The powerful toy with reason, the powerless need it, for by definition it is their only weapon.

Just as the American story recounted in Chapter 2 is an ideal that can teach us how to live in accord with our noblest ambitions and liberate ourselves from the abuses of our actual history, so reason is an ideal that can teach us how to live in comity and free ourselves from the incivility that always attends reason's failure. When reason is polluted by interest and power, the remedy is not to jettison but to cleanse it. The remedy for hypocrisy is not less but more reason. Rationalization is evidence of reason abused, not proof that there is no reason. The object of questioning is to test and strengthen rather than to annihilate the idea of the rational.

Education is a training in the middle way between the dogmatic belief in absolutes and the cynical negation of all belief. On the fringes where dogma or nihilism prevail, force is always master. Well-taught students learn to suspect every claim to truth and then to redeem truth provisionally by its capacity to withstand pointed questioning. They learn that somewhere between Absolute Certainty and Permanent Doubt there is a point of balance that permits knowledge to be provisionally accepted and applied (science, modestly understood, for example) and allows conduct to be provisionally evaluated in a fashion that makes ethics, community, and democracy possible. There is much illusion in this fragile middle ground. Civilization, Yeats reminded us, is tied together by a hoop of illusion. It would be dangerous to pretend that the illusion is real, but it is fatal to dispense with it altogether. Justice and democracy are the illusions that permit us to live in comity. Truth and knowledge are the illusions that permit us to live commodiously. Art and literature are the illusions that make commodious living worthwhile. Deconstruction may rid us of all our illusions and thus seem a clever way to think, but it is no way at all to live.

The educator's art is to prompt questions that expose our

illusions and at the same time to tether illusion to provisional moorings. The teacher must know how to arouse but also how to mollify the faculty of doubt. Her special art is moderation. She will question whether the statements "This is good! This is beautiful! This is justice!" mean something more than "I control the discourse! I define art! I am justice." But her aim will be to distinguish the counterfeit from the real rather than to expunge the very ideas of the good, the beautiful, and the right. There are illusions and there are illusions. "We the People" as a description of a slave-holding society is an illusion that needs to be exposed; "We the People" as an aspiration that permitted, even encouraged, the eventual abolition of slavery is an illusion worth keeping, even worth fighting for, along with such illusions as natural right and human reason on which the concept relies. The ability to discern the difference between these two forms of illusion is what good education teaches. Such judgment can come neither from inculcating fixed canons nor from deconstructing all canons.

The educator cannot teach when offered only the choice between dogma and nothingness; between orthodoxy and meaninglessness; between someone's covert value hegemony and the relativism of all values. The first business of educational reformers in schools and universities—multiculturalists, feminists, progressives—ought to be to sever their alliance with esoteric post-modernism; with literary metatheory (theory about theory); with fun-loving, self-annihilating hyperskepticism. As pedagogy these intellectual practices court catastrophe. They proffer to desperate travelers trying to find their way between Scylla and Charybdis a clever little volume on Zeno's paradoxes. They give to people whose very lives depend on the right choices a lesson in the impossibility of judgment. They tell emerging citizens looking to legitimize their preferences for democracy that there is no intellectually respectable way to ground political legitimacy.

OVERDIFFERENTIATION AND HYPERPLURALISM

Just as skepticism has been too much of a good thing for American educational reformers, so has the sometimes obsessive focus on difference: in pursuit of a wieldy multiculturalism, there have been excesses that can be called overdifferentiation and hyperpluralism. Achieving the fine balance required to preserve a union rooted in difference has always presented a formidable dilemma. To unify a culture that comprises many cultures is a task at which neither politicians nor educators in the United States have been consistently successful. The challenge facing modern proponents of a just and inclusive America remains how to hold the elephantine conglomeration together without surrendering the diversity of groups and liberty of individuals that define it. An underdifferentiated America pretends to a unity that actually excludes many groups from participation; an overdifferentiated America falls to pieces, sacrificing what it means to be an American to a passion for inclusiveness.

Traditional societies generally were more uniform and homogenous to start with and were bound together by traditional ties: common traditions, national customs, a single tongue, above all a common and unifying religion. America has never been a traditional society and must do without the comfort of such bonds. As described in Chapter 2, it was created from the jetsam of many nations, a self-consciously new society that urged immigrants to forget their pasts and create a new and common future.

The world has long since been disenchanted (Max Weber's term), and even were America to be less sectarian and confessionally splintered than it is, Christianity no longer has the power to hold even Christians together—if they speak different tongues, come in different colors, or belong to different classes. Forty years ago, when William Buckley, Jr., wrote a startling book about the demise of man's relationship to God in the setting of Yale's liberal pedagogy, he was only confirming Alexis de Tocqueville's worst fears about the effects of secularization on America's sense of community.[15] Buckley wrote well before the muckraking students of the sixties had begun probing the liberal consensus and the limits of authority; but the subtitle of his book was "Superstitions of Academic Freedom" and included a section called "The Hoax of Academic Freedom," in which Buckley assailed the "neutral" pretentions of the university in the same critical language used by later countercultural critics. "I believe it to be an indisputable fact that most colleges and universities, and certainly Yale," Buckley wrote, "do not practice, cannot practice, and cannot even believe what they say about education and academic freedom. I am not saying they do not utilize the rationale of academic freedom to obtain license when and where they desire it."[16] Part of Buckley's case against academic freedom was that it undermined social cohesion and opened America to the disintegral forces of atheistic communism (this was the 1950s!). More than a century earlier, after a visit to these shores, Tocqueville had warned that a society predicated on liberty and equality, more than any other, required an unusually strong glue to hold itself together: "How is it possible," asked Tocqueville, "that society should escape destruction if the moral tie is not strengthened in proportion as the political tie is relaxed?"[17] Traditional societies were held together naturally and needed little artificial help; despotic nations possessed powerful political bonds and required less in the way of conventional ties. But artificial societies governed by weak, liberty-granting governments needed all the help they could get from moral and religious institutions.

Our schools today can aspire to provide artificial civic and cultural bonds, but they cannot revive natural ones. Living in a disenchanted world without Sunday schools to inculcate religious community or Monday schools to teach us the meaning of civic community, we risk disintegration. No catechism or canon can fix that. Reaching nostalgically back into time for some mythic village community that may or may not have existed will do nothing to repair our unraveling society. Tocqueville knew that.

He feared the loss of cohesion that emancipation brought in its train, but unlike the modern conservatives he understood that the process was inevitable. He knew that creeping moral anarchy could not be avoided in a society organized around freedom. He worried that the emerging egalitarianism of America's vibrant local democracy could nourish envy, conformity, and a fatal leveling, but he also realized that equality was the currency by which the Americans had purchased their freedom and was understandably of great value to them.[18]

Modern conservatives share Tocqueville's fears but have neither his dialectical hopefulness (grasping the rose that springs from within the cross) nor the realism that permitted him to recognize the ineluctability of the modern age—even in its more noxious manifestations. Where Tocqueville saw in "the gradual development of the principle of equality . . . a Providential Act,"[19] Bloom, Bennett, and company are moved by anxiety, sometimes, it almost seems, by terror, and rush forward to reclaim a vanished past. Where Tocqueville called for "a new science of politics" to fit the "new world" of democracy, they urge curricula modeled on a golden age (an age that never actually existed, since the "great books" of the eighteenth and nineteenth centuries were not necessarily ours), then scapegoat teachers for having *created* the brave new world teachers are trying (in the spirit of Tocqueville) to help students learn to challenge, to overcome, or, when necessary, to inhabit.

We live today in Tocqueville's vast new world of contractual associations—both political and economic—in which people interact as private persons linked only by contract and mutual self-interest; a world of diverse groups struggling for separate identities through which they might count for something politically in the national community. This is a poor social mortar at best, and the fragmentation of free societies increasingly looks like an inevitable by-product of their fractious liberties and resolute individualism. Or, to turn the problem around as Dewey did, with the welcome growth of diversity and difference come new problems of grounding social cooperation: "How are we going to make the most of the new values we set on variety, difference, and individuality," asks Dewey, "how are we going to realize their possibilities in every field, and at the same time not sacrifice that plurality to the cooperation we need so much? How can we bring things together as we must without losing sight of plurality?"[20] Arthur Schlesinger, Jr., asks pretty much the same question in his new polemic *The Disuniting of America*, where he challenges radical advocates of ethnic and racial and gender difference to show how, when they finish turning America into a "quarrelsome splatter of enclaves" with their "cult of ethnicity" and their "Europhobic" reforms, there will be a nation called America left standing.[21] Nor is it only critics of the new multicultural agenda who make this point. Catherine R. Stimpson, a fair-minded advocate of curricular change, recognizes in conservative responses the presence of "a profound moral and political question: What are the commonalities that a multicultural society must have if it is to be a society?"[22]

By the 1960s, Tocqueville's concerns and Buckley's anxiety began to look prophetic. Pluralism's liberties were on a runaway course. Radicals exalted in the very tendencies that conservatives associated with a society undergoing decomposition. From the radical perspective, to disenchant the world was not to steal its romance or loosen its religious underpinnings, but to expose its elites and demystify the theological and political rhetoric once used to justify an invisible hegemony. What students of Tocqueville regarded as a betrayal of the idea of an integral national community held together by constitutional ideals, educational progressives regarded as a welcome new stress on diversity, difference, and pluralism. The traditional emphasis on the whole had only monumentalized WASP phallocentric culture and marginalized everyone else. To focus on difference and to celebrate multiculturalism was to liberate the oppressed from silence and to move them from the periphery into the vital center where monolithic elites had for so long enjoyed a monopoly.

The story we rehearsed in Chapter 2 was a story of unity from diversity (*E pluribus unum*), of a nation held together by common ideals and republican principles even where elites had wanted to use those ideals to exclude others. It was a story whose multiple metaphors each suggested ways the parts come together to constitute a whole: separate pieces patched together into a quilt, distinctive colors arranged in a luminous rainbow, individual tiles set into a mosaic, different identities melted together in a common pot, unique threads woven into a single cloth. Even in its early years of Anglo domination, America was by the standards of Europe exceedingly diversified. There were thus reasons beyond the self-interest of elites to seek sources of unity in institutions and rhetoric—in republican principles and democratic practices—reasons that seemed eminently sensible for a society likely to feel burdened rather than liberated by its diversity and likely to be fractured rather than united by its pluralism.

Today's radicals continue to see the American story as one of actual exclusion as well as aspiring inclusion. This critique, which offers an accurate enough account, does not, however, solve the problem of a heterogenous society's need for integration. Certainly critics can demonstrate that excluding people who are different is not an acceptable remedy to liberty's disintegral tendencies. Historically, the attempt to maintain unity by preserving "purity" legitimized injustice and slavery, and in time led to a fracturing of the Union that precipitated a bloody civil war. The war reunited but hardly unified the nation.

In 1855 and again in 1865, the United States was not so different from Yugoslavia in 1991 before it disintegrated, its parts being forcefully held together by military might in the name of a universal citizenship that to many Americans was an excuse for the oppression of one part of the nation by another. The experience of Yugoslavia suggests how fragile such legal and political ties can be in the face of a heritage rooted in distinctive ethnic identities.

Oddly, it is today's progressives who take the position of the

Old South following the Civil War, seeing in the idea of national union and a national community an excuse for the dominion of some over the rest. Radical differences have been papered over by a (to radicals) specious unity—distinctive cultures buried by a hypocritical call to universalism that, they believe, can only be a cover for well-entrenched ruling groups. This angry and scornful version of the American story depicts the fragments and shards not as vital pieces, which are made whole through integration into the larger community, but as distinctive entities that can best be made whole by being spun off and treated independently: thus the specter of secession again haunts America. The aim is no longer to rescue integration; it is to delegitimize it altogether. It is to dignify the parts apart from the whole; to speak not of gay Americans and African-Americans and Italian-Americans and Hispanic-Americans in terms of the common "American" suffix they all share, but only of gays, of Afrocentrism, of Latino culture, of Catholics or Women or physically challenged (a.k.a. handicapped) or Jews as radically distinctive, sharing so little that they may not be capable of comprehending one another at all. Thus, Jews may think Gentiles cannot understand the Holocaust, African-Americans that whites cannot direct films on black subjects, Asian-Americans that no Occidental actor can believably portray an Asian character.[23]

From this narrowing perspective, difference becomes the sole insignia of identity and the common story of America vanishes into a plethora of particular tales of particular peoples with particular histories, genders, colors, or sexual orientations. Teaching becomes a matter of pedagogical narrowcasting: each group gets its own texts, its own stories, its own subject matter. Outsiders are not invited to participate since they cannot possibly be expected to understand. In confronting the European discovery and early settlement of America, African-Americans learn about slavery, Hispanic-Americans about glorious empires, Native Americans about colonialism and plunder, native South Americans about European-caused plagues and the annihilation of a civilization, Anglo-Americans about how other Europeans beat them to it, and Italian-Americans alone about Christopher Columbus.[24] Common ground ceases to exist; without common ground there can be no common teaching. And without common teaching, there is no American story and so no America, only the pieces. How exactly democracy is supposed to survive in such a setting is not altogether clear.

These excesses are what have led Tocqueville's critics among the conservatives such as Peter Berger, Michael Novak, and Richard John Neuhaus to argue that hyperdifferentiation threatens attachments to nation (patriotism), to God (religion), to family (marriage), and to children (motherhood). Because these attachments have already been severely eroded by the historical forces of secularization, commercialization, disenchantment, and radical individualism, they are especially vulnerable to those versions of multiculturalism that are committed to what we might call hyperpluralism. By creating a mood of interior skepticism toward the nation's own history, and an attitude of uncritical fascination with alternative cultures and values, hyperpluralism has left the generation that will inherit the American Union awash in diversity, cultural relativity, and corrosive self-doubt and with little sense of a common community or, indeed, of the value of or even the need for a common community. Made over into a curriculum, this penchant for overdifferentiation destroys the civic mission of the nation's schools and universities and deprives students of safe, ethical moorings in a threatening and chaotic world where others may have far less scruple about the value of their norms and the power of their patriotism. Inviting the young to take seriously the culture of poverty, the culture of women, the culture of the third world, has led them to ignore, neglect, even to derogate the culture of Americans—presumably the culture to which all might aspire in the ideal, since the ideal (if not the practice) is precisely aimed at rooting out discrimination and oppression based on such differences.

These hyperpluralist excesses carry the more obsessed among

its champions out of the circle of moderation. The lack of balance is striking. Evan Carton, in his contribution to a symposium on "The P.C. Struggle" in the liberal Jewish monthly *Tikkun*, is unyielding in his insistence on "the primacy of social relations over individual autonomy"; he is certain that "knowledge and the organization of knowledge are products and instruments of power."[25] Not "sometimes." Not "under some circumstances." Not "in part." There is no dialectic, no acknowledgment that if knowledge is implicated in power, it may also constrain power; that if the American story has given aid and comfort to the American establishment, it has also been a consolation and a source of legitimation for those who challenge it; that if the story has sometimes kept the revolutionaries out, it has also kindled the revolution; that if diversity is to serve its constituents, it must be a way station to tolerance, mutual respect, and free community, as well as a value to be cherished in its own right.

In the late 1980s, the California school system adopted a new "framework" for social studies and history curricula that, compared with the framework it replaced, was genuinely multicultural. Textbooks that meet the new standards have been adopted in over half of California's schools.[26] But in cities with large minority enrollments, there has been an ongoing battle over adoption in which students and classrooms seem forgotten, and rhetorical excess prevails. The liberal historian Gary Nash, who is responsible for one of the new textbook series, is flabbergasted by the protests: "I had never heard of the Bantu migration and the rise of the Zimbabwe state when I got my Ph.D. at Princeton. We have 80 pages on African history for 12-year olds ... [yet the critics] ... continue to say this is a Eurocentric series." Apparently to blame is the new framework's persistence in talking about American commonalities—such as democracy.[27] Once again, the goodwilled teacher is left hanging between desperately polarized ideological alternatives: teach your students English only, Western Civ only; teach them that the English story of America must be their story too—whatever their ethnic origin, race, or gender; or teach them that all integrating stories are bogus and that difference is essence, diversity is all, and honorable values are whatever values *your* people (as defined exclusively by difference) have. In the fall of 1991, the children of the Oakland Unified School District, representing a 91 percent minority enrollment, found themselves with no social studies textbooks at all, because adults continued to wrangle over the abstract principles of an appropriate curriculum.

Is there no middle ground? Must we define the alternatives in so skewed and skeptical a fashion? The critics of integration and common community read the numbers and the numbers are incontrovertible: In an America that is more and more nonwhite, demographics must necessarily become the engine of pedagogy. After all, how much learning can possibly go on among Americans who are cast as "different" and then taught stereotypical stories about American sameness that pointedly exclude them? We encounter the numbers here over and and over again. Sometime toward the middle of the next century America will become predominantly nonwhite. The University of California system already is. Many inner-city schools have been for decades. Yet the demographics of increasing diversity cannot resolve the dilemma; as the Oakland Unified Schools show, the problem is only magnified. The figures point to the need to educate with a sensitivity to difference *and* to the need to educate to overcome difference. How about a middle way? Can differences be celebrated without precluding union? Is a national community possible that encompasses diversity? Hasn't that always been the dream?

MODERATING EXCESS: DEVELOPMENTAL PEDAGOGY AND MULTICULTURALISM

There are two moderating strategies that help mediate difference and unity and thus build a bridge between multiculturalism and monoculturalism. The first strategy rests on the pervasively developmental character of education and moral growth and results in a focus on differences now that acts to secure unity later. The second focuses on the roots of multiculturalism in a particular monocultural tradition and reminds us that the virtues of pluralism, tolerance for difference, and respect for diversity are themselves the product of a particular culture that—if we wish to teach either multiculturalism or liberty—we must continue to impart. Both strategies enjoin flexibility and warn against neat ideologically correct solutions, whether radical or conservative.

The developmental perspective is crucial to education because it softens tough binary choices enjoining A-alone or B-alone and suggests instead a first-A-then-B (or first-B-then-A) approach that recognizes the changing needs of different stages of growth. Most teachers know that the road to liberty passes through a wood of rigid structure and imposing authority; for freedom is tested and nurtured by a confrontation with limits, and liberty emerges only out of a willed casting off of constraints. We were never so free, said Jean-Paul Sartre in a conundrum that will puzzle only those who misunderstand liberty, we were never so free as during the German Occupation. Similarly, the road to responsibility winds its way through and out of a forest of constraint. We learn that responsibility is a condition of freedom by experiencing the seductions of servitude—where others rule, I have no obligations. Pursuing the same logic, we realize that spontaneity may issue from a long acquaintance with discipline. Because its subjects are human beings who grow, evolve, and change, education necessarily invokes strategies that are deeply developmental. In their apprenticeships, the grand artists like Picasso and the paradigm-smashers like Max Ernst first mastered the genres whose boundaries they eventually exploded. A mastery of technique—the discipline of rules—is the instrument of liberation in life as well as in the arts.

When teaching the uses of difference, a developmental strategy may be employed to emphasize separate and distinct identities in order to afford minorities sufficient self-confidence to become participants in a community that takes them beyond their separateness. An emphasis on difference may be an essential step on the road to self-respect and thus to overcoming discrimination based on difference. First the many and only then, the one. I criticized Asante earlier for believing it was a sufficient justification for Afrocentrism to say that it helped preserve African-American sanity. But as a developmental strategy rather than as a self-sufficient argument, it is perfectly reasonable to say that African-Americans, having inherited the legacy of centuries of oppression and facing racism today, will never be full participants in the great American community until they are fully free; that to be free they must first treat one another with respect; and that respect is possible only in a climate of sanity missing in many inner-city ghettos. If Afrocentrism reinforces sanity, dignity, and self-respect, it becomes liberty's ally and in time contributes to the fashioning of a stronger national community. Henry Louis Gates, Jr., the W. E. B. Du Bois Professor of Humanities at Harvard, makes the case for developmental strategy this way: "It is only when we're free to explore the complexities of our hyphenated culture that we can discover what a genuinely common American culture might actually look like."[28]

Much the same applies to the cultivation of a native language in classrooms where English is the only permissible—and, ideally, preferable—common tongue. Teaching children to learn means teaching them language and literature—not just language skills, but a love for language. It may be that the only way Hispanic-American children are going to become learners of liberty and citizenship is for them first to learn in their own native language and about their own native language. In time they will have to learn English, but first they must learn to learn.

This is anything but a rule, however. Developmental strategies vary; they are experimental and evolving. Gender-blind curricula that work for third graders may fail for preadolescent seventh graders for whom gender has become a highly personal matter, and then may work again in graduate school where students are already well aware of the impact of gender issues and need not be reminded of it every time they confront a canonical writer like Milton or Shakespeare or Woolf. College-level creative writing assignments that encourage improvisation and stream of consciousness will seem foolish, even dangerous, in a junior high school English class where the essentials of grammar and composition need to be established. African history may be pedagogically useful in instilling a sense of identity and pride in African-American youngsters, involving them in history as a serious discipline; it may also serve the quite different purpose of extending ethnic horizons for white youngsters, suggesting different teaching strategies. Moreover, African history may make sense only if it is preceded or followed by courses in European history and culture (not just European colonial history), just as canonical Western civilization courses may make sense only when they are set in a comparative framework. Martin Bernal's extraordinary argument using literary, archeological, linguistic, and historical sources to make a case for the influence of an at least partially black-African Egyptian culture on the classical Greek roots of Western civilization will be meaningful only to those who emulate Bernal and study classical Greece itself, the nineteenth-century German interpretation of Greek civilization, and classical Middle Eastern and African civilization.[29]

Multicultural literary criticism requires genuinely multicultural reading habits. Chinua Achebe's perspective-wrenching essay on Joseph Conrad's *Heart of Darkness* is provoking only if we have already read, appreciated, and perhaps lionized Conrad's book. Here the canonical work must be taught before it can be challenged; and, by challenging it and not some other work, the challenger reinforces the target's place in the canon.[30] Achebe himself must in turn be challenged by bold teaching so that the dogmas of classical English literature are not simply replaced by novel dogmas of reductive ethnicity. In a course of mine where both works were taught, some students reacted with a callow self-indictment along confessional lines: "When I first read Conrad, I thought it was really a great book, but now that I've read Achebe I realize it is just a Eurocentric racist tract." Education must be consistently rather than selectively subversive: "Ah yes, there is more to Conrad than meets the eye; Achebe reveals how an English author reads from the perspective of one of his subjects who is not of his own race or culture. But, ah yes, Achebe himself represents only one standpoint, and there is more to Achebe than meets the eye! He too has an agenda!" Conrad cannot be dismissed as an artist simply because, from Achebe's standpoint, he is also a racist, for every culture has its biases and to reduce literatures to biases ultimately requires that we deny literary significance to all literatures everywhere. The mind is meant to expand in a series of ever-larger concentric circles, taking in new perspectives to supplement and clarify the meaning of earlier ones. It is not a binary switch that must be in an A or a B position, on or off, Conrad or Achebe, English or African, dead white male or quickening Afrocentric female. Multiculturalism as method can actually lead to transcultural standards and thus back to a convincing universalism. Beyond the biases and limits of singular cultures lies a territory of commonality where root meanings of the idea of "civilization" can be found.

In John Singleton's film *Boyz N the Hood* (1991), an earnest white teacher is seen lecturing sixth graders in an L.A. ghetto school on the subject of holiday menus. As she goes on about Pilgrims and turkeys and the spirit of charity, her class wriggles and frets and yawns and giggles. I can imagine first graders and college sophomores alike responding the same way to such hopelessly well-intentioned efforts to inculcate the canon of a Western civilization that, on its surface, has no resonance for many children. For reasons to be explored, I believe that the old Western canon should be taught, but it probably cannot be taught effectively until students are provoked to caring. And that will not happen unless there is a hook. At some moment later in the educational process, the sources of Thanksgiving in Pilgrim ceremonies that were at once paternalistic and generous, manipulative and ingenuous, tokens of colonial commerce yet also tokens of the Christian impulse to brotherhood, can be the subject of a lesson. But only after stories are told that strike closer to home, only when a link is established to the neighborhood (the "hood" in the film's title) from which the kids come. When Singleton's young hero tries to inspire the kids his teacher couldn't reach by offering them his own rap on Africa, they remain just as placid and cynical. For them, Africa isn't yet the "hood" either. Where is the hook to snatch these potential young dropouts from their indifference, anger, and despair? That is the crucial question for a developmental pedagogy.

In a country where young black males are being decimated and conventional pedagogies are proving useless, why not experiment? In educational arenas where children are being abandoned as if brain-dead (which they soon become), why not look to developmental strategies? Even if they contradict some ultimate goal of education or contravene some respectable rule of procedure, they may initiate or aid a process that will eventually serve both our goals and our rules. Separate schools for young black boys? An alternative monoculturalism on the model of aggressive Afrocentrism? Military-style academies to raise "wilding" young men up to civility? Even an emphatic and polemical method that may distort history as it is taught in graduate school in the name of instilling pride, curiosity, self-respect, and an interest in learning among kids who normally don't finish junior high? Semi-mythologized tales of George Washington's cherry tree epiphany and Abe Lincoln's boyhood cabin life were offered for a very long time as "hooks" to teach the young ethics and patriotism. No one thought graduate history seminars would replicate these myths, but they had a useful place in the developmental curriculum. I regard the strategies suggested here as not only permissible but laudable—just as long as they are understood to be elements in a developmental and experimental pedagogy that, in time, moves beyond or to more sophisticated and inclusive perspectives.

Conservatives fear that teaching multiculturalism breeds relativism and then cynicism. But seen dialectically, the lesson of other cultures or of voiceless subcultures within a dominant culture need not do so. The knee-jerk nativist reaction to Margaret Mead's style of anthropology (if we acknowledge that *they* practice polygamy without falling into villainy, *our* devotion to monogamy will be undermined!) is silly. Acknowledging that there is more than one form of "the Truth" does not necessarily entail the demise of all truth. That prudence is contextual or that practice takes different forms in different societies does not make prudence unvirtuous or practice immoral. In the "great books," in different religious principles, and in other distinctive artifacts of a great many different societies are to be found the common threads of a common spirit. Universalism—to the degree it is possible in a pluralized world—must be a matter of parallel, complementary, or mutually nonexclusive principles and processes rather than of identical or unitary values and customs. To read the Mahabharata is not to desecrate the Bible. The case for reading Virginia Woolf does not turn on the case for not reading Shakespeare. The real lesson of books like Bernal's is not that Western civilization is actually Egyptian and Egyptian civilization is actually black African, so that everything finally is exclusively black African—although there are some who would try to misread that lesson from it. Rather, it is that "Western" civilization is civilized in generic ways that draw on East and South as well as West, ways that suggest an underlying *human* preoccupation with science, math, literacy, culture, and government.

Cultural values are not locked in a zero-sum game, where the validation of one requires the devaluation of another. This may be the imperialist's game, but it should not be the educator's. Anthropology reveals that values and practices from one culture often reflect underlying concerns evident in the values and practices of another. Taboos may vary in their content, but humans seem to find a need for limits that leads them to regard certain behaviors as taboo. The war of good and evil, the dialectic of the one and the many, the struggle between the earthly and the transcendental, the tension between individual and community, the contest of liberty and power, the striving for eternity and universality pitted against the reality of mortality and particularity, the quest for unity in the face of plurality, the need to protect difference in the face of the impulse to unity, the unending battles of men and women, of parents and children, of public and private, of brother and brother and of sister and sister, are all features of a common global condition; just as the disenchantment of the world—the eroding of authoritative values by scientific "progress" and the secularization of societies under conditions of industrialization and prosperity—appear to be a common global fate.[31] To deny the reality of this fate is to substitute power for judgment and to try to conceal our own forms of particularity (Western or white or male or propertied—or African or black or female or colonized) behind a mask of universalism.

Yet the idea of the universal, if it is to survive modernity's many skepticisms, will have to be an encompassing rather than a restricting idea, taking in and making sense of contradictions and differences rather than trying to make cosmic claims for one particular culture. Perhaps that has always been true, even where differences were less widespread and obvious and unity appeared within our grasp. This is why the only tenable form of universalism has been dialectical, a play of many particularisms rather than a projection of our own. Whether in Socrates or Hegel, whether in ancient Egypt as a bridge between the old African civilizations and the new European culture or in modern America as a bridge between an Anglo-European monoculture and the new multiculturalism of immigrants from all over the world, the quest for a universal has been an attempt to encompass rather than deny difference, and it has made a coming to terms with otherness the condition for the forging of identity.

Earlier I generalized about freedom and responsibility. Let me be concrete and equally dialectical here. Liberty is not learned by turning second graders loose to do as they please. Responsibility is not taught by letting college sophomores devise their own educational curricula any way they choose. Democracy will not be the outcome of classes in which majorities decide who will talk as well as on what subject and from which point of view. The final object must be liberty, responsibility, and democracy; the eventual outcome of the process must be a demonstrated capacity for intellectual criticism, a feel for cultures other than one's own, an ability to discover common ground and from that ground establish common communities.

In education, though, not everything can happen at once. The outcome is not identical to the process; what it takes to bring children and young adults to learn is not always synonymous with what we want them to learn. Students are beings in transit (as we all should be)—never in the same place from one day to the next, let alone one year to another. Every stage calls for a different strategy, just as each group, as defined by its own special needs and shortcomings, demands a different approach. Teach the child what she needs to know, but also teach her what she is ready to learn. We may want to point her in some direction, but we still have to start from where she stands. Of course, like the weary traveler asking for directions who receives the cranky advice: "Trouble is, son, you can't get there from here," we might sometimes want to say to those students focused exclusively on present circumstance, "From where you seem to be standing, you can't get to power and voice and a role in America at all!" Programs that start from the ghetto may become "ghettoized," indulging and celebrating a particularity that is actually powerlessness, making kids safe and secure only by protecting them from the real competition and society they will eventually have to confront, teaching them pride by celebrating a black English that will obstruct achievement outside the ghetto.[32] Will the flourishing new field of "women's studies" bring gender into university curricula generally, or will it marginalize both the topic and the women and men who care about it by drawing them

142

away from standard "power" curricula like social science and history? I do not have the answer, but the question needs to be asked.

In the end, each battle must be fought experimentally and individually, with decisions based on particular children in particular schools. As Katha Pollitt has reminded us, "While we have been arguing so fiercely about which books make the best medicine, the patient has been slipping deeper and deeper into a coma."[33] In a society where nobody reads, except when required to, the battle for culture of any kind may already have been lost. Where ghetto culture and power culture are alike illiterate, what's the difference between black English and white English?

There can and must be universal ends such as truth, community, and service, even if they are measured exclusively by how unrealized they remain, but there is no universal pedagogy. The road leading to these ends is circuitous and involves educational blind turns, useful cul-de-sacs, and prudent detours that may seem at times to be leading away from the goal. In some places, just drawing kids into school and keeping them there long enough to awaken their potential for learning is the primary educational mission. In others, the aim may be to shake up a complacent acceptance of mainstream doctrines. In still others, the challenge will be to overcome a too-facile skepticism, a too-promiscuous cynicism, a too-complacent relativism. University teachers may be faced with first-year lecture courses in which all three aims must somehow be combined because of a stupefyingly heterogenous enrollment. Introducing a class of 400 to American history or political science becomes an educational nightmare when enrollment includes 85 prep school graduates, a couple of hundred graduates of public high schools (most from cities and suburbs, but some from rural areas), 40 adults (including 14 senior citizens), and nearly 100 minority students, of whom half come with serious deficiencies in their previous training but another 20 percent are America's highest-scoring test takers—Asian-Americans. There is no single developmental strategy appropriate to groups in so many diverse developmental stages. Ideal models—canonic or multicultural—cannot survive. Real teaching involves too much experimentation, too many pragmatic adjustments, too little success with any single strategy or method to lend itself to policy generalization of the kind that issues so easily from ideological or intellectual debates.

MODERATING EXCESS: MONOCULTURAL ROOTS OF MULTICULTURALISM

The preceding argument suggested that multiculturalism can be part of a pedagogy of commonality when it is seen in developmental terms. It is also the case that monoculturalism has multicultural consequences, at least in one important instance. Pluralism, tolerance, and multiculturalism have distinctive Eurocentric roots that justify the special place of "Western civilization" in the multicultural curriculum.

In the attacks on Western culture and the canon, there is a certain confusion about exactly what is at stake in public education in a multicultural democracy. This confusion also envelops the relationship between the many peoples who make up our society and the one sovereign people that constitutes our nation as a political and legal entity. The motto *E pluribus unum* is actually a little misleading, for the great *unum*—although it once arose out of an early "many"—is in political practice the premise and not the outcome of diversity. In our constitutional regime, diversity and difference are relegated to the private sphere, where they can be promoted and enjoyed, but they are prudently barred from the public sphere, whose object is precisely to ensure the impartiality of citizenship by securing a universal personhood for all citizens. Personhood is intentionally acultural, aiming at a legal formalism in which differences are dissolved.

To take one example, the United States historically celebrated its openness to religion by building a wall between it and govern-

144

ment. American Catholics may celebrate Catholicism and American Jews Judaism, but what American citizens celebrate is religious freedom: religious tolerance and the separation of state and church. Much the same is true of race. When, in the Civil War years, America began to try to live up to the putative universalism of its founding ideals (making good on the promise of "We the People"), it did so not by extending the civic compass from whites to blacks but, in the extraordinary words of the Fifteenth Amendment, by proclaiming that the rights of citizens cannot be denied or abridged "on account of race, color, or previous condition of servitude." It did not read the Negro race into the Constitution; it read race itself entirely out. Difference, an occasion for pride in the private sphere, becomes in the public an occasion for prejudice, and hence is prohibited.

The controversial 1991 New York State Social Studies Review and Development Committee report "One Nation: Many Peoples" is but one example of a form of multiculturalism that seems insufficiently attuned to commonality. It focuses on the plural "peoples" of New York State to ground its multicultural inclinations, but about the "nation" alluded to in its title it is earnestly opaque—as Arthur Schlesinger, Jr., Diane Ravitch, and other critics have noted.[34] The report takes a seemingly moderate attitude, claiming to "balance" difference and citizenship, as if they were two sides of a single coin, and in doing so meets the dialectical standards emphasized in the last section. But there is a sense in which a dialectical balance is hard to come by. Understood as incommensurable virtues of quite separate public and private realms, difference and citizenship are finally "balanced" only by keeping them apart—the one, personal and private; the other, public and civic.

This raises a question about public education's civic mission and its public agenda (to be taken up in detail in later chapters). Like some of the conservatives we have been criticizing, the New York State committee's report neither acknowledges sufficiently the overriding interest of public schools in the public education of democratic citizens (which requires an emphasis on the commonality of democratic civic ideals) nor recognizes fully the cultural roots of those ideals in the "dominant culture" it is so impatient to delegitimize. Mimicking those conservatives who want to privatize education, radical multiculturalists sometimes seem anxious to let the "public" fall silently out of public education. Despairing of the private domain, they seem to want education to assume the private duties of cultural socialization traditionally discharged by family, religion, and tradition—by private groups and voluntary associations.

Conservatives want to teach the canon, critics want to teach multiculturalism: Who wants to teach democracy? Private agendas abound: Who will teach the public agenda? Like other universals, the very notion of a public can be rendered illegitimate by a too-critical multiculturalism that insists on seeing American culture as nothing more than a disguise for the hegemony of a single class. Public education (most education in America) is necessarily about the education of public persons, of democratic citizens devoted to a common set of legal and political principles that work both to ameliorate and to transcend difference. These principles are the water in which individuals and distinctive groups swim without colliding. To teach these democratic principles means in turn to teach democracy's history and supporting culture—along with its defects and manifold hypocrisies.

Formally speaking, as an abstract system of laws, democracy's constitutional and civic framework is independent of culture; genealogically, it is neither free-floating nor culturally undetermined. The principle of universal citizenship, the primacy of law over human whim, the aspiration to civic participation—above all, the crucial idea underlying multiculturalism that all humans are created equal and have equal rights as individuals and as members of ethnic, gender, religious, and other groups—these are all ideals that can neither be plucked from thin air nor selected at random from some global inventory available to all peoples at all times. As observed above, many cultures evince universal ten-

146

dencies, but not all tendencies can be universally found in all cultures.

Think for a moment about the ideas and principles underlying anticanonical curricular innovation and critical multiculturalism: a conviction that individuals and groups have a right to self-determination; a belief in human equality coupled with a belief in human autonomy; the tenet which holds that domination in social relations, however grounded, is always illegitimate; and the principle that reason and the knowledge issuing from reason are themselves socially embedded in personal biography and social history, and thus in power relations. Every one of these ideas is predominantly the product of Western civilization. Science, technology, mathematics, literacy, literature, and scores of other cultural artifacts have origins that can be traced to a wide variety of civilizations, including those of Africa and Asia. Democracy has had a narrower provenance. Multiculturalism as an ideal has flourished mainly in the West. There were in Africa magnificent ancient cultures—in Benin, in Zimbabwe, in Mali, in Ghana, and (as is better known) in Egypt—from which Westerners have much to learn; moreover, these civilizations have influenced the early shaping of Western civilization itself.[35] But liberal democracy and its supporting ideology of rights, equality, and autonomous community do not belong to their generic legacy or largesse. They are rooted in Europe and become stronger as European civilization advances. The democratic idea is born in a delicate condition in Judeo-Christian Western Asia and in the civic republicanism of Hellenic Athens and the republican legalism of Rome; it grows in medieval Christian Europe and emerges in the free principalities of Italy, Switzerland, and Germany in early modern Europe. In the new nation-states of France and England, it is tested in the quest for religious freedom from repressive church-related monarchies and in the struggle for self-government in the face of despotism. America's unifying political principles emerge in turn as hard-won spoils of this violent, frequently hypocritical, and always powerfully ambivalent history. These unifying and just ideals alone are what privilege "Western civilization" courses and whatever principal texts (the canon) might be associated with them in America's classrooms.

Put simply, multiculturalism has monocultural origins. As a society, we are a rich tapestry of peoples from every part of the globe, each with its own proud history and cultural roots. We need curricula attuned to that variety and capable of drawing marginalized peoples into learning. But as a constitutional system offering to these multiple peoples a regime of democratic tolerance, stable pluralism, and mutual respect that (to the degree the ideal is made real) can protect all these constituent cultures, we have a particular, even unique, cultural history. For many, perhaps even most, societies, multiculturalism and the celebration of difference have meant prejudice, persecution, fratricide, tribal war, and anarchy. America is the exception, Yugoslavia more nearly the rule. Current examples of unstable multicultural societies can be found almost anywhere one looks: not just Yugoslavia but in Romania, in India, in Nigeria, in Sri Lanka, and of course in the disintegrated ex–Soviet Union. Even in liberal multicultural societies such as Switzerland, Belgium, Spain, and Canada, cultural minorities exist in various degrees of distrust, animosity, and open rebellion with respect to the dominant majority.

Our own European brand of multiculturalism, before it was modulated by liberal democracy, gave rise not to tolerance and stability but to the War of the Roses, the Inquisition, and the Thirty Years War. And then there was a tragic history of colonialism and imperialism that paralleled the rise of liberal democracy. Where democracy failed in Europe, it produced two centuries of intranational fratricide, several world wars, and the Holocaust. It was refugees from these multicultural conflagrations who sought in America what they believed was a unique brand of political comity: a comity that, they believed, was afforded by a constitutional system devoted, in the ideal at least, to universal equality and rights. The liberal democratic ideals that permit, even encourage, cultures rooted in difference to coexist and cooperate rather than persecute and annihilate, that afford celebration of difference without producing discrimination and internecine warfare, must then be regarded as both rare and precious.

Radical teachers—reductionist, relativist, deconstructionist, postmodern—are children of a predominantly Western tradition and a tribute to its procreative diversity. Critics of the canon are the canon's latest interlocutors and proof of its evolving character. The canon has always had critics; indeed, it is constituted by a series of radical critiques, each one widening the compass of debate and enlarging the pool of debaters. The role of "outsider" coveted by modern critics was invented by some of the greatest "canonical" writers, including Machiavelli, Hobbes, Rousseau, Marx, and Nietzsche, right down to Arendt, Foucault, and Derrida.

The history that defines multicultural ideas would then seem worthy of special attention in a society that, precisely in the name of its variety, wishes to succor and preserve its unity. It is neither Eurocentric arrogance nor white male hegemony that pleads for special attention: it is a self-reflective and honest multiculturalism bent on exploring its own genealogy. Indeed, it is only the sense of commonality that can kindle common responsibilities that oblige Americans to care about the needs and aspirations of groups other than their own.[36]

The West defined by its dead white male protagonists has brought many ills to the modern world: colonialism, paternalism, expansionism, imperialism, and an unsavory taste for hypocrisy that permitted the toleration of slavery in the midst of freedom and still permits poverty in the midst of plenty. Of course, the East and the South do not necessarily look much better when their stories are told by dead brown males (try reading the Hindi Bhagavad-Gita for its multicultural and transgender perspectives!) or by live yellow males (the Greater East-Asian Co-Prosperity Sphere was a melting pot in which distinctive peoples were melted in a rather more literal sense than they might have wished) or even by live white females (are the fringes of the pro-life or pro-choice movements any less monomaniacal and intolerant than the macho-man gun lobby?). Still, with or without the comparisons, the history we teach our children must report and critically debate and perhaps even distribute blame for the consequences of elitist hegemony. But in the shadowed train of its many vices, the Western tradition also brought with it one great set of virtues, a gift of its dialectical history: the ideal of democracy and the rule of law, of personal liberty secured by popular sovereignty. It has given us the democratic tools with which democracy's hypocrisies and disguised hegemonies might be challenged and dismantled. And it has produced those vital ideals of pluralism, tolerance, and the separation of private and public that have permitted American multiculturalism to function democratically rather than destructively.

It would be a terrible irony if one of the results of democracy's American success were to be an erosion of education for American democracy; if the critical perspective parented by Western philosophy were to turn patricidal; if the principles of universal inclusion and tolerance for diversity that have drawn and continue to draw so many different cultures to this land and are the essence of what it means to be an American were to be shoved aside because of a refusal, in the name of difference, to teach their unique history and, along with its vices, the virtues of the culture that produced them.

CHAPTER 5

CONSERVATIVE EXCESSES AND

ALLAN BLOOM

In the last chapter I urged radical multiculturalists to better understand the cultural roots of their critical methodology and egalitarian ideals. Conservative critics of multiculturalism have their
own lessons to learn. They first need to better understand the
Western monocultural tradition in whose name they raise so
many alarms. While radicals have fallen into excesses in their
zealous pursuit of reform, conservatives, in trying to service a
nostalgic vision of excellence past, have turned on democracy
present with a mean-spirited excess of their own.

Of all the cultural conservatives who have assailed democracy, none makes a case as profoundly rooted in philosophical
argument as Allan Bloom. No relevant book has been so widely
read or seriously engaged as *The Closing of the American Mind.*
Bloom has kept Americans up nights worrying about the perils
of value relativism and aggressive post-modernism. He seems to
share Senator Barry Goldwater's belief that excess in pursuit of
virtue is no vice. Nonetheless, I intend in this chapter to take

issue with his excesses, for they turn out not only to be conservatism's excesses but a blight on democracy.

Among all the discussions of curricula, none is more wedded to the idea of a classical canon than Bloom's. He begins with Socrates and descends to the Enlightenment and then on down to Nietzsche, Heidegger, and their final victims, the modern American professoriat. No one has been quite so ready to blame progressives, radicals, multiculturalists, and the sixties for the corruption of the canon. No one has paid less attention to the sins of the elders, or more attention to the foibles of the children and their tutors. The "P.C." label (political correctness) had scarcely been coined when Bloom wrote, but certainly there is no pejorative aspect of the term that Bloom did not anticipate.

Bloom's book has had a peculiar history in this land, for America, land of paradox, often makes heroes out of equality's severest critics. To those who condemn its popular virtues, it offers popular success; to those who disdain its materialism, it offers riches. Allen Bloom has been a beneficiary par excellence of this paradox. In *The Closing of the American Mind* we confront a most astonishing, a most enticing, a most subtle, a most learned, a most invidious tract—an extraordinary and adept exercise in the Noble Lie aimed at persuading Americans that philosophy is superior to ordinary life and philosophers superior to ordinary citizens, and consequently that higher education ought to be organized around the edification of the Few who embody philosophy rather than the Many who embody democracy. As this book is committed to the idea of the inherent compatibility of democracy and excellence, Bloom's book is committed to the idea of their incompatibility.

Like *The Lonely Crowd* in the fifties or *The Greening of America* in the sixties, *The Closing of the American Mind* is one of those books that, by synopsizing and eloquently voicing the colloquial mood of an era in a formal academic language, endows its age with a higher legitimacy. In a famous talk at Harvard skewering his critics, Bloom proclaimed: "I am not a conservative—neo- or paleo-."[1] Nonetheless, *The Closing of the American Mind* is nothing less than a vindication of the age of reactionary Reaganism, as seen by a Man of Reason wedded to the tradition of Socrates (as explicated by Plato). Bloom's critical temper is an erudite and seductive philosophical version of Colonel North's: outrage at a nation in which a knowing and self-appointed Few are compelled to dwell in a society governed by the tastes and prejudices of the Ignorant Many whose only possession is an unlovely freedom.

What is perhaps most remarkable about *The Closing of the American Mind* is its celebrity among men and women its author clearly despises, and its commercial viability in a popular culture for which he has expressed contempt. Its success—and here is a dense and difficult book of nearly 400 pages, which, though sometimes polemical and always readable, is also an academic treatise on the history of political thought—can only astonish its creator. Bloom has conceived what must be regarded as one of the most profoundly antidemocratic books ever written for a democratic audience, certainly a book as hostile to egalitarianism as any since Ortega y Gasset's *The Revolt of the Masses* or perhaps Nietzsche's *Thus Spake Zarathustra*. Nietzsche's dazzling work alluded to bourgeois democratic men as "last men" (a phrase subsequently borrowed by Francis Fukagama)—pygmy insects who hop foolishly about and grin as civilization crumbles. Bloom sees the young as craven boors, "nice" to their crass and callow cores.

Although Bloom is at war with democratic morality, with all such "leading notions of modern democratic thought, absolutized and radicalized, [as] equality, freedom, peace, [and] cosmopolitanism," his book has reaped popular praise, not simply from conservative critics but also from mainstream commentators. It was praised in the *New York Times Book Review* as "an extraordinary meditation on the fate of liberal education in this country," although in this case the reviewer was far more conservative than Bloom himself.[2] It was hailed in the *Los Angeles Times Book Review* as a work in which readers receive "an explanation of the meaning of liberal democracy . . . and the fundamental attitudes, ideas and institutions it requires."[3] Another magazine offered reverent attention in a three-part cover story that called the book "the most penetrating analysis of the United States to appear in many years."[4] Five years after its publication, it continues to set the terms of the debate in America over higher education and civic morality.

For provoking the debate, Bloom deserves firm credit. Indeed, he first did so in two essays in the 1960s, "The Crisis of the Liberal University" and "The Democratization of the University," where he laid out the major themes that were to occupy him in *The Closing of the American Mind*. But for the terms in which he has set that debate, he deserves still firmer criticism. I intend to scrutinize Bloom's book closely, for in it can be found most of the arguments and not a few of the excesses that are conservatism's program for education. That this program is not democratic will be quickly apparent. Exactly how undemocratic it actually is will be my subject for the balance of the chapter. That such a profoundly antidemocratic, antimodernist tract should have been welcomed and embraced by reviewers who are otherwise presumably content with American democracy, and that it should have become the indispensable guide for people who like to talk about (rather than engage in or pay for) education, is more than a little ironic. To me, the irony reveals deep and troubling fissures in the justifying structures of our democratic life. Bloom's views are perfectly consistent with the position of a philosopher steeped in Platonism and distrustful of democracy; they are wildly incompatible with modern democratic education. Yet many democratic educators have become their champions.

CLOSED MINDS OR CLOSED UNIVERSITIES?

Bloom is distressed by democracy in part because of its insouciance in the face of declining cultural excellence. But the success of *The Closing of the American Mind* suggests that democracy's

real vice may be its incorrigible lack of self-confidence, its deference to European-style elitists who proclaim the natural superiority of their standards or their styles of education or their
pristine philosophies.[5] In the conservative 1950s, the historian
Louis Hartz observed that the much-feared great American majority was in fact a toothless puppy dog forever tethered on a
lion's leash. Bloom still fears the lion, worried that it may devour
philosophy and its ardent practitioners. To date only the puppy
dog has appeared, but Bloom is sufficiently anxious to pull his
punches in his campaign against democracy.

The Closing of the American Mind is in fact as smooth and
painless a polemic as we are likely to see from a critic of democracy, for it is written by a philosopher for whom rhetoric is "the
gentle art of deception,"[6] a disputant who regards himself as the
heir to a tradition of philosophical discourse beginning with Socrates and running through Leo Strauss (Bloom's own teacher at
the University of Chicago) that believes political writing in a
democratic society is necessarily an act of concealment and deception. To say exactly what you mean about liberty and equality
when you live in a liberal democratic state and must depend on
its tolerance is perilous for philosophy and may even be suicidal
for the philosopher, as the story of Socrates so vividly demonstrates. Philosophical writing must therefore be layered writing,
ambiguous writing, writing packaged for the "Cave" of shadows
where ordinary men and women live steeped in prejudice and
myth. Philosophy may refuse to be an anodyne of the kind represented by religion or its modern surrogate, psychotherapy, yet
it must nonetheless eschew full candor. The philosopher, Bloom
reminds his more attentive readers, does "love the truth . . . but
he does not love to tell the truth."[7]

This suggests that the leading characteristic of *The Closing of
the American Mind*, this ostensible paean to the virtues of open
discourse, is a commitment to closed communication, to esoteric
meaning and rhetorical ambivalence. In the rhetoric of this school
of philosophy, nothing is quite as it seems. Plato, for example,

may seem to advocate the rule of philosopher-kings in his *Republic*; but according to Bloom (in the introduction to his translation, which readers who are serious about understanding Bloom's argument ought to consult), Plato conceals himself in a mantle of irony. His true meaning, which will be apparent to his true readers, is to warn philosophers against the temptations of rule, which they are likely to attain and which will turn the impassioned denizens of the Cave against philosophy. In the same manner, *The Closing of the American Mind* to unsophisticated readers may appear to be a companion volume to E. D. Hirsch's *Cultural Literacy*,[8] with which it seems to have in common a yearning for a more civilized culture and an affection for the so-called great books (although Bloom has little affection for the idea of a "canon"). The appeal to great books is in Bloom's school of thought an appeal to a tradition of elite discourse that considers genuine literacy a preserve of the few, and regards illiteracy as an intractable condition of the many. "The university," Bloom suggests in an essay from the sixties, "is supposed to educate those who are more intelligent and to set up standards for their achievement which cannot be met by most men and women. This cannot but be irritating to democratic sensibilities."[9]

If we are to understand Allan Bloom on his own terms, it is necessary to pull back the curtain on his art of rhetoric, to tell outright the truths that he believes must be concealed, to uncover the practices his skillful art of rhetoric-as-palliative depends upon. This means moving beyond the superficial structure of Bloom's argument. The first section of his book, "Students," is a passionate trashing of the sixties with its (as Bloom would describe them) adolescent uprisings, mindless music, and psychotherapeutic self-indulgences. It is this entertaining and fearsome part of his indictment that has attracted much of the critical praise—after all, this is an era in which it is fashionable to whip the young for the ills of their elders, and Bloom manages to associate most of democracy's vices with the excesses of youth.

The second section, "Nihilism: American Style," is a more

scholarly meditation on the corruption of American values by a vulgarized German ideology made up in equal parts of Nietzsche, Weber, and Freud. This discursive journey into historical political thought has left several otherwise admiring reviewers complaining they cannot argue with Bloom since they cannot follow him. The final section, "The University," brings together the legacy of German philosophy with American university culture in a biting attack on the sellout of the American academy, under the baleful influence of German positivism and cultural relativism, to the material needs of the nation's soulless democracy. This sellout is likened to Heidegger's notorious Rectorial Inaugural (*Rektoratsrede*) at Freiburg University, in which he dedicated himself and his university to the service of the new Nazi state. It is typical of Bloom's rhetoric that, having esteemed American liberal democracy in the abstract, he can then assert that an American university that pledges itself to serve democracy's needs resembles a German university that dedicates itself to the service of Nazism.

Bloom is deeply and quite rightly concerned with the connection between Heidegger's assault on rationality and the rise of fascism. Yet he himself risks aping some of Heidegger's less attractive intellectual traits. The German democratic philosopher Jürgen Habermas draws a portrait of Heidegger that is oddly apposite to Bloom. Habermas decries in Heidegger the

> claim that a few people have a privileged access to truth, may dispose of an infallible knowledge, and may withdraw from open argument. . . . the same attitude suggests, finally, detaching philosophical thinking from the egalitarian business of science, severing the emphatically extraordinary from its roots in ordinary everyday experience and practice, and destroying the principle of equal respect for all.[10]

As we shall see, these attitudes sometimes attend the "Straussian" standpoint, which Bloom champions. More often, Bloom is simply carried away by polemics, as when he draws a startling analogy between Woodstock and Nuremberg, as if flower children and pleasantly stoned hippies listening to Jimi Hendrix and Janis Joplin were clones of black-shirted fascists organizing a new epoch of genocide.

The superficial divisions that separate one section of *The Closing of the American Mind* from another conceal a deeper structure, however, one consisting of a heavily layered rhetoric that penetrates from political to philosophical ground, revealing arguments intended for more and more selective audiences. Contrary to what one might suspect, it is a rhetoric that grows more antidemocratic as it grows less polemical, grows more severe as it moves away from its more obvious passions. Bloom's deeper analysis is Socratic and grows out of his commitments as a gifted philosopher—a man who lives apart from others because of his taste for reflection.[11] These commitments lead him to believe that democracy for the many (those not like him) and education for the few (those like him) proceed from radically incompatible premises that can never really become congruent. Moreover, they persuade him that society ought to be arranged to achieve the education of the few even if it means some compromise for the many. "Never did I think," he writes, "that the university was properly ministerial to the society around it. Rather, I thought and think that society is ministerial to the university."[12] Unless we understand the university in terms of the few, the "theoretical life falls back into the primal slime" (democratic society presumably) from which it "cannot re-emerge." Finally, Bloom wishes to restore the relations between philosophy and the political regime idealized by Socrates in Plato's *Republic*, where the preeminence of philosophy over mundane life is guaranteed and the preeminence (if not the guardianship) of philosophers over ordinary men and women is secured. For the philosophical life is alone truly civilized, alone truly human, and the "intellectual virtue" it embodies is of greater worth than the "moral virtue" that attends living well for ordinary women and men.

There is much to admire in Bloom's fine-souled attachment to intellectual virtue, but I retain sufficient faith in the American commitment to egalitarianism to believe that if Bloom's readers and critics understood that this was his position, it might be a lot less popular. The man who believes that higher education should serve higher souls and democracy should be subservient to the university rather than the other way around raises vital questions about our political culture. They are questions worth raising; they go to the core of many of this book's central controversies and offer a test of our democratic commitments. Surely if we wish to make our democratic convictions more than a pretense, we owe such a philosopher not just a laurel wreath but an argument. To argue with Bloom, however, we must understand him, and to understand him we must penetrate through the layers of rhetoric to the antidemocratic lodestone at their core.

THE GUNS OF CORNELL

The first layer of Bloom's rhetoric is polemically diverting but really little more than an exercise in overheated autobiography. It is the story of what I will call the Guns of Cornell. April 1969, Ithaca, New York: At Cornell University the sixties were captured decisively in a grim and, to many, terrifying photograph published on the front pages of every newspaper in America: there they stood, arrogant, unforgiving, angry—armed black students emerging victorious from negotiations with the university administration, wearing bandoliers, flashing a V sign or black power salute with one hand while clutching a gun in the other. This spectacle took place in the pacific sanctuary of the academy (the student union building) while the president of the university stood numbly by, keeping the police at bay in the name of academic autonomy. The famous photo scrambled together many troubling and persistent educational issues: racial mistrust, affirmative action, academic freedom, curriculum reform, the crisis of professorial authority, student rebellion, white backlash, and the meaning of the ivory tower in a society where objectivity and impartiality were increasingly seen as covers for the prejudices of a highly politicized society.

A number of Cornell faculty never fully recovered from the trauma, and some would say that it was the beginning of the end for the American university. The political science department at Cornell was particularly hard hit, with some "liberals" as heavily targeted as "conservatives."[13] Resignations were to ensue, including those of the eminent political scientists Alan Sindler and Walter Berns, as well as that of a young political theorist named Allan Bloom.

Certainly the incident at Cornell has weighed heavily on Bloom for the past two decades. Many of his colleagues found themselves divided, drawn to the long-standing historical grievances of black Americans who had for centuries associated their victimization with white institutions that included the university. Yet they were drawn equally to the claims of the academy, *their* academy, which, after all, depended for its operation on tolerance, goodwill, and freedom of inquiry. Not Allan Bloom. He had then and has now not the slightest doubt that the student demonstrators were all "thugs" and the faculty who supported or gave in to them were cowards and traitors to both truth and their vocation. The moral dilemmas of racial prejudice, the ethical complexities of Vietnam, the issue of university-sponsored secret research, and the possibly subjective character of educational "standards" could not excite his wrath in the way those gun-toting black students did in April 1969. In as much as Bloom has neither forgotten nor forgiven, *The Closing of the American Mind* is his single-minded revenge on those colleagues and students, and the America that made them possible. So unpopular have the sixties become that few critics have commented on the pugnacious and bullying tones of *The Closing of the American Mind*, which make Bloom seem a far less compassionate teacher than his admirers may care to think.

Teaching and getting even do not have much in common. High-minded, rigidly unquestioning calls to action are unlikely to produce loving guidance or empathetic coaching. Indeed, the tone of Bloom's polemics against students signals many of the vices both conservative and liberal critics of "political correctness" have rightly worried about in the radical orthodoxies examined in the previous chapter.

In fact, although Bloom is obviously devoted to the tiny minority of elite students he has taught at institutions like Cornell and the University of Chicago, his book overflows with contempt for the young: disdain for the unwashed mass of adolescents and for their tastes, their pastimes, their sexual practices, their "niceness," their music, their reading habits (he both condemns them for not reading and excoriates the authors they choose—Hermann Hesse, Thomas Mann, J. D. Salinger), and their defects of character, of which the absence of nobility is to him the most alarming. Bloom comes to the young as Thomas Mann's hero Gustav von Aschenbach comes to Venice, looking for an imagined eros but finding infidelity, corruption, and death. Bloom sees in Mann's tale "a Freudian vision" unlikely to instruct "the finer spirits";[14] yet there is something of Aschenbach in Bloom's disenchantment with the young, those "flat" souls with "defective eros"[15] who "do not experience love."[16] With the artful and worshipful interlocutors of Socrates perching as archetypes in his imagination, Bloom can hardly be other than appalled by the average American eighteen-year-old, who is more than a little artless and never very reverent, particularly toward teachers. No wonder he complains that "Harvard, Yale and Princeton are not what they used to be—the last resorts of aristocratic sentiment within the democracy."[17]

As a consequence, there is much passion but little conviction in Bloom's account of the Guns of Cornell. He alludes to connections between the evils of rock music and Plato's theory of the soul, which makes reason sovereign over the passions and condemns music as a siren song of anarchic impulses that reason must control. But the connections are strained and Bloom's unrelenting sixties bashing finally sounds more like the exasperation of an aging parent aghast at his daughter's purple hair or his son's mysterious bathroom habits than the observations of a detached cultural critic. His account of the Cornell incident leaves out vital contextual details—not simply the institutional history of racism in America, but the particular background of the event, which lasted hardly more than twenty-four hours and ended peacefully with the evacuation of the black students from the student union, carrying unloaded, open-breeched weapons displayed in an unsuccessful effort to camouflage the fact that the protesters had in fact folded. This background also included such racist provocations as a cross burning in front of a black coed dorm and an attempt by white fraternity students to "liberate" by force the student union that blacks (originally unarmed) had occupied. These white liberators came in a back window while negotiations were proceeding, scuffled with the occupiers, and were ejected, at the cost of a long delay in further negotiations. The immediate cause of guns being brought into the occupied union, however, was an explicit threat (monitored by campus security) from armed local vigilantes to clean out the union with guns of their own.

Such background events do not justify the violation of the academy by guns—an egregious infringement of the discourse of liberty—but they do provide a relevant context and suggest why administrators who worked out a peaceful solution might have thought they were doing well to avoid the kind of slaughter that was to come to Kent State University. I cannot believe Bloom would have preferred a bloodbath in which the integrity of the academy would have been purified by human sacrifice, but he does not seem to have thought much about such a possibility, for he is little interested in context or the broader political issues.

Are the historical grievances of ordinary men and women of color not to be compared with the rights of philosophers to an intellectual sanctuary?

LEGITIMIZING REAGANISM

Yet to leave Bloom as an angry victim of the Guns of Cornell is to understate the seriousness of his claims and the extent of his antipathy to democracy. What happened at Cornell was merely one instance of democracy's "totalitarian" tendencies. Like the champions of the new conservatism, Bloom is hostile not only to what he deems the moral decline of the university in the face of student activism and rampant egalitarianism, but to much of what democrats, liberals, and progressives have accomplished in the last fifty years. He does not simply oppose feminism or the abolition of the double standard in the abstract, he condemns them because they destroy the old sexual arrangements where a man could "feel he was doing a wonderful thing for a woman and could expect to be admired for what he brought."[18] What need is there for liberated women, when in a true family, "the husband's will is the will of the whole"?[19] Feminists are not merely destroyers of the family, they are "the latest enemy of the vitality of classic texts"[20] and thus, since classic texts are the touchstone of a philosophical society, of education itself.

Bloom offers useful criticisms of modern value relativism, but his critique of the young is finally not about relativism. If, in his caustic commentary, they seem to possess no values at all, they also seem guilty of having far too many of the wrong values. To him a concern for nuclear survival is bogus posturing; a belief in tolerance is a sign of moral flabbiness; to be "nice" and "without prejudices" reflects shallowness rather than conviction. Relativistic democrats presumably cannot hold moral convictions, so whatever "values" they possess are so many diversions occasioned by the conspiracy of therapists and their divorced (female) patients. If this sounds too odd to be true in a book celebrated for its nobility, listen to Bloom's own voice: "There are big bucks for therapists in divorce, since the divorcés are eager to get back to persecuting the wretched who smoke or to ending the arms race or to saving 'civilization as we know it.' "[21] Bloom condemns not merely equality and the struggle for rights (a struggle that he believes has, in any case, been "won") but the notion of rights itself—a commitment to "life, liberty, and the pursuit of property and sex" that is summed up in Bloom's version of Lady Liberty's plea: "Give us your poor, your sexually starved. . . ."[22]

For Bloom, rights theory turns out to be a legitimation of the pleasure principle, a justification for individuals to indulge themselves. Underlying redistributive social justice (the distribution of goods based on need rather than worth), strategies of self-examination and self-realization associated with psychotherapy, and ideologies of feminist liberation, of affirmative action, and of equal educational opportunity, is a dangerous and false belief in equality. Bloom complains that "almost no one wants to face the possibility that 'bourgeois vulgarity' might really be the nature of the people, always and everywhere."[23] The true villains, then, are neither Abbie Hoffman nor Tom Hayden, but Erich Fromm and John Dewey—not the armed prophets of Cornell, but the far more dangerous unarmed prophets of therapeutic salvation and the brotherhood of man.

Again, one can only be astonished at a democratic society that receives these aristocratic strictures without a murmur of protest. The dominant stance of the book is "interrogative not prescriptive," reports Roger Kimball in his *New York Times* review. Bloom cannot be a rightist, reasons Frederick Starr (the president of Oberlin) in the *Washington Post's Bookworld*, because "he does not consider [the conservative] position sufficiently serious even to warrant a critique."[24] Is it that the deeply reactionary flavor of *The Closing of the American Mind* is lost against the background conservatism of our era? Just as *Platoon* and *Full*

Metal Jacket, which did as much to celebrate as to condemn the violence and anarchy of war, were praised as realistic "antiwar" films, so perhaps a book that assails democracy and egalitarian education can only be welcomed by guilty college presidents as a contribution to the reform of democratic education.

What is perhaps most curious about Bloom is that while his appeal is to great souls, his readiest comrades in arms (though they will hardly have read him) are likely to be of a more common garden variety. Had his sampling of modern popular music moved beyond the throbbing mindlessness of hard rock to encompass the soft moralism of country-western, he would have discovered a highly popular sentimental imagery retelling unhappy tales rooted in his own version of traditional values: of fidelity promised though unkept, sin proffered but declined, patriotism noble and uncompromised, true love given if unrequited, blood feuds settled by manly duels to the death. He also could uncover among the nation's growing population of religious fundamentalists vibrant soul partners in his quest for a less relativistic and material life. In truth, Bloom's political views accord much more convincingly with those of the commoner "rabble" he despises than with those of the refined but overcivilized and corrupted aesthetes who are our nation's artists, writers, philosophers, and university teachers. When Bloom observes crankily that kids nowadays "just don't seem to have prejudices against anyone" and that "there are no longer schools of thought that despise equality and democracy,"[25] one wants to urge him to abandon the civilized confines of Hyde Park for a week on the southside of Chicago just beyond and the ethnic environs to the north and west, where whole tribes of Americans stand ready to make manifest the resilience of spite, prejudice, and hate in modern America. Like so many college teachers, Bloom spends too much time in hushed classrooms and hallowed libraries where civility blankets bias and discourse displaces combat, and where violence generally refers to words rather than deeds. But the truth is close at hand. Even without leaving campus, Bloom can find on lavatory walls racial and sexual graffiti suggesting that students are not really so "nice" and value-free after all.

Bloom would certainly be uneasy if his civilized conjectures about the inadequacies of egalitarianism were taken as rationalizations for the bigotry of racists or religious zealots. The philosopher longing for an ancient nobility of soul is hardly likely to identify with a rabble that insists it too is confronting runaway modernity when it votes for David Duke, or with zealots who yearn in three-quarter time for a lasting love or cry out in tongues for Jesus to enter their lives or dump blood on women trying to enter an abortion clinic.

In truth, Bloom's conservatism is of a fundamentally different stripe. He opposes democratic values not as an advocate of religion and myth, but as a philosopher wedded to reason in a world in which reason is under siege; even (he would insist) as an old-fashioned antistatist suspicious of the "tyranny of the majority" and untrusting of the all-too-sovereign people. It is not really the last twenty years that disturb Allan Bloom, but the last two hundred years. The last two thousand, for that matter. For the problem finally is not just American democracy run amok, but the Enlightenment run amok, Machiavelli's Renaissance gone wild. The problems go back at least to the French Revolution and to those aspects of the philosophy of Enlightenment that caused it.[26] In fact, if we read Bloom carefully, we realize nothing has been quite the same since a court composed of distrustful Athenian freemen put a noble Socrates to death for the crime of being a truth-speaking philosopher in an opinion-governed society. The great divide is less between modern conservatives and modern democrats than between ancients and moderns. This theme of ancients and moderns leads us to a deeper layer of Bloom's rhetoric, back to his mentor and teacher, the great University of Chicago political philosopher Leo Strauss.[27]

IN THE FOOTSTEPS OF THE MASTER

Behind Allan Bloom's aspiration to intellectual excellence lies the political philosophy of Leo Strauss, a philosopher who, although he eschewed political influence, exercised an enormous authority over American higher education and the society beyond academe. Today his ardent disciples hold sway over extended segments of the academic world, where they constitute a tightly knit and clannish community with its own journals, its own conferences, and its distinctive scholarly methodology and pedagogy. You would not know from conservative handwringing about the takeover of the university by leftists how many tenured Straussian teachers ply their wares. On the whole, this is a good thing, because their values commit them to education (if most often in an elitist mode), and their passionate adherence to the canon makes them genuinely effective and affecting teachers of the Western tradition. They can also be found in plentiful numbers beyond the academy, often in the upper reaches of the nation's value-conservation bureaucracies: the Department of Education and the National Endowment for the Humanities. They have found their way to the State Department, to the White House domestic staff, even to the office of Vice President Dan Quayle, whose chief of staff, William Kristol, is as much an apprentice of Strauss as of his father and mother, neoconservative scholars Irving Kristol and Gertrude Himmelfarb.

As with any set of disciples, Straussians are divided on many questions, but they share certain principles: a conservative disposition to modernity born of an attachment to the ancients, especially as incarnated in Socrates; a preference for virtue (sometimes called ancient liberty) over equality and individualism (modern liberty), as well as for excellence over inclusiveness; and certain common convictions about scholarly method, which, although they are drawn from the ancients, are of powerful political consequence for moderns. These convictions reveal an atttiude

167

toward the great books that has little to do with the democratic humanist's call for enhanced cultural literacy or improved liberal education. To Straussians, great books are great, not as popular guides to a philosophical life for the unphilosophical masses, but as secret codes for a tribe of initiates—esoteric and multilayered texts to be read by the prudent conservators of values, often against the obvious meanings imputed to them by less careful readers (those who have not studied with Strauss).

The origin of this cabalist belief in secrecy and conspiracy can be traced back to the trial of Socrates, which, if it taught philosophers anything, taught them the imperative of prudence, even duplicity, in philosophical argument. Speak to the envious and impetuous masses in one tongue, and speak to fellow philosophers and their gifted apprentices in another. To the first audience, the philosopher must speak in soothing riddles and noble lies that deceive in order to placate; to the second, he dares speak the unvarnished truth. Voltaire once suggested that wise gentlemen ought to send their servants from the room before discussing the improbability of God's existence. Strauss seems to urge that the children of Socrates send the modern masses from the (class)room before engaging the terrible truths of our own times— the death of God, the sleep of reason, the erosion of truth's foundations in metaphysics, the intractability of power in a world that is supposed to be governed by virtue. Succor the children with bread and circuses, but keep them out of the Ivy League. Give them palatable half-truths that tell them what they need to know to live decent and compliant lives under the leadership of the wise, who alone can risk staring full-truth in the face. This is the essence of Strauss's political teaching as derived from his philosophical teaching. As a moralist, he was a great man. As a democratic educator of citizens, his teaching left something to be desired.

Does this make any difference to our understanding of Bloom? Are the doctrines of esoteric interpretation and antimodernism found in Strauss really linked to Bloom's express attack on democratic education? If this view seems too academic, too parochial, too conspiratorial by far, it may help to compare *The Closing of the American Mind* with Leo Strauss's perennial text *Natural Right and History*, written in 1953 when Allan Bloom was a student of Strauss at the University of Chicago. In this classic text, written fifteen years before the Guns of Cornell and nearly thirty years before the onset of the Reagan era, can be found Bloom's central themes enunciated in language Bloom must feel proud to borrow. There are the same leading villains— Machiavelli, Hobbes, and Rousseau (modernity as encapsulated in the Enlightenment and the French Revolution)—who are responsible for devaluing the ancient world's concept of soul, and transforming nature from a source of guiding Truths into a legitimizer of animal impulses. There are the same secondary miscreants, above all those relativistic social scientists of our own era along with their German teachers Nietzsche, Weber, and Heidegger. To Strauss, this menagerie of hedonists, positivists, relativists, and nihilists is held together by a discontent with the ancients and by a dogmatic insistence that facts and values are wholly incommensurable (see Chapter 3).

Strauss's teaching challenges the modernist orthodoxy frontally and with both courage and insight. It denies every conclusion reached by philosophy and science since the Enlightenment, and in doing so buries a fair amount of garbage. Fans of postmodernism and deconstructionism could benefit from even a brief encounter with Strauss's work. Yet finally, Strauss buries too much that is not garbage; along the way he resurrects a metaphysic that is simply untenable in light of the intellectual evolution and practical history we have experienced. For Strauss, and thus for Bloom, Truth exists and can be known to men through reason. In destroying the ideals of nature and nature's gift to men of reason, modern thought has destroyed the ancient understanding of philosophy as the quest for and the love of Truth, replacing it with a debased and debasing historicism. In Leo Strauss's account:

While abandoning the idea of natural right and through abandoning it ... German thought has "created the historical sense," and thus was led eventually to unqualified relativism. What was a tolerably accurate description of German thought twenty-seven years ago would now appear to be true of Western thought in general.[28]

Through the spread of positivist social science, this relativism has spread to America, where the "the rejection of natural right is bound to lead to disastrous consequences."[29] Strauss's "disastrous consequences" set Bloom's polemical agenda. His task is to catalog and elaborate upon trends alluded to by Strauss. Strauss writes that "American social science has adopted the very attitude toward natural right which, a generation ago, could still be described as characteristic of German thought."[30] Bloom has only to put flesh on this Straussian skeleton.[31]

The basic argument of *The Closing of the American Mind*, then, is an amplification of the argument of *Natural Right and History*—that value relativism and the nihilism issuing from it come to America courtesy of "The German Connection" (the title of Part 2, Chapter 1 of *Closing*), or what both Strauss and Bloom see as the Americanization of Nietzsche, Weber, and Freud. All of the vices of adolescent selfhood and individuality assailed by Bloom result in the first instance from this illicit transfer of Continental despair to the new world. In Strauss's words: "[T]he contemporary rejection of natural right leads to nihilism— nay, it is identical with nihilism ... [moderns] had to make a choice between natural right and the uninhibited cultivation of individuality. They chose the latter."[32]

Strauss is prelude, Bloom is fugue in this dance of despair. The result of the rejection of natural right as narrated by Strauss is for Bloom the vulgarization embodied in the romantic culture of self-realization, creativity, and an unbounded selfishness: "Modern psychology has this in common with what was always a popular opinion, fathered by Machiavelli—that selfishness is somehow good. Man is self, and the self must be selfish."[33] This leaves life feeling like what Strauss calls a joyless quest for joy and what Bloom agrees is a material quest by flat souls for de-eroticized sex and unnoble pleasure.

Allan Bloom's critique is interchangeable with Leo Strauss's. It is much more than a critique of rock music or armed blacks in the academy; nor is it just a critique of the sixties or an assault on America's meretricious mass democratic culture. Rather, the target is modernity itself. As with Strauss, it is both a critique of Rousseau and Nietzsche and at the same time a Rousseauean and Nietzschean critique of modernity. It is a critique of what happens when Rousseau's radical vision is trivialized as the French Revolution; or what happens when Nietzsche is corrupted and transformed into an excuse for noncommitment and pleasurable all-American nihilism; or what happens when the death of God is turned into a justification for the deification first of men and, in time, of the basest among men.

The road leading back to Leo Strauss quickly takes a more radical turning, then, a turning that leads back to Strauss's villains and the esoteric methodology by which conscientious modern philosophers can ensure that ordinary men and women are spared philosophy's unhappy truths (including the truth that there may be no truth).

SAVING (STUPID) AMERICA FROM A (TOO-SMART) NIETZSCHE

The two strands of the Straussian argument come together to resolve what is one of the more impenetrable puzzles of *The Closing of the American Mind*: Bloom's simultaneous praise for Nietzsche's analysis (Nietzsche is "an unparalleled diagnostician of the ills of modernity") and his indictment of the trivialized American version of Nietzschean philosophy as a primary factor in the closing of the American mind. Nietzsche is at once hero and villain, astute cultural critic of bourgeois culture in the abstract and nefarious corrupter of American youth in practice.[34]

To unravel this paradox, we need to consult Strauss's esoteric theory of text. We return to Voltaire's advice about banishing servants from theological discussions. Nietzsche is palatable for Bloom and perhaps, if Bloom is their cautious guide, a handful of his more gifted students at a "first-class" university like Chicago. But in the watered-down form of relativism, positivism, or psychotherapy, Nietzsche is absolute poison for the American masses. The danger is not philosophical relativism, but pop relativism; not Nietzsche, but the "doctrinaire Woody Allen" whose way of looking at things "has immediate roots in the most profound German philosophy."[35] If Woody Allen as a pop Nietzsche seems farfetched, Bloom himself often seems like a slightly paranoid Tocqueville who, although burdened by an aristocratic background and Continental manners, finds himself inexplicably residing in the state of Illinois among barbarians he at once dotes on, patronizes, and despises. In his reading of *Death in Venice*, Bloom offers a nuanced interpretation that dwells on "the relation of sexual sublimation to culture." He is quick, however, to add, "I do not think it was received that way by Americans."[36] As with other texts, "Americans" (and here Bloom prefers not to count himself as one of them) misread and distort Thomas Mann's classic, noticing "the sublime less than the sex." Readers get texts wrong, and philosophers must thus write with foreknowledge of their readers' frailties: hence, the casting of philosophy as a "gentle art of deception." From the perspective of Bloom's jaundiced eye, ordinary Americans just can't get anything right—least of all the meaning of the Death of God or the uncertainty of Truth in the post-Enlightenment world.

As a modern, Bloom cannot really deny that the credentials for both absolute Truth and a Supreme Being have become philosophically suspect: Nietzsche was merely the messenger. The trouble is not really in the message, however. Nietzsche knew and Bloom agrees that the philosopher's nobility is to be found precisely in his fearlessness when faced with the most shattering cosmic news. Only the souls of great men can confront the death of God or the transvaluation of all values without terror. The masses, on the other hand, though "educated" in democratic public schools, are unequipped to absorb such grim tidings. To strip them of their myths and their religious comforts, when they are constitutionally unfit for philosophy, is to leave them defenseless *and* to render them dangerous. Faced with the news of God's death and Truth's uncertainty, mass man in America has simply put his soulless self in God's place, to the peril of learning, philosophy, and civilization. The Betrayal of the Intellectuals engenders the Revolt of the Masses, whose trivialized mass culture is at war with everything noble and good.[37] Virtue gives way to utility, reason to passion, and the good to the merely self-interested. Theories of government are constructed around economic interests and power relations rather than obligations and civic virtue, and regimes, transferring their legitimacy from virtue to right, begin to license the passions they once tried to contain.

In these arguments there is much conviction and more than a little truth. Indeed, as argued in Chapter 3, it was exactly this stance, from which Straussians could stage attacks on social science positivism and liberal neutrality, that gave conservativism its decidedly radical flair back in the 1960s. In France, Leo Strauss is read as fervently by the left as by the right, for he is correctly seen as a critic, not just of modernity but of modernity's vices. In this he is not so far from left-leaning critiques of Enlightenment.[38]

The trouble for Bloom is that however convincing the arguments, ordinary men must be handled carefully, addressed in a manner that spares them horrors they cannot bear: their own mortality, for example (not to speak of God's!). There is a solution, although Bloom can only hint at it. Remember, the philosopher cannot speak honestly and expect to be tolerated in a democracy of mass opinion. That solution is not to inundate ordinary mortals with books they cannot understand and are likely to misconstrue, but to send them—like Voltaire's servants—out of the room. The open mind may function best in the closed university. To the educable, an education; to the rest, protection from fearsome truths through inoculation by half-truths: a diet of noble lies such as may be required to insulate the university from mediocrity and democratic taste. Through Bloom's eyes, affirmative action puts into the classroom young men who can learn from Hobbes and Nietzsche only the lesson of the rightfulness of their appetites; feminism puts into the classroom young women who can learn from Dewey and Freud only the lesson of their equality with, nay their sexual superiority to, men. Philosophy is not finally to be saved by handing out big books to little boys, but by locking the library doors.

This is strong medicine, and will be disbelieved by those who insist *The Closing of the American Mind* is only an impassioned plea for traditional liberal education and more reading of the great books. Yet for a philosopher who believes in the gentle art of deception, Bloom is remarkably candid about the nature of "the real community of man," which "is the community of those who seek the truth, of the potential knowers." To be sure, this community "in principle" includes all men "to the extent they desire to know. But in fact this includes only a few, the true friends, as Plato was to Aristotle . . ."[39] We are back, then, to the community of true knowers against the mass of feelers and doers who constitute the rest of humankind. We are back to Socrates facing his ignorant accusers. As democratic Athenian citizens, they possessed the right to judge him and the power to condemn him; but how trivial the right, how paltry the power, when compared to the Truth that belonged to Socrates alone.

Finally, Bloom's rhetorical journey begins and ends with Socrates. How much misery might have been spared, what revolutions, what prejudices, what myths, what armed braggarts might have vanished from the historical landscape, had the Athenians loved and followed Socrates, instead of executing him.

IN THE BEGINNING: THE TRIAL OF SOCRATES

Socrates occupies the place of honor in the Straussian pantheon of great philosophers, not simply because he was the first, but because, ironically, he was also the last—the last (in Plato's account) to think that Truth existed in nature and could be known by men of reason. When he was tried and executed by free citizens for thinking freely (and teaching what he thought), a somber warning was sent out from the cradle of Western civilization to all subsequent cultures. Philosopher beware! Equality is your enemy. The ethics of the Many (the morality of action, or what the Greeks called moral virtue) will always be the fiercest foe of the ethics of the Few—the Best (the virtue of the mind, or what the Greeks called intellectual virtue).

Plato, a student and chronicler of Socrates, had already learned the lesson. Socrates had been an aristocrat who believed in the aristocracy of reason. In Plato's amplification of the Socratic theory of knowledge, Truth was identified with an underlying Nature (*physis*) accessible to reason. As reason ought to rule the passions in a single man, so the rational ought ideally to rule the passionate: this is the theme of *The Republic*. Plato treads carefully, however, with the example of Socrates before him. Though denizens of the Cave who live in the shadow of opinion and prejudice cannot rule themselves rationally or well, they are also unlikely subjects of philosophical rule. If they are to live justly, under the guidance of reason but not under the overt rule of philosophers, they must be fed myths and stories, "noble lies" that correspond to "true opinion" rather than pure Truth. The philosopher disguises such lessons as he might wish to teach. His primary goal is to preserve philosophy (his way of life) from the depredations of the Cave (the way of the Many).

Whether the philosopher actually wishes for power is a central puzzle of Plato and of Straussian scholarship. Most classicists have assumed that Plato's *Republic* is the philosopher's bid for and justification of philosophical rule, not because the philosopher lusts for it but because philosophy alone secures just government, and thus the possibility of a secure life for philosophers. The Straussians, on the other hand, preoccupied with the vulnerability of philosophers in an open society, have insisted that Plato pointed to the ideal republic ironically, as a warning against philosophical rule. He wished to show how ridiculous philosophical rule was and thus both to dissuade philosophers from undertaking it and to let the masses know they were in no danger from philosophy, with which they could thus afford safely to coexist.[40] Yet knowing that, for Bloom, philosophy is a gentle art of deception, we must ask whether the imputation of irony is not itself a tactical ploy, a noble lie to protect the politically ambitious philosopher from retribution. The trouble with noble lies is that we never know quite when we are being lied to and when we are getting the truth. Is the philosopher lying when he says philosophers must often lie? Is the philosophical state a lie or are those like Bloom who say it is themselves lying?

Either way, what Socrates teaches modern philosophers is that reflection and action are often at war with one another, that the philosopher can never trust equality (which denies his nobility) or the morality of action (which denies the priority of reflection over action in defining the human essence). Truth exists for the few who know how to seek it. It is poison for the rest, who can only confront it as myth and prejudice, but who when confronted with it directly will always trivialize and distort it (as happened with the Americanization of Nietzsche) or turn it against the philosophers (as happened with Socrates).

Most dangerous of all is the truth promulgated by Nietzsche: the truth that there is no truth. Some philosophers would even say this was the truly subversive message of Socrates, and that it was for this skepticism that he paid the ultimate price. In any case, for Allan Bloom, the mischief caused by the vulgarization of this lesson is called America. What is the lesson of the American story we portrayed earlier other than that there is no eternal truth, no natural order on which to pattern politics, than that a people must invent its own constitutions and create an order open to variety and difference? The lesson, for Bloom, is everywhere evident in the flat-souled kids who people America's colleges and universities. Facing death in an era after God (Alasdair MacIntyre's era "after virtue"), these little people, equal in their common dwarfishness, are too smart for the comforts of religion, but too stupid for the consolation of philosophy. With the help of psychotherapy, they become arrogant anarchists, self-proclaimed kings, worst of all, democratic citizens. As citizens, they become claimants to God's throne, each one a purveyor of his own subjective little "truth" now defined by communities of deliberation where each counts as one and only one, and where one person's opinion is worth as much as the Truth of an ancient master. Socrates' nightmare has come to pass: desire rules reason, the impulsive govern the prudent, and mass man rules philosophy. The name of this nightmare is democracy.

The citizen of a democracy who understands what Bloom intends in the honor he pays Socrates will be wary in the face of Bloom's modern claims. Like all critics of modernity, Bloom captures significant weaknesses in modern democratic culture. Nonetheless, the citizen has every reason to mistrust the philosopher who mistrusts him. The modern challenge to those who affirm absolute Truth is rooted less in democratic ideology than in critical epistemology (metaphysical claims to truth cannot be validated by science or rationality) and in the historical experience with Dogmatism (the tyranny of "Truth" politicized as the Divine Right of Kings, the Inquisition, Revolutionary Terror, or

Totalitarianism). The Straussians' claim that classical texts have fixed if esoteric meanings known only to an elect comprised by students of Leo Strauss is simply one more example of this dogmatism. As the contentious domain of textual interpretation suggests, texts are human artifacts for which no Rosetta Stone can be found; as such, they are even more resistant to "true" interpretation than historical events or metaphysical claims. We need not accept deconstruction's excesses to appreciate the social contexts that help give texts their meanings. Although one would hardly know it from reading Bloom, Plato's *Republic* itself has meanings as numerous as its interpreters, who are both learned and legion. The Straussian claim that it can only be ironic and hence must be read exclusively against the grain is silly. Ultimate interpretations will always remain contested. That is philosophy's strength.

The final lesson for democrats of the trial of Socrates ought to be that a dogmatism of philosophical certainty is no less dangerous to democracy than a dogmatism of democratic relativism (every claim is as good as every other claim) is dangerous to philosophy. If the open philosophical mind really depends on the closed society—the pacification of the masses for their own good and the exclusion of the Many from the best universities—then citizens of the open society have as much right to defend themselves in the name of their convictions, as philosophers do in the name of theirs. Their best democratic defense turns out to be an educational strategy aimed at reconciling excellence and equality. As no one who has read to this point will be surprised to hear, that is precisely my strategy.

OPEN MINDS FOR SOME, OR AN OPEN SOCIETY FOR ALL?

When all is said and done, *The Closing of the American Mind* is a Straussian challenge to the Open Society, which for Allan Bloom

presents a permanent threat to the open mind and thus the philosophical life. Bloom may not be arguing that "the old forms were
good or that we should go back to them,"[41] but he has two crucial
quarrels to pick with America: the quarrel of the philosopher
with democracy and equality and the quarrel of the ambivalent
cosmopolitan with both the European decadence he fears and the
American philistinism he loathes. The quarrel between philosophy and democracy is the quarrel between Socrates and Athens,
and we have seen how deeply that struggle affects Bloom. The
quarrel between America and Europe is a more complex affair,
and here Bloom seems torn.

As a champion of an innocent America corrupted by the
tainting cynicism of Europe's antiphilosophies (for that is what
Nietzsche and positivism represent), Bloom conceives himself as
a loyal but knowing son of the American Republic, anxious to
protect its less sophisticated citizens from the old world's new-
fangled nihilisms. If it is true that God has died (and there are
times when Nietzsche's bad news seems also to be Bloom's), don't
tell the Americans! They already have a penchant for the vulgar,
the novel, and the experimental, and will seize on God's with-
drawal in order to claim the seat of cosmic sovereignty themselves. In lieu of one Great and True Master, they will install
themselves as multiple mini-masters. In place of tragic acceptance, the typical stance of the ancients toward malice and mis-
fortune, they will deploy ideologies of reform, growth, progress,
and revolution. With their hands clasping computers and spliced
genes, and their heads bursting with progressive ideologies from
Marxism to welfarism, feminism, and radical egalitarianism, they
will set out to replace their vanished Creator and improve upon
His handiwork. In this role, Bloom appears as America's Rousseau,
trying to preserve it from modernity's noisome arts and sciences,
hoping that if it can only be kept in a state of glorious innocence, it
may preserve something of its religious and constitutional foundations in nature, and rekindle its deference for rational authority and
for the universities where that authority is celebrated.

Yet even as Bloom cherishes America's insularity from the contagion of European cultural relativism, he cherishes Europe. An inveterate visitor to Paris, a connoisseur of French manners and mores, he is not just Rousseau, but Rousseau *malgré lui*, Rousseau dazzled by the cosmopolitan culture he decries, seduced by the Seducers against whom he warns his fellow countrymen. Allan Bloom is an American Puritan thundering against his Continental mistress as he takes her in his arms.

Yet from within her embrace, he cannot help but appreciate the deficiencies of America's unsullied purity. As a partisan of Europe, he may be suspicious of its nihilistic intellectualism (after all, where did post-modernism and deconstruction get started?), but as an American he is even more suspicious of America's self-righteous anti-intellectualism. With innocence comes a simple-minded disdain for ideas that, as the historian Richard Hofstadter noticed, inures us to books and debases our souls.[42]

We are much too practical a people for Bloom's taste: philosophy enjoins reflection, but for Bloom the "hidden premise of the realm of freedom [America] is that action has primacy over thought."[43] Where Americans want to see man as "a problem-solving being," he is (or ought to be) a "problem-recognizing and problem-accepting being."[44] In light of his Continental disdain for the commonplace, it is easy to see why Bloom abhors America's only homegrown school of philosophy: for pragmatism turns out to be a school of the commonplace. Although it is quite untainted by Nietzsche, it makes a fetish of action and renders reason subservient to ends and consequences. Bloom can only regard the Pragmatists' attempt to distill a philosophy out of American practicality as a sellout of genuine philosophy. This aristocratic hostility to America's spirited practicality, to its optimism about change, to its belief in the second chance, to the very things in the American story that multiculturalists distrust and which one might suppose Bloom would defend—America as the "new" world, the second Eden, the City on the Hill—blinds

Bloom to certain central strengths of the American polity, as well as to the relationship of ordinary human beings to books. Perhaps because he earns his living reading and writing (the European vocation, as it were), he makes just a little bit too much of books and what they can teach us. Rousseau liked to say he preferred the Sparta that knew how to act aright to the Athens that knew how to think aright: he probably would have preferred a just America that knew how to conduct itself to a learned America that did not. Not that the two must collide; in Ben Franklin and Thomas Jefferson, as well as in John Dewey and Walter Lippmann, the practical and the profound converged.

Nonetheless, America's true philosophers have, on the whole, not been bookmen or academicians or theorists. They have been poets like Emily Dickinson, Walt Whitman, and Woody Guthrie, essayists like Henry Adams and Ralph Waldo Emerson, lawyers like James Madison and Hugo Black, and moral leaders like John Brown, Susan B. Anthony, and Martin Luther King, Jr. They are represented by Ben Franklin in Philadelphia rather than Ben Franklin in Paris, Jefferson at Monticello adapting his contraptions to the architecture of his home rather than Jefferson writing his inaugurals. Bloom can argue with Dewey while Strauss argues with the positivists, but America's great historical teachers prefer to make their points in the domain of deliberate action and common purpose. The founders borrowed certain ideas from Harrington and Locke and the Scottish economists to be sure, but they were first of all inventors, innovators, and men of action; their strength lay in practice, and the constitution they wrought was not a theory rooted in ideas but an experiment rooted in practice. As the story they told suggests (retold here in Chapter 2), this was an adventure in self-invention, a tale of doers rather than of talkers.

We continue to learn the most—the good and the bad, the lessons and the warnings—from our doers, from Jefferson and Franklin, Eugene Debs and Robert Taft, Harry Hopkins and

Martin Luther King, Jr. Bloom yearns for heroes and condemns us for having none worthy of the name, but the nation democrats aspire to is not the country that has no heroes but (in Bertolt Brecht's distinction) the country that needs no heroes. At its best, Americans have been their own heroes, their nation a creation of anonymous settlers, cattlemen, garment workers, grade school teachers, factory laborers, entrepreneurs, farmers, longshoremen, inventors, and just plain folks. These common people saw in America a place where they might govern themselves free of the dominion of the dogmatists and truth-knowers, who in concert with Europe's monarchs had established a noble civilization on the backs of illiterate and powerless masses—just as Socrates had gone down to the port of Piraeus to lecture Athenian youths on virtue while slaves dug the silver on which his leisure depended.

Bloom simply gets America wrong. Being a book man, he assumes that pragmatism is an *idea* that molds and thus misdirects Americans. In fact, Dewey and James are attempting as much to capture as to influence the practical temper of the American spirit. Rather than imposing ideas on practice, they try to distill ideas from practice. If Americans distrust Truth or the pretentions of certain noble souls to possess it, it is neither because they have read Nietzsche nor because they have gone to school with soulless positivists or have been taught by value-neutral social scientists or radicalized child-professors of the sixties. It is because, having banned rank and title from their constitution, they do not trust teachers who tell them "smarter" means "better," or who propound a correlation between the nobility of a soul and its right to an education. If they lack confidence in those who claim to possess Truth, it is because they are the descendants of immigrants who fled such Truth-sayers. They knew the truth as it was purveyed by inquisitors, prosecutors, and king's counsellors—dogmatic believers who impressed their Truths by impressing the men for whom their Truths were intended. Bloom actually confesses to longing for the days in which Protestants and

Catholics, by hating each other, demonstrated they were "taking their beliefs seriously."[45] Is the average American to be faulted for preferring the frivolous shallows of religious tolerance to the seriousness of the Salem witch-hunts? A very wise American once remarked that to be roasted alive on account of one's beliefs is perhaps to have them taken just a little bit *too* seriously.

Americans are practical people, with practical vices no less than practical virtues. If they lack a tragic sense, it is in part because of the story they have told themselves about themselves, because they conceived of America as Europe's exit from tragedy. If Americans refuse to accept things as they are, it is because they are the refugees from things as they were elsewhere. If American education is not steeped in the sorts of rich prejudice prized by Bloom as an emblem of passionate commitment, it is because the schools have been factories of Americanism in which generations of immigrants have learned to be free.

Like all women and men great and small, Bloom yearns for community. But to his community only committed truth-seekers are to be admitted, those for whom reflection alone constitutes the good life. Unhappily, there are precious few lovers of reflection, and as the ancients have taught us, a community of philosophers is an oxymoron, for reflection is finally a divine and solitary occupation. Political community is what distinguishes human beings from both the animals and the gods—as well as from the philosophers who would be gods. The ancient philosopher with whom Americans have most in common is in fact Aristotle, not Plato. In the infinite variety of their associations—their fraternal clubs and church bazaar committees and hospital benefit associations and neighborhood political clubs, their PTAs and Granges and cooperatives and charities—Americans are the true communitarians who give life to Aristotle's definition of man as a *zoon politikon*, a political animal par excellence.

There is much to be admired in Bloom's philosophical temperament, in his aspiration to a nobility of soul. Yet this cannot mean that we must measure our own souls by the aspirations of philosophy. Souls are deep in many different ways, and reading is hardly the only road to virtue. I have witnessed in the ardent talk of an inspiring teacher a powerful nobility of soul, but in the eyes of an impoverished mother suckling a child at her breast I have seen the same thing. The Olympic athlete shines with an excellence no less luminous than the Olympian philosopher's. The search for knowledge is a vital project for the human race, but it is only one project among many, and it cannot be permitted to intimidate or awe us, nor to impede our evolution toward democracy and justice. Souls are not made to be sized, and to speak of one as larger or better or more deserving than another is to deny the soul's essential universality.

BLOOM'S AMERICAN REPUBLIC: THE RULE OF THE PEOPLE OR THE RULE OF VIRTUE?

We return, then, to Bloom's queries, which are also ours: Is quality education possible in a democratic society? Can a virtuous society be achieved by educating everyone well? Or only by educating the virtuous to rule over the rest? How deep does Bloom's distaste for egalitarianism and modernity go? Does he finally aspire not only to education by and for the wise, but to government by and for the wise?

Disclaimers abound in *The Closing of the American Mind*. Bloom absolves Socrates from any lust for power, even in the name of preserving wisdom, and certainly he would extend the same exoneration to himself. Nonetheless, egalitarians who read him with care must at least contemplate the possibility that philosophical modesty about philosopher-kings, whether in Plato or in Bloom, may itself be one more gentle deception, the greatest of the noble lies necessary to protect philosophers from the society whose tolerance they require—at least until they can rule it.

We have observed how tortuous is the path of Straussian philosophical rhetoric in a democratic society; and we know from Bloom's own impassioned diagnosis how insidious the revolt of the masses appears to the philosopher. Bloom even acknowledges how useful it is to philosophers to have "well-placed friends,"[46] and conservatives can hardly complain they lack friends in the Washington of the 1990s. We might be forgiven for wondering, when Plato assured us that philosophers had little wish to be kings and no lust at all for power, how it is that so many students of Strauss have found their way into the Platonic caves of shadows along the Potomac.[47]

Even if philosophers were to retain their modesty, even if there is no deception in Bloom's political disclaimers, even if the tension between democracy and philosophy is productive as well as perilous, even if democratic politics are safe from aristocratic rationalism, Bloom's analysis still poses profound problems for democratic education. If with Bloom we understand philosophy as the love of pure knowledge—as a cult of reflection and reason, a rationalization of hierarchy in human essences, a celebration of excellence, as an activity of the Few, a skepticism about life in the Cave, a chasing after the gods, a destroyer of religion and mores, an exposer of myths, and a foe of normality, mundanity, and equality—then philosophy cannot become the central discipline of democratic education without undermining equality and citizenship.

Some interpreters have tried to make Socrates into the political villain of his own trial, not a pedagogical subversive but a traitor to democracy who endangered the Athenian republic by supporting its aristocratic detractors. But the more suggestive question for us is whether Socrates was a sound teacher for everyone. In the Socratic hagiography, this is the most heretical question of all. Yet the trial of Socrates was not simply the trial of a freethinker by know-nothing democratic thugs in a close-minded democratic city run by a rabble. It was the trial of a friend and relative and possibly a sympathizer of Critias' Thirty Tyrants, who had used the excuse of the Peloponnesian War to impose a brief and terrible tyranny on Pericles' once-free city, the trial of an aristocratic critic of equality, the trial of a teacher of the Few who disdained the Many.[48] Socrates loved the truth, and he certainly loved Athens (he chose death over exile); but he did not love democracy, and he saw in equality the conceit and envy of ignorant, debased souls. Nor did he believe that men had a right and a responsibility (let alone any capacity) to govern themselves in common. That a man might be better off ruling himself badly than being ruled wisely by another more prudent man—the central tenet of democracy—was simply beyond the philosopher's ken. That a man's essential humanity might lay in his commonality with others rather in than a unique rational faculty of his own was not a conclusion a philosopher of reason could accept. This may not make Socrates a political traitor to Athens, but it does make him a dubious model for teaching in a democratic polity.

The lesson Bloom's encounter with Socrates teaches Americans, once they penetrate the gentle deceptions, is that the philosopher's ideal of the open mind flourishes best in a closed society where, if philosophers do not rule, those who do rule defer to philosophy. Where education is less for than against democracy, and students are selected not by their need or their right to learn but only by their mental capacity, the smart will learn only to be wise and no one—not even the wise—will learn to be free. We can understand why a philosopher of noble intentions may be aghast at a society moved by the suspicion that one man is as good as the next, a society convinced that the Puerto Rican sixteen-year-old with two babies and no library card is as deserving of an education as the Choate graduate who has enrolled in a seminar at the University of Chicago. But will we want such a philosopher to educate our children. I mean *all* our children?

What most astonishes me is not that Allan Bloom wrote a book on education in America that makes democracy wisdom's primary adversary, but that so many Americans greeted it with cheers. We are being asked to choose between the open mind and the open society, being asked to close the university to the Many in order to secure it for the Few, being asked to make reflection and its requisites the master of action and its requisites. How we respond will not only effect what kind of education we will have, but whether we will remain a free and egalitarian society devoted to justice, or become a nation of deferential tutees who have been talked out of our freedom by a critic of all that has transpired since the ancient world yielded to the modern.

It should not be forgotten that we have had societies in which Truth and those who held it were deemed superior to the common sense of common men. The Society of Jesus in its early incarnation was one such association, and so passionately did it believe in its Truth that it conducted a century-long Inquisition in its name. Protestants in turn invented their own forms of inquisition. What John Locke and those other proto-moderns with whom Bloom associates the decline of ancient virtue preached was that a too-firm belief in religious or philosophical Truth with a too-large *T* was a recipe for costly intolerance and lasting injustice. Only when the quest for Truth gave way to the possibility of doubt were human beings safe from persecution in the name of dogma.

Disenchantment has its uses. Modernity's main gift to us has been the open society, where men and women treat one another as equals and believe all have an equal right to govern themselves, even if unwisely, to live their own lives, even if unnobly, and to be fully educated, even if that education is devoted to making them adequate self-governing citizens rather than great philosophers. The open society insists that nobility of soul is no better a title to special treatment than a beating heart, and that the differences between homo sapiens can never be the basis of allocating goods among them—whether those goods are material, political, or intellectual.

Allan Bloom clearly does not accept these modern notions. His problem would seem to be that in an era after virtue, after the death of God, after the regime of reason, it is hard, so very hard, for rationality's disciples—for men of true virtue—to live. The ideology of democracy is a sound, one might even say noble, response to the dilemma: it permits us to live with our uncertainty, our agnosticism, our doubt, our sense of abandonment, our isolation, without murdering one another; to live even with a certain modicum of justice made up of equal parts of compassion and tolerance. But it is not a response to Bloom's liking, because he does not believe most men and women are up to it; he worries that democracy will never be more than a disguise for the rule of irrationality and prejudice, and thus not an alternative to but a surrogate for anarchy or organized mayhem. The most apt response to Bloom's attempt to teach the Few how to be noble might then be for all of us to teach him not only the virtue of democracy, but how he himself might learn to be democratic. He might even be the better for the exchange.

If Bloom's canon, rooted in aristocratic reason and a few men's noble souls, is the only canon offered to democratic schools, democratic schools will have little choice but to complete their crude demolition of the very idea of a canon as an authoritative guide to learning. My own claim for the worthiness of the Western tradition as a teacher of liberty is that it is an open, self-critical, subversive, and encompassing tradition that invites everyone into the conversation, even where those already in it might prefer to keep newcomers out. The canon is not the enemy of modernity: for the canon spawned modernity, as well as its rebellious post-modern children. Socrates' first refusal to accept an answer to a question he asked, his first insistence on posing still another question, began the fatal unraveling of orthodoxy, and today's dilemmas—skepticism, nihilism, post-modernist excess—are thus in a certain sense also *his* doing.

The conservative antipathy to democracy in the name of philosophy is actually rather peculiar, for democracy is how women and men emancipated from the consoling certainties of authority (religious, political, and metaphysical) try to govern themselves in a world that has been disenchanted to no small degree precisely by philosophy. We did not disenchant the world, and we are democrats only because we are trying to live in it—to nurture values such as tolerance, mutual respect, and common problem-solving in the face of uncertainty; to hold people together in artificial and egalitarian communities that the decline of traditional and religious ties have weakened. In the end, democracy is more a response to the terrors of modernity than it is modernity's monstrous creation.

Allan Bloom, Alasdair MacIntyre, Roger Kimball, and others like them call for an impossible restoration of the world we have lost, a resurrection of the sort of philosophy that philosophy itself has undone. The prudent democrat, on the other hand, teaches how we might survive the passing of orthodox values in a world that provides neither escape routes back into the authoritarian past nor ladders leading up into the aeries of the philosophers' republic. The democrat may even promise more: the possibility of transforming survival into a virtue; for with a truly democratic education, it becomes possible to forge an art of politics that can allow us to survive the modern and the post-modern, and even flourish in their spite.

The condition of modernity is above all America's condition: that is both our brave boast and our tragic fate, and it is what gives democracy its powerful American resonance. Student rebels, educational reformers, and all those other children of Dewey who helped produce the educational revolution of the sixties got a good many things wrong. They indulged in excesses corrosive to their ideals. But they got a few things right as well.

They saw that to expose the power biases of conventional science and "neutral" scholarship was less to undermine the pursuit of genuine truth than to clear hypocrisy from truth's way. And they appreciated that by including studies of and by women, blacks, and other dispossessed groups within Western society, they were not narrowing but enlarging the notion of Western culture.

Along with Bloom, we may weep at how queasy we feel living in a world after virtue, at how difficult it is to discern the good in a world no longer shadowed by the authority of an eternal God or guided by a metaphysician's account of the eternal verities. Indeed, even modernity's fans may shudder a little at a world where modernity's great teacher—science—has been demythologized and forced to seek legitimacy. Even scientists must now appear before the bar of sociology and prove that their latest theories can withstand a critique of "dominant paradigms." Even Einstein and Newton must prove it is not just their power that legitimizes their science. Nonetheless, it is this dismally disenchanted world for which educators must prepare the young—a world of doubts and puzzles; a world of too much materialism and too few great books, of more than enough selfishness and not enough civic education; a world where culture must encompass the globe and universalism must encompass particularism if either are to survive.

Clinging to values that have lost their resonance, blaming outsiders for the loss of what the culture has failed to preserve from within, assailing the teachers for failing to teach the young what the old clearly do not want them to learn, is more than just hypocritical: it is dangerous. One generation's excesses can perhaps save another from its own. From all those endless teach-ins, from the campus riots and student rebellions, from the campaigns against secret research and the anti-ROTC demonstrations, from the foolish innovations and the curricular novelties, from the free speech movement and the free university ideal, have come some saving truths. Equality is not the enemy of freedom;

power must not be the determinant of culture; pluralism is not a recipe for nihilism; the opening of the schools to all need not spell the closing of the American mind; democracy does not automatically disqualify excellence; to acknowledge the plurality of culture is not to deny the universality of cultural aspirations; the rise of progressive education is not the same thing as the fall of Western civilization; and finally, all education is and must remain radical, subversive, critical, yet at the same time comforting, unifying, integrating—a reminder of the past, a challenge to the present, a prod to the future.

These are small but precious truths capable of securing an American future in a world that, however much the cultural conservatives curse it, is not going to be exclusively American or white or male.

CHAPTER 6

WHAT OUR FORTY-SEVEN-
YEAR-OLDS KNOW

John Dewey had no doubt that "the measure of the worth of the administration, curriculum and methods of instruction of the school is the extent to which they are animated by a social spirit. . . . in the first place, the school must itself be a community life."[1] Where once this was a common assumption, the debate about the nature of liberal education has in recent years rendered it controversial. In challenging traditional curricula, the canon, and the story we tell about our past, we have to a large degree forgotten about the fundamental context of teaching liberty: the civic role of America's schools and colleges in fostering citizenship and preparing the young for life in a democratic culture. Dewey's argument was less an innovation than a summary of the historical practice of American public schooling. Colleges and schools, public and private, religious and secular, land grant and traditional, were united in their conviction that among the preeminent ends of education was a training in democracy. Citizenship was not merely a matter of voting (and acquiring the information required to vote intelligently); it was a way of life thought to be distinctively American. Read the early "mission statements" of Harvard or William and Mary or Princeton: typically, Queens College (which was Rutgers in the eighteenth century) announced itself prepared to "promote learning for the benefit of the community."

What was once obvious has now become so opaque that for many there is a question as to whether there should even be a question. Does the university as the highest stage of schooling have a civic mission? Does it have any discernible mission at all? The evidence is far from clear. Nor is it just conservatives like Bloom who are suspicious of universities too committed to equality, democracy, and citizenship. There are plenty of ivory-tower purists and quite enough professional academics who dispute the direct relevance of education—especially higher education—to democracy, willing to make a powerful case against the idea of a civic mission for our schools even if the conservative critique is put aside. Asked about its civic role in a "free" society, the college establishment seems at times to know neither what a free society is nor what the educational requisites of freedom might look like. Nonetheless, both administrators and their critics have kept busy, for, like zealots (classically defined as people who redouble their efforts when they have forgotten their aims), they have covered their confusion by embellishing their hyperbole. They wring their hands and rue the social crises of higher education—apathy, cynicism, careerism, prejudice, selfishness, sexism, opportunism, complacency, and substance abuse—but they hesitate when faced with hard decisions and prefer to follow rather than challenge the national mood, which throws a few bones to the radicals in the way of curricular reform and then screams in horror about how the radicals have taken over academe.

Students, reflecting the climate in which they are being educated, are, well, a mess. In its annual report on *The State of America's Children*, the Children's Defense Fund continues to play Cassandra: Every thirty-five seconds a baby is born into poverty. Every night 100,000 children go to sleep homeless. Almost twice a day a kid under five is murdered. Every year nearly a half million drop out of school. Every day 135,000 kids show up at school with guns instead of books. "It is a morally lost nation," comments the Defense Fund, "that is unable and unwilling to disarm our children and those who kill our children in their school buses, strollers, yards, and schools. . . ."[2]

Insulated from much of the violence, our colleges and universities breed attitudes no less destructive. At the very moment minority students at Dartmouth are receiving anonymous hate letters from their peers, and feminists at Dartmouth are being sent notes enclosed in condoms reading "You disgust me," students at the University of Utah are voting members of the "Who Cares?" party into student government, embracing their promises to pay their way by "panhandling, and running strip bars, raffles and prostitution." Youthful hijinks, perhaps: after all, a decade earlier students at Wisconsin had elected the "Pail and Shovel" party into office (its platform: stealing and wasting as much money as possible), and panty raids of one kind or another have been campus staples for a century. "Boys will be boys," say the boys of an earlier generation. The critics are often themselves part of the problem. At least one of the more celebrated compilers of complaints against the young—Dinesh D'Souza in his *Illiberal Education*—was himself on the staff of the race-baiting, right-wing *Dartmouth Review* (financed by rightist sources outside the university), and hence himself part of the anarchic puerility he has sold so many books reviling.

I worried earlier (in Chapter 4) about excesses of the reformers' curriculum. But far more worrisome and a good deal more toxic is the wave of racism, overt sexual discrimination, and homophobia that is sweeping America's campuses in the wake of the conservative permissiveness of the Reagan-Bush years. As liberal permissiveness afforded the young the opportunity to express sexual, political, and cultural desires repressed in more traditional times, so conservative permissiveness affords the young the opportunity to express sexual, political, and cultural prejudices repressed in more liberal times. Thus, D'Souza can presumably speak for a whole liberated generation of white males (though he is nonwhite) when he allows as how "nobody will say so, but the truth is that a large number of students and faculty [need he say *which* students and faculty?] have simply *had* it with minority double standards and intimidation."[3] Which is another way of saying what so many exasperated Americans are saying: that they have *had* it with the homeless, with minorities, with feminists—in other words, with equality.

Things look still worse when these attitudes are correlated with national patterns of student political apathy: less than one-fifth of the eighteen- to twenty-four-year-old population voted in recent congressional elections, which is less than half of the 47 percent of the general population that voted. In the 1988 presidential election (such elections typically draw higher turnouts), the eighteen to twenty-four youth vote fell to 18 percent. Student lethargy is mirrored by administrative paralysis. Having abjured the infantalizing tactics of in loco parentis, which once made college presidents into den mothers (without, however, offering a clue on how to deal with their unruly wards), administrators are left without meaningful pedagogical strategies outside the classroom. The outcome is often a thin layer of oversolicitousness in small matters covering an elephantine indifference in larger ones: carefully purveyed substance abuse information programs coupled with nonchalant acquiescence to residential halls and fraternities that often seem held together mainly by booze, sex, and bigotry; a perilous intervention on behalf of minorities complaining about "racially insensitive" teachers coupled with a willingness to see 60 or 70 percent of minority students, heavily recruited for public relations purposes, drop out of school once they are no longer in the limelight.

Critics howl about what is or is not being taught, but in reality the issue is whether anyone is *teaching* at all nowadays. In his *Profscam*, Charles J. Sykes makes far too many wild charges against the professoriat; but he is not wrong to note that "contemporary academic culture is not merely indifferent to teaching, it is actively hostile to it."[4] How can any young faculty member spend very much time debating whether to teach Wordsworth or Woolf, Milton or Jim Morrison, Thomas Jefferson or Clarence Thomas, when she will get tenure only through research in a process that marginalizes teaching—radical or conservative, multicultural or canonical—and makes publication the only serious consideration? College presidents will tell you, quite correctly, that great teachers are usually ardent researchers, and pioneering thinkers make the most inspiring classroom pedagogues. But good teachers need to spend at least a few hours a week in a classroom. No matter how gifted the educator, she cannot practice the teaching craft in front of her computer, in her laboratory, or at the library, let alone while speaking at a professional conference or traveling to a research archive. To talk about the "balance" needed between research and teaching is, at best, an exercise in wishful thinking. At worst, it is a lie. The dirty little open secret of American higher education, known to every faculty member who manages to gain tenure, is this: No one ever was tenured at a major college or university on the basis of great teaching alone; and no one with a great record of research and publication was ever denied tenure because of a poor teaching record. Teaching is the gravy, but research is the meat and potatoes.

Most of the disputes examined in these pages, most of the quarrels I have picked with colleagues, are about pedagogy. But this new battle of the books is being carried on by a minority of faculty united by a deep concern for education. I have little reason to feel a kinship to Allan Bloom, and he has less to like me. But we are as blood brothers when compared to the vast apathetic mass of faculty who do not much give a damn one way or another about what goes on in America's classrooms. Too many faculty members on too many campuses either do not care or cannot afford to. Certainly university administrators give them neither reason nor incentive. They have become "employees" of university corporate managers; they have turned their trade association, the American Association of University Professors, into an adversarial labor union interested in worker equity rather than excellence, and willing to strike classrooms and abandon students when their economic interests are in jeopardy. Necessarily so. The demeaned status of teachers in the modern university gives scholars little reason to measure their career progress other than by how quickly they get tenure, how much they get paid, and how little time they have to spend in the classroom.

At Rutgers University we have spent the past fifteen years successfully competing both for talented junior faculty and for world-class scholars by promising them minimal teaching schedules. I know of junior colleagues who have been on the faculty roster for two years and have scarcely seen the inside of a classroom. An Ivy League university, disturbed by the disrepute into which teaching has fallen, recently offered its faculty a teaching prize. The reward? A course off the following year! Is this some scandalous profscam? Far from it; it is a natural reaction to the university incentive structure.

We may moralize about the virtues of education, but higher education has come to mean education for hire: the university is increasingly for sale to those corporations and state agencies that want to buy its research facilities and, for appropriate funding, acquire the legitimacy of its professoriat. I do not mean the university in service to the public and private sectors; I mean the university in servitude to the public and private sectors. I mean not partnership but a "corporate takeover" of the university.[5] The president of the University of Maryland recently announced, with apparent pride: "We've finally recognized that there's an awful lot a university can learn from a corporation."[6] One thing it can learn is how to stay solvent: In 1982, the Monsanto Company gave over $23 million to the medical school of Washington University, not as a gift, but to "fund research leading to marketable biomedical discoveries" over which Monsanto would retain "sweeping rights."[7] A faculty member at the University of

California at Davis turned over patent rights to the fruits of his invention to the Allied Corporation for $2.5 million dollars. Allied then bought $2 million worth of shares in a firm the professor had founded. In 1989, a Harvard faculty committee proposed that researchers be prohibited from holding stock in companies for which they develop drugs; the proposal was overwhelmingly defeated in a raucous faculty meeting.[8]

In involving itself with primary school as well as college pedagogy, corporate America has quite naturally expressed a concern with education in strictly utilitarian terms: "Education isn't just a social concern, it's a major economic issue," proclaimed the chairman of IBM in a full-page advertisement in the *New York Times Magazine*.[9] The chairman's anxiety had to do with competition: "If our students can't compete today, how will our companies compete tomorrow?" The question is, are these concerns and anxieties valid criteria for internal school reform? Should faculty members subordinate free inquiry to guided research? Should results be freely promulgated or sold to corporate sponsors? This entire discussion takes place in an era of the hegemony of markets. Chester Finn, Jr., once William Bennett's deputy at the Department of Education, calls for a consumer-oriented education in place of the producer-centered system organized around "those who are employed by the education system."[10] When Russell Jacoby writes about "The Greening of the University," he is talking not about national parks but about industrial parks.[11] Hannah Grey, while president of the University of Chicago, was, Jacoby reminds us, on the board of directors of ARCO, J. P. Morgan, and Morgan Guaranty Trust. And Benno C. Schmidt, Jr., Yale's president renowned almost exclusively for his fundraising success, has just been snatched from his post by Whittle Communications to head up (and lend a little Ivy class to) a new $60 million, one thousand school education-for-profit venture. So it is that autonomous pedagogical standards are displaced by market pressures from both immediate consumers (students) and long-term consumers (the private and public sectors). Perhaps schools shackled to the market will change or even reform it. More likely, they will become pawns of the tastes, values, and goals of society at large.

The impact of these changes on faculty are everywhere evident. Faculty who play ball share in the spoils. Those who do not may find themselves on second-class career tracks or even unemployed. Harvard prizes teaching, so it offers the Levenson Award for Outstanding Teaching. In both 1986 and 1987, the prizewinners were fired—denied tenure and told to take their outstanding teaching somewhere else—apparently because their research was not up to Harvard's standards. Yet both found jobs immediately in other leading universities, and some students were left wondering whether the two were *penalized* for their teaching excellence. Research, publications, and grants brought in from the outside are what count. Where commerce encroaches on education so blatantly, can teachers really be faulted for thinking like capitalists, or more modestly like proletarians? There has been some complaint about the unionizing of faculty members who, administrators argue, ought to regard themselves as professionals, but unionization has been a reactive process and reflects simple market realities.

The market, in fact, has been invading the classroom with increasing shamelessness. Well before its new venture, Whittle Communications introduced "Channel One" into America's high school classrooms. Channel One is a short news program aimed at teenagers that is squeezed between commercials. In return for $250 million worth of hardware, selected schools are now making advertising an integral part of the learning process. Not the study of advertising, but the basic message of commercials—buy, buy, buy. Some brave states like New York have refused the bribe, but many have succumbed and there are currently over ten thousand schools in the hoop. Meanwhile, Whittle has moved on to the book market—an arena of the autonomy and integrity of intellect—to publish titles whose revenues come primarily from advertising run in along with whatever wisdom appears on the pages. More than a little ironically, one of Whittle's more interesting books is Arthur Schlesinger, Jr.'s attack on radical multiculturalism in defense of the neutrality and sanctity of the classroom.[12]

The privatization and commercialization of schooling continue apace, with the connivance of the new research-driven scholasticism. College presidents talk pleasantly about the synergy of teaching and research, and in simpler, more pristine times, the two could perhaps be mutually reinforcing. But more recently, as Jacques Barzun has noted, research and scholarship have not only become ever more narrow and specialized—and thus remote from teaching—but have also taken the very culture that is their putative subject and held it hostage to their reflexive scholastic concerns. Where commercialization fails with direct bribes to draw scholars into the marketplace, scholasticism triumphs and isolates scholars from any relationship to the real world.

"Since William James, Russell, and Whitehead," Barzun reminds us, "philosophy, like history, has been confiscated by scholarship, and locked away from the contamination of cultural use." And from the contamination of educational use. The new scholasticism that is academic specialization has turned the study of culture into the study of the study of culture—self-conscious preoccupation with method, technique, and scholarship displacing a broad humanistic concern for culture itself. This applies to the new champions of democratic education no less than to others, as the preceding discussion of hyperskepticism revealed. We no longer simply read books, we study what it means to read books; we do not interpret theories but develop theories of interpretation. We are awash in what the biographer W. Jackson Bate of Harvard calls "self-trivialization," pursuing an intellectual quest that takes us away from students and the world which they are supposedly being educated to inhabit.

The oddest thing about much of the new radical scholarship on feminism and race is how inaccessible it is to its purported constituencies. At least Marx's *Manifesto* was a good and popular read. Conservative prose is intelligible to nonspecialists: perhaps that accounts for some of its success. Liberal culture defenders of the old school, like Edmund Wilson and Lionel Trilling and Irving Howe, were also gifted stylists, as are such younger critics as Carol Gilligan, Catherine Stimpson, Michael Wulzer, and Louis Gates, Jr. But a good deal of post-modernist criticism is intelligible only to insiders and their graduate students and, trapped in its own metacritical jargon, is no less elitist than the canon it challenges. Undergraduates are left to fend for themselves. Whether universities sell themselves shamelessly on the open market or withdraw into a cocoon of self-obsessed solipsism, students are betrayed. These tendencies manifest themselves in two unacceptable models of the university, neither of which acknowledges the place of schooling in a democracy or the place of democracy in schooling.

TWO CULTURES, TWO UNIVERSITIES

Thirty years ago, C. P. Snow registered a classic complaint about the cultural illiteracy of scientists and the scientific illiteracy of the cultured, warning that between science and the humanities was growing "a gulf of mutual incomprehension—sometimes (particularly among the young) hostility and dislike, but most of all lack of understanding."[13] Our students have bridged the gulf with indifference and universal shallowness. By their ignorance of both science and culture, equity between the two cultures is achieved. Illiteracy and innumeracy meet at ground level to create a splendid egalitarianism of ignorance. Whereas Snow worried about "Luddite intellectuals" turning their backs on the technological future and unreflective scientists ignoring the temporal contexts of history and literature, today's students are given little reason to care for past or future. Society assures them that a prudent sense of today, as gauged by dollars, is sufficient education in today's ubiquitous present. Scholars either mimic students aiming for maximum economic advantage by rushing precipitously into the marketplace, or turn their backs by retreating into scholasticism.

No wonder that students capable of much more, students who have even been known to demand much more, have wallowed complacently in cynicism, privatism, vocationalism, avarice, and know-nothingism. No wonder cynics beyond the ivy walls have had little use for the teachers, their students, or the stolid administrators who oversee the unsettled relations between them. Clark Kerr (once the chancellor of the University of California system) was only half kidding when, in answer to a question about what his university constituents really wanted, he replied that as far as he could make out students were interested in sex, alumni were interested in football, and faculty were interested in parking. Kerr, prophet of the multiversity—vocational education's granddaddy—was being unfair. The not so amusing truth is that students are interested in credentials rather than what they represent, alumni are interested in buildings rather than what goes on in them, and faculty are interested in research rather than in the scientific and humanistic cultures that both nourish and are nourished by research. Perhaps that is why, *mutatis mutandi*, we can still sympathize with H. L. Mencken's quip that the best way to reform the university is to burn down the buildings and hang the professors. Many of today's professors might prefer hanging to a four-course per semester teaching load.

Not every critic is a cynic, however, and today there are two positive models of the university being purveyed to address the current crisis in education. These are models not of the competing curricula fought over by faculty (the topic in earlier chapters), but of the university itself, as fought over by administrators, boards of governors, and politicians. The two models are mirror images of each other and embody the tendencies alluded to in the introductory discussion. One model is scholastic and calls for refurbishing the ivory tower and reinforcing its splendid monastic isolation, while the other apes the marketplace and calls for tearing down the tower and overcoming isolation by forging new associations with—a new servitude to—the market's whims and fashions, which pass as its aims and purposes. Neither model satisfies.

We may call the first the purist model and the second the vocational model. The first, an embellishment on the medieval university, is favored by nostalgic scholastics. In the name of the abstract pursuit of speculative knowledge, it calls for insulating the university from the wider society. Learning for learning's sake: not for career, not for life, not for democracy, not for money; for neither power nor happiness, neither career nor quality of life, but for its own pure sake. To the purist, knowledge is radically divorced from time and culture, from power and interest, from ordinary language and commonplace speech; above all, it eschews utility. It aspires to reconstruct Aristotle's Lyceum in downtown Newark, catering, however, to the residents of New Athens rather than Newark. It knows a social context exists but believes the job of the university is to offer sanctuary from that context. The purist model is in many ways the old-fashioned liberal model of academe as a neutral domain in which free minds engage in open discourse at a cosmic distance from power and interest and the other distractions of the real world. It has many virtues, which often include a genuine love of teaching; but it suffers from all of those illusions that, as suggested in Chapter 3, were exposed and challenged by 1960s critics of liberalism and positivism.

Since the purist understands the teacher as someone who "transmits" a fixed tradition to the young, he must regard cultural critics who question the paradigms underlying the great tradition as subverters of education and traitors to their profession. Since he understands the student as someone who "acquires" knowledge as he might acquire his grandfather's Vermont farm, he must regard students who look for critical relevance in their studies and for clues to civic responsibility and the arts of living as dilettantes or philistines or worse. There may be both liberals and conservatives among the purists: relevance is their common enemy.

The vocational model abjures tradition no less decisively than the purist model abjures relevance. Indeed, it is wildly alive to the demands of the larger society it believes education must serve. Where the purist may reject as so many diseases even the victories of modernity (equality, social justice, and universal education for the conservative purist; capitalism and bourgeois culture for the liberal purist), the vocationalist accepts even the ravages of modernity as so many virtues—or at least as the necessary price of progress.

The vocationalist wishes to see the university prostrate itself before modernity's new gods. Service to the market, training for its professions, research in the name of its products are the hallmarks of the new full-service university, which wants nothing so much as to be counted as a peer among the nation's great corporations, an equal opportunism producer of prosperity and material happiness: All-American High, a wholly owned subsidiary of Whittle Communications, itself a partly owned subsidiary of Time-Warner, the communications behemoth, which is now entering a still more global partnership with Toshiba Corporation and C. Itoh and Co. under the umbrella of Time-Warner Entertainment. All-American U, a branch of Xerox Corporation, Dutch Royal Shell, Nissan Motor Company, and your state government, dedicated to serving stockholders first and students incidentally, if at all. Forging dubious alliances with research companies, All-American U plies corporations for program funding and stalks the public sector in search of public "needs" it can profitably satisfy. In each of these cases, it asks society to show the way and compliantly follows. As with the purist model, there are virtues in this model. There is some attempt to justify the association with society as a form of service, and no doubt significant service can be performed when a state university agricultural station works with local farmers to improve their crops, or a hi-tech center draws industry, thus increasing the tax base on which the university ultimately depends for its funding.

Yet whether as service or sellout, the focus on research adapted to the needs of the larger society can obviously corrupt. Advocates of "the Entrepreneurial University" seem impervious to these dangers. If it requires that teaching be subsumed to research, and research itself sometimes reduced to product-oriented engineering, too bad. If basic research is slighted, with devastating consequences for the link between science and the humanities (a link that depends on a conception of science rooted in fundamental intellectual inquiry rather than technological payoffs), that is the price that must be paid. If to be adequately funded means taking in advertising that privatizes and commercializes education in ways wholly inconsistent with learning, the realist will do what is necessary. If it requires that education take on the aspect of vocational training, and that the university become a kindergarten for corporate society where in the name of economic competition the young are socialized, bullied, and brainwashed into market usefulness, then the curriculum must be recast in the language of opportunism, careerism, and professionalism—in a word, commerce. Every course is affixed with a "pre-" (as in premedical, prelaw, prebusiness, and preprofessional). Academic departments hem in students' intellectual lives with a bevy of technical requirements, which leave no room for liberal or general education and which assume that education for living is in fact education for making a living. When education is about learning to do business in a market world, advertising ceases to be inappropriate. Enter Whittle Communications. Where the philosopher once said that all of life is a preparation for death, the educational careerist now thinks that all of life is a preparation for business—or perhaps, more bluntly, that life *is* business.

The first of our two models is aristocratic although liberal, humanistic but poignantly nostalgic—not merely Luddite in Snow's sense, but also, at least in one of its incarnations, profoundly antimodern. In its conservative mode, it wishes to educate the few well and perceives in the democratic ideal an insuperable obstacle to academic and cultural excellence. Harvard and Yale and Princeton are simply not what they used to be, complains Allan Bloom—and loudly may he complain with Benno Schmidt on his way to Whittle! Opening school doors to fashionable minority programs, opening school curricula to trendy feminism, opening the classroom to chic civic education is to close the mind to the higher calling of scholarship understood as the contemplation of a wisdom already discovered, set down, and consecrated.

Alan C. Kors, a University of Pennsylvania historian who is among the founders of a newly formed National Association of Scholars (not, please note, of Teachers), does not mince words: "The barbarians are in our midst," he warns. "We need to fight them a good long time. Show them you are not afraid, they crumble."[14] Stephen H. Balch, the director of the new association (whose members include John Silber, Oscar Handlin, James Q. Wilson, James Coleman, Robert Jastrow, Lucy Dawidowicz, and a host of other large-caliber pistols called in on behalf of the Big Canon), assumes a loftier tone, calling on scholars "to redeem American higher education from intellectual and moral servitude to forces having little to do with the life of the mind or the transmission of knowledge."[15]

Balch's language is studied and precise, and deserves attention: "Life of the mind," he writes, posing it as an alternative, a way apart from mere life. "Transmission of knowledge," he writes: education not as creative or critical thinking, but as the transmission and absorption of truths already discovered, known, and handed down. Assemble the young at the ivory tower and have them sit passively while the Canon imprints itself on the tabula rasa of their young minds, well away from the sprawling modern towers of babble where active participants in learning create only cacophony; let them worship at the altar of True Learning as monks and nuns cloistered from the seductions and responsibilities of lives that must eventually be lived.

The vocationalist regards this point of view as dangerous and unrealistic. For better or worse, to him education and its institutional tools are embedded in the real world. His pedagogical tasks are socialization, not insulation, integration, not isolation. This is hardly to say he is some radical sociological critic of liberal learning. The point is not to plumb and reveal the academy's hidden linkages to class, gender, and power; only to acknowledge and follow them—"There is an awful lot a university can learn from a corporation"—wherever they lead. In the sublime marketplace, where demand is king, it is society that leads, education that must follow: support it, ape it, reinforce it, chase it, undergird it, affirm it, preserve it. Whatever society wants and needs, the university tries to supply. Society says I need doctors, I will pay lawyers, and students rush to acquire medical skills and legal credentials. Education as vocationalism in service to society becomes a matter of socialization rather than scrutiny, of spelling out consequences rather than probing premises, of answering society's questions rather than questioning society's answers. Where once the student was taught that the unexamined life was not worth living, he is now taught that the profitably lived life is not worth examining. Where the radical democratic critic points to power in order to liberate liberal learning from it, the vocationalist points to power in order to track its course and follow it to its source.

The conflict between these two models gets expressed everywhere—in curricular disputes, in conflicts over admission and graduation requirements, and in debates over the role of civic education and its instruments (community service, for example) in university life. The purist wishes the free society well, but sees no connection between higher education and training the young to live responsibly in such a society; even when she admires democratic culture, she may deny its legitimacy in the academic domain. "I believe in democracy and trust that my students will somehow become good citizens, but that is neither my specialty nor the proper provenance of a university's curriculum, and so I must leave it to other institutions," she might say. Happily insulated from the seductions of profit and the lure of the unexamined life, the purist remains smugly cloistered, certain that those who challenge her are conditioned by ideology and fashion.

The vocationalist, on the other hand, seeks a total and uncritical relevance, as dictated by whatever society considers prudent or profitable. Courses must reflect the highly competitive global market, and programs must be designed to reinforce disciplinary and paradigm boundaries rather than examine or break through them. There is a place for philosophy and ethics to be sure, but only in a course called "Ethics and the Law" or "The Ethics of the Medical Profession," and more often than not taught by an anthropologist or sociologist, if necessary a philosopher, but probably not a theologian. Arts culture perhaps, but only in a seminar on "Managing the Arts for Profit." Basic science, maybe, but only inasmuch as it can demonstrably benefit applied science. For the purist, life is wholly subordinated to mind, which exists independently as a disembodied abstraction; for the vocationalist, mind is wholly subordinated to life, which is taken as a given in whatever forms it happens to manifest itself.

A THIRD MODEL: A CIVIC MISSION?

Neither extreme recognizes that education is a dialectic of life and mind, of body and spirit, in which the two are inextricably bound together. Neither acknowledges how awkward this makes it for a liberal arts university at once to serve and challenge society, to simultaneously "transmit" fundamental values such as tolerance, responsibility, and love of learning *and* to create a climate in which students are not merely conditioned by what is transmitted (transmission tends toward indoctrination). Such a university must stand apart from society in order to give students room to breathe and grow free from a too-insistent reality. At the same time, it must stand within the real world and its limits in order to prepare students for real lives in a society that, if they do not mold it to their aspirations, will mold them to its conventions. Students must be both protected from a precipitous engagement with "real life" and prepared for responsible and critical real-life roles.

The school, the college, and the university must all be guardians. Students require protection from a world for which their education is meant to be a training. They also need protection from their own not yet mature selves, achieved by exposing them to the reality of limits, the necessity of discipline, the benefits of deferred gratification; by asking them, by requiring them, even by demanding of them, things they would not necessarily require of themselves, precisely because they are not yet the educated women and men the process seeks to produce. Education is about learning to be free, and means ultimately setting students free from their teachers too. But there is a great deal of difference between setting them free and leaving them alone; between cultivating their autonomy and annihilating all limits; between helping them to make free choices and pushing them into free-fall.

Like all of us, the young are as inclined to run from as to embrace real freedom. Rousseau, who knew so much about the paradoxes of liberty, observed that freedom is a food easy to eat and hard to digest. The young have a tendency, in the cafeteria and in the classroom alike, to eat without digesting: it is the latter process that often requires the delicate but unwavering intervention of educational authority. No, you cannot make someone love literature, but you can make her take courses that in time, with gifted teaching, may give her the necessary skills, the patience, and the resources to do so. This may even turn an apathetic cultural illiterate into a spirited book reader. No, you cannot force someone to take Benin civilization as seriously as French civilization or an Aztec poem as seriously as *Don Quixote,* but by widening the scope of general education courses you can let him know that Africa has civilizations worthy of attention or that before their demise, the Aztecs wrote poetry. No, you cannot force someone to volunteer, but you can teach her what volunteering means by requiring community service as part of a basic civic education curriculum under the guidance of critical readings and teacher mentors, and thus in time perhaps turn a complacent and selfish cynic into a spirited volunteer, even an involved citizen.

If the young were born literate, there would be no need to teach them literature; if they were born citizens, there would be no need to teach them civic responsibility. But, of course, educators know that the young are born neither wise nor literate nor responsible—nor are they born free. The consequences of this argument, first advanced in the prologue, now become apparent. If women and men are born at best with the potential for wisdom, literacy, and responsibility, with an aptitude for freedom, however, that is matched by an aptitude, even a deep need, for security and domination and thus a disposition toward tyranny, schooling matters deeply. The educator must know how to exploit, challenge, coerce, or seduce these potentials into flowering. Education is about change, and change often hurts. That is why discipline, rules, and requirements always play a role in cultivating autonomy, spontaneity, and freedom. That is why the teacher must sometimes, precisely in the sense that Rousseau suggested in his most famous paradox, force students to be free; which is to say she must guarantee their eventual freedom as responsible adults and citizens by imposing on their freedom as students. She must respect their aspiration to freedom sufficiently to curtail its abuses wherever they stand in the way of its own growth. She must sometimes thrust liberty upon them when they do not want it, and she must sometimes wrest it from them when they want it most but it seems to her likely to endanger them.[16]

Neither the purist nor the vocationalist seems fully to appreciate the dialectical character of learning: how it both grows out of and challenges society, how it may extend the canon by sub-verting it, how it can enhance autonomy at the moment it limits it. Neither fully understands just how troublesome and unsettling and painful learning can be. To speak the language of education is to speak in a voice that is always subversive, radical, critical, and unsettling to young people who, like the rest of us, also yearn for certainty and safety. It is hard to move, easier by far to stay put; painful to accept fully the responsibility of freedom, easier to let someone else (the teacher, the administrator) assume it and then, secure in one's irresponsibility, cry "Tyranny!"—when it is exactly tyranny one is craving. On the other side, there is the danger that, as courage vanquishes fear and the mind finally lurches into motion, momentum will overcome prudence. As it accelerates, mind will be unable to find a resting point short of confusion, anarchy, or nihilism.

If learning is painful and costly, it is also an activity rooted, like all activity, in experience: an overly theoretical and insular approach, or one that encourages passivity, separates knowledge from experience and thus diminishes the capacity to learn. As John Dewey wrote in *Democracy and Education*,

> In schools, those under instruction are too customarily looked upon as acquiring knowledge as theoretical spec-tators, minds which appropriate knowledge by direct en-ergy of intellect. The very word "pupil" has almost come to mean one who is engaged not in having fruitful expe-riences but in absorbing knowledge directly.... the inti-mate union of activity and undergoing its consequences which leads to recognition of meaning is broken; instead we have two fragments: mere bodily action on one side, and meaning directly grasped by "spiritual" activity on the other.[17]

You cannot prepare the young to think critically while train-ing them to adjust to and work efficiently within an unexamined professional paradigm. Law school is not where the justifying norms of Western legalism are held up to scrutiny. Medical schools do not assign Ivan Illich to help would-be doctors understand that the grounding norms of medical science can be challenged and that what we call good health may be subject to different interpretations.[18] It is in the autonomous general education environment that such fundamental teaching is likely to occur; yet it is precisely here that professionalization is beginning to take its toll.

Yet I have already suggested (see Chapter 3) that academic autonomy cannot nourish our critical faculties by segregating our cognitive from our affective and sensory faculties and dumping them in a black box labeled DO NOT OPEN WHILE ACTUALLY LIVING. The space into which educators invite the young is not strictly cognitive, but it is not identical with everyday space either. It is inner space turned inside out, experience turned upside down. It is hypothetical space situated in a real world, an arena that permits experimentation free of consequences and thought free of responsibility—in the name of learning the meaning of consequences and the discipline of responsibility.

In education's pedagogical laboratories, mistakes are allowed with penalties no worse than a half-grade off. That is why penalizing bigoted classroom speech without regard for its context generally violates the autonomous academy no less than does the slur it is meant to redress. In protecting learners, we need to protect the ignorant and the informed, the reactionary bigots and the zealous radicals alike. Radicalism is protected even though we know that the radical art of digging deep to uncover roots can imperil the plant above; subversion is encouraged, even if the premises being challenged are sacred and the challenges offered implausible. In such rarefied space, breathing is difficult and the air is heady and intoxicating, as on a mountaintop. The danger is always hyperventilation or suffocation: too much air, or the asphyxiating terror of too little.

The ancient canon choking on its dusty claims to legitimacy

can suffocate. It denies on principle the proposition that knowledge is always socially constructed, always conditioned by power and interest. Although it rests on a discourse that has gone on for millennia, it cannot imagine itself as a product of communities whose rules include some and exclude others and whose paradigms are often obstacles to new knowledge even as they codify the old. The thinkers who comprise the canon often saw themselves as engaged in a conversation with one another; Michael Oakeshott has called political philosophy a conversation with eternity. What is striking is that the canon's conservators fail to recognize the inherently discursive and interlocutory character that is its very essence.

This is not to say that knowledge is never more than a conditional cultural construction. It is only to say that knowledge in all its forms is initially produced in this fashion: a guess, a dream, a hunch, a hypothesis, a gentlemen's agreement, a working premise, a "let's for a moment assume that . . ." Its truth value cannot be measured by the standard of some independent epistemological foundation, nor by the authority of the originator, nor by the longevity of its reign as an agreed-upon convention, for these measures explain the origin but not the status of knowledge. Its status depends instead on consensus, which in turn depends on the nature of the community in which it qualifies as knowledge. In other words, what will count as true knowledge will depend on a community's discursive rules, the deliberative or conversational conventions to which it is subjected, the inclusiveness or exclusiveness of its membership, and so on.

Communities, rules, and conversational conventions vary, which is to say that while all knowledge is social, not all knowledge is equal in its truth status. That there is a sociology of knowledge is precisely what makes it possible to legitimize (or delegitimize) truth claims. We have seen how cultural conservatives like Allan Bloom insist that unveiling the social and power bases of knowledge must necessarily relativize or trivialize it. They think that to construe knowledge as social is to indulge in reductionism, to believe that all truth claims are equally contingent and thus, in their common cognitive impotence, equally invalid. An equivalence of zeros. But to construe knowledge as social is in fact to facilitate and legitimize distinctions: it is to distinguish knowledge claims and truth claims by appeal to the standards of discourse by which they are formulated, debated, and agreed upon or refuted. Canonical truth implies that the epistemological claims of knowledge are to be justified on the basis of their authoritative origins: they are a product of revelation, or nature as read by reason, or of wise philosophers in possession of a unique rational faculty. Knowledge understood as socially constructed, on the other hand, has a genuine validity, but it is a validity that is conditioned and thus conditional. It will be more or less persuasive to the degree the community from which it arises can be shown to be more or less democratic, more or less rational, more or less open, more or less critical, more or less self-reflective, more or less inclusive. The only truth the modern school can have is produced by democracy: consensus arising out of an undominated discourse to which all have equal access.

A canon that cannot be reinvented, reformulated, and thus reacquired by a learning community fails the test of truth as well as of pertinence, and is of no use to that community. Thomas Jefferson regarded habituated belief as an enemy not only of freedom but of usable conviction, and argued that every constitution and every law naturally expires within nineteen or twenty years. Canons, like constitutions, are also for the living, and if they do not expire every nineteen years, they surely grow tired and stale and begin to feel not like our own but like somebody else's imposed on us. Which is not to say they must be discarded: only that they must be repossessed anew, reassessed, relegitimized, and thus reembraced by each new generation. A canon is no use if it is not ours, and it becomes ours only when we reinvent it—an act impossible without active examination, criticism, and subversion. That is why teachers cannot teach the canon properly without provisionally subverting it. Their task is not to transmit the canon but to permit, even to help, their students reinvent it. Paradoxically, only those "truths" founded on abstract reason that students can make their own, founded on their own reasons and their own experience of the world, are likely to be preserved. Waving *The Republic* at the young will do nothing to restore literacy or extend the truths of the old. Much canonical teaching actually undermines belief by turning interesting arguments into unapproachable monuments. Shoved to their knees before a monument, kids may salute, yawn, wink, or giggle, but they are unlikely either to learn or to acquire belief.

In a society as contradictory as ours, experiential education has a problematic side as well. We look to education to modify the real world, but the real world also impacts on education. As students learn explicitly from the classroom, the lessons of the larger world in which the classroom exists also seep in. When the latter contradict at every turn what is taught in school, an attitudinal fissure can open up which students will experience as hypocrisy. Psychologists might call it cognitive dissonance: two powerful but contrary sets of impressions contained within a single mind, neither of which can be discarded but each of which denies the other.

Nowhere is this dissonance more visible than in the high-volume controversy over cultural literacy. Many education specialists, neutral about the ideological debates reviewed here but persuaded that American students are generally illiterate, emphasize cultural illiteracy. Their criticism of students in general opened this chapter. But the charge of cultural illiteracy brings with it a special indictment of both students and teachers: the former are made to seem lazier, stupider, more selfish and self-serving than earlier generations; the latter are slandered as politicized, radicalized, and utterly unsuited to teaching literacy. But what are we to make of a society that deploys rigorous standards of culture and learning in its schools which are nowhere to be found in the practices and behavior of the society itself? Why are students, with their keen sense of the hypocritical, so cynical about the preaching to which they are subjected?

THE SOCIETY BEYOND SCHOOL

The cultural literacy literature asks no such questions. In *What Do Our Seventeen-Year-Olds Know?*, Diane Ravitch and Chester E. Finn, Jr., (the former a current key player and the latter a former key player in the Department of Education), ask what the young know. Their answer is emphatic: not much. E. D. Hirsch has not only exposed the decline of "cultural literacy" but has offered his own version of a basic cultural vocabulary of the kind once provided by Homer, Shakespeare, and the Bible—a vocabulary that he believes is indispensable to any civilization worthy of the name.[19] American students—our kids—have been variously berated by latter-day critics as boring, vapid, lazy, selfish, complacent, self-seeking, materialistic, small-minded, apathetic, greedy, and, of course, illiterate. Allan Bloom also thinks they are soulless, valueless, and "fair" to the point of lacking all taste and belief.[20] How might we describe their parents then? Ourselves? Is there really any difference?

It has been fashionable to blame progressive education and graduates of the sixties-tainted teacher corps for the ignorance of the young. The legacy of the sixties is supposed to be the valuing of skills over substance, participation in learning over authority, creativity over memorization, social justice over high standards, and relevance over the timeless classics (see Chapter 3). So obvious were the villains that early in William Bennett's tenure as President Reagan's Secretary of Education, Bennett's primary charge seemed to be to destroy their protective covering by the dismantling of the Department of Education. It was almost as if the implicit message was supposed to be that if the schools were doing more harm than good, closing down the schools might actually improve cultural literacy. With the complicity of the kids themselves (seduced by sex, drugs, and rock 'n' roll, which to Bennett and Bloom remained the primary corrupters), Dewey-eyed school teachers were creating a generation of cultural morons. The problem was schools that did not live up to the high standards of society, teachers who had failed their mission, and students who had betrayed the adults from whom they were to inherit a precious legacy.

Yet there is ample evidence to suggest that whatever problems our schools have, they pale in comparison to the cultural defects of our society; that the "illiterate" kids are smart, not stupid, smarter than given credit for. But they are society-smart rather than school-smart, adept readers, but not of books. What they read so acutely are the social signals emanating from the world in which they will have to make a living. And their teachers in this world, the nation's true pedagogues, are television, advertising, movies, politics, and the celebrity domains they define. If children spend 900 hours a year in school and 1,200 hours watching television, which teaches more, and what is likely to get taught? The first lesson kids learn is that it is much more important to heed what society teaches implicitly than what school teaches explicitly. Isn't this an intelligent assumption?

What our seventeen-year-olds know is exactly what our forty-seven-year-olds know, and teach by example. Ravitch and Finn devised an ingenious instrument to test literacy, but they tested the wrong generation. What, then, do our forty-seven-year-olds know? To plumb the preceding generation's knowledge, we cannot imitate Ravitch and Finn and inquire after the author of the *Iliad* or the dates of the French Revolution or the identity of the philosopher David Hume. Readers, especially if closer to forty-seven than seventeen, might try on this fifteen-question test for size.

What Do Our Forty-Seven-Year-Olds Know?
A Multiple-Choice Test[21]

1. One third of Yale's 1985 graduating class applied for positions as (a) kindergarten teachers (b) citizen soldiers in the volunteer army (c) doctoral students in philosophy (d) trainees at First Boston Corporation.

2. The signals coming from television and magazine advertising teach you that happiness depends on (a) the car you drive (b) the clothes you wear (c) the income you pull down (d) the way you smell (e) the books you read.

3. The American most likely to have recently read the *Iliad* and written a poem, while sitting alone listening to Palestrina, is (a) a member of Congress (b) an arbitrageur (c) a real estate developer (d) a cosmetic surgeon (e) one of those illiterate students who can't read or write.

4. The Republican administrations of 1980 to 1992 have worked to get government off the backs of the American people through deregulation and privatization in order to (a) unleash business (b) encourage market competition (c) increase productivity (d) foster trickle-down prosperity by helping the rich to get richer (e) give the young plenty of private space in which to paint, sculpt, and read the classics.

5. To be hired by a top corporation, the most important credential you can have is (a) a doctorate of divinity from Harvard (b) an honors degree in classics from Oxford (c) a Yale Younger Poets award (d) a comparative literature degree from the Sorbonne (e) an MBA from just about anywhere.

6. If you were running for president, you would devote many hours of study to (a) the Bible (b) Shakespeare's plays (c) the *Federalist Papers* (d) Plutarch's *Lives of the Romans* (e) the paperback version of *How to Master Television Makeup*.

7. To sell a screenplay to Hollywood, you should (a) adapt a play of Ibsen (b) retell the story of Jean Jacques Rousseau's dramatic encounter with David Hume (c) dramatize the *Aeneid*, pay-

ing careful attention to its poetic cadences (d) novelize the life story of Donald Trump, paying careful attention to its fiscal and sexual cadences.

8. Familiarity with *Henry IV, Part II* is likely to be of great importance in (a) planning a corporate takeover (b) evaluating budget cuts at the Department of Education (c) initiating a medical liability suit (d) writing an impressive job résumé (e) taking a test on "What Do Our Seventeen-Year-Olds Know."

9. Book publishers are financially rewarded today for publishing (a) cookbooks (b) cat books (c) how-to books (d) popular potboilers (e) critical editions of Immanuel Kant's early writings.

10. Universities are financially rewarded today for (a) supporting bowl-quality football teams (b) forging research relationships with large corporations (c) sustaining professional schools of law, medicine, and business (d) stroking wealthy alumni (e) developing strong philosophy departments.

11. In preparing to interrogate a Supreme Court nominee at a Judiciary Committee hearing, a senator should (a) read Laurence Tribe's *Constitutional Choices* (b) review the candidate's judicial history and job résumé (c) discuss procedure with the committee's chief counsel (d) familiarize himself with pornographic movie titles.

12. In assessing the cultural value and social significance of a new work of art, a museum committee should (a) compare the work in question with the masters (b) read a primer in aesthetics (c) develop independent critical standards (d) enroll in a college philosophy of art seminar (e) find out whether it has been funded by the National Endowment for the Arts.

13. The best way to teach critical thinking in a media-manipulated society is (a) to offer critical courses on the media (b) to increase home reading assignments so that students will be less tempted to watch television all the time (c) to read Aristotle on rhetoric (d) to place a television set in every classroom showing canned news and plenty of ads.

14. To help the young learn that "history is a living thing," Scholastic Inc., a publisher of school magazines and paperbacks

aimed at adolescents, recently distributed to 40,000 junior and senior high school classrooms (a) a complimentary video of the award-winning series *The Civil War* (b) free American history textbooks (c) an abridgment of Tocqueville's *Democracy in America* (d) Billy Joel's single "We Didn't Start the Fire."[22]

15. A major California bank that advertised "no previous credit history required" for Visa cards to Berkeley students turned down one group of applicants because (a) their parents had poor credit histories (b) they had never held jobs (c) they had outstanding student loans (d) they were humanities majors.[23]

For extra credit: Name the ten living poets who most influenced your life, and recite a favorite stanza. Well, then, never mind the stanza, just name the poets. Okay, not ten, just five. Two? So, who's your favorite running back?

My sample of forty-seven-year-olds scored extremely well on this test—as did the seventeen-year-olds who took it. (In every case the correct answer is the last, or all but the last; I think you will be able to figure out which.) Test results (nobody did the extra credit question) reveal a deep strain of hypocrisy in the lamentations of the educational and cultural critics. They want our kids to know things the country at large doesn't give a hoot about. But the illiteracy of the young is our own, reflected back at us with embarrassing force. We honor ambition, we reward greed, we celebrate materialism, we worship acquisitiveness, we commercialize art, we cherish success, and then we bark at the young about the gentle arts of the spirit. The kids know that if we really valued learning, we would pay teachers what we pay lawyers and stockbrokers; if we valued art, we would not measure it by its capacity to produce profits or to produce intolerance in prudish government funders; if we regarded literature as important, we would remove it from the celebrity sweepstakes and spend a little money on our libraries so adults could read too.[24] If literacy were truly an issue, we would start addressing the one in five American adults who are completely illiterate—and perhaps pay some attention to the additional 34 percent who are functionally illiterate.[25]

Much of this book has dealt with the crisis of our schools, but underlying the educational crisis is a crisis of our society at large. Schools can and should lead, but where they confront a society that in every instance tells a story exactly opposite to the one schools wish to teach, their job becomes prohibitively costly. I am not being utopian. There is always a space between where we are and where we hope our children may lead us. Ideals being aspirations, adults never live up to the ideals they wish to inculcate in their young. But adults must at least appear to believe in those ideals. If they organize society around a contrary set of beliefs and fail across the board to practice what they preach, the young will quite naturally ignore the talk and follow the practice. They will watch a man with a rubber arm who can throw a ball consistently at 95 miles per hour easily earn a hundred times as much as a primary school teacher, and they will eschew careers in teaching. They will notice that their government spends $80,000 a year keeping young blacks behind bars and only a quarter of that keeping them in school, and they will write off school (and probably young blacks as well). The young are not blind. This is not just the difference between ideals and reality.

Kids just don't care much for hypocrisy. If they are illiterate, their illiteracy is merely ours, acquired by them with a scholarly ardor. They know what we have taught them: There is nothing in Homer, in the Bible, in Shakespeare that will benefit their climb to the top of our competitive society. While the professors argue about whether to teach the ancient history of Athens or the ancient history of Egypt, the politicians run political campaigns based on mindless image mongering and inflammatory, studiedly ahistorical polemics. While school teachers debate the ethics of caring, the country turns its back on the homeless. And so our students dismiss talk of civilization, whether Eurocentric or Afrocentric, and concentrate on cash-and-carry careers, a tribute not to their ignorance but to their adaptive intelligence. Although we can hardly be proud of ourselves for what we are teaching them, we should at least be proud of them for how well they have learned it.

Teachers, however, will not be content with such a cynical outcome. They will still look for ways to build community in the face of an indifferent society. They will still hope to teach seventeen-year-olds what forty-seven-year-olds have refused to learn, and will still try to teach them liberty. To do so, they will have to employ a model of education much more dialectical than is currently available.

DEMOCRATIC EDUCATION: THE PLACE OF COMMUNITY

A dialectical model of education will refuse to prostrate itself, its back to the future, before the ancient gods of the Canon, but will be equally reluctant to throw itself uncritically into the future, as envisioned by the new gods of the marketplace. If schooling merely imitates society, it can only replicate and reinforce its weaknesses. That is why I am arguing not that the university has a civic mission, but that the university *is* a civic mission, is civility itself defined as the rules and conventions that permit a community to facilitate conversation and the discourse upon which all knowledge, and thus all community, depends. Where society offers little in the way of cultural literacy, the school can offer much. Where society is indifferent to democracy, the school can be its nurturer. On this model, education is a social activity that can take place only within a learning community bringing together reflection and experience. On this model, knowledge is an evolving communal construction whose legitimacy rests directly on the character of the social process. On this model, education is everywhere and always an ineluctably communal enterprise.

I mean to suggest much more than that democracy and education are parallel activities, or that civic training and the cultivation of knowledge and judgment possess a parallel structure. I am arguing that they are the same thing. That what distinguishes truth, inasmuch as it is ours to possess, is not conformity to society's historical traditions or the standards of independent reason or the dictates of some learned canon, but conformity to communicative processes that are genuinely democratic and that occur only in free communities.

In a world in which truth is no longer to be mined from extraterrestrial bodies labeled God or nature or reason or metaphysics, the conditions of truth (such as "truth" is in this residual post-modernist form) and the conditions of democracy are one and the same: As there is freedom, as the community is open and inclusive and the exchange of ideas thorough and spirited, so there is both more democracy and more learning, more freedom and more knowledge. Knowledge is always provisional: ideas conditionally agreed upon. And just as no argument will be accorded merit because of its source alone, so no individual will be privileged over others simply because of who he is (white or male or straight) or where he comes from (old money, the wrong side of the tracks, the United States of America).

Once this is understood, we can move beyond the old instrumental arguments on behalf of democracy that rest the case for citizen training inside the university on the instrumental need to shore up democracy outside the university. It may not be the school's primary responsibility, but someone has to teach civics, runs this argument. And it is a powerful argument: neither education nor research can prosper in an unfree society, and schooling is the only way we are likely to be able to produce citizens who will uphold freedom. But it is also an exclusively prudential argument. The prudent Jefferson is known for his wise linkage of education and democracy. If, as Jefferson argued in his *Notes on Virginia*, the people are "the ultimate guardians of their own liberty," then we had best "render them safe" via a thorough education. "The only sure reliance for the preservation of our liberty," he wrote to James Madison in 1787, is to "educate and inform the whole mass of the people." My argument here, however, goes well beyond Jefferson's instrumental formula making education "the guarantor of liberty." It suggests that liberty is the guarantor of education; that we not only have to educate every person to make him free, but we have to free every person to make him educable. Educated women and men make good citizens of free communities, but without a free learning community you cannot educate women and men.

Mary Wollstonecraft pointed in this direction when she wrote in the *Vindication of the Rights of Woman* that "in order to open their faculties [children] should be excited to think for themselves; and this can only be done by mixing a number of children together, and making them jointly pursue the same subject."[26] It is exactly what Dewey means when he suggests not merely that education is crucial to democracy, but that democracy itself is

> more than a form of government, it is a mode of associated living, of conjoint communicated experience. The extension in space of the number of individuals who participate in an interest so that each has to refer his own action to that of others to give point and direction to his own, is equivalent to the breaking down of those barriers of class, race and national territory which kept men from perceiving the full import of their activity.[27]

Walt Whitman, who refused to wall off democracy from life, or life from poetry, or poetry from democracy, mocks those who try to cut the fabric of democracy to the sorry measure of their own tiny imaginations. Was it the first Political Scientist or the first Great Books Man, the first Purist with no room for democracy in his academic specialty or the first Vocationalist with no time for democracy in her training program Whitman had in mind when he wrote:

Did you too, O friend, suppose democracy was only for elections, for politics, and for a party name? I say democracy is only of use there that it may pass on and come to its flower and fruits in manners, in the highest forms of interaction between men, and their beliefs—in religion, literature, college and schools—democracy in all public and private life.... [28]

The point where democracy and education intersect is the point we call community. If democracy is a mode of associated living, then it is also true, Dewey has written, that "in the first place, the school must itself be a community life." Dewey is framing a careful philosophical argument rather than just a provocative metaphor. He is insisting that the "realization of the meaning of linguistic signs ... involves a context of work and play in association with others."[29] He is saying that in the absence of community there is no learning; that language itself is social, the product as well as the premise of sociability and conversation.

We need to reread Dewey, recomprehend him, for underlying the pathologies of our society and our schools—beneath the corruptions associated with alcohol and drugs, complacency and indifference, discrimination and bigotry, and violence and fractiousness—is an affliction of community: its corruption, its fragmentation, its breakdown; finally, its disappearance. We can no more learn alone than we can live alone. And if little learning is taking place in American schools and colleges it may be because there is too much solitude and too little community among the learners (and their teachers too). Schools that were once workshops of intimacy have been transformed into factories as alienating as welfare hotels and as lonely as suburban malls. The best lack neither facilities nor resources, neither gifted teachers nor able students; but they are for the most part devoid of any sense of community. And without community, neither the almighty canon nor the almighty dollar can do much to inspire learning or promote freedom.

Dewey's conception of education is often deemed "progressive," yet in fact it harkens back to classical and neo-classical models of *paidaeia* and *Bildung*. Paidaeia was the term the Greeks used to encapsulate the norms and values of public life around which citizenship and learning were organized. To be an educated Athenian was to be a free and participating citizen. These were not two distinctive roles, two parallel forms of training; they were a single identity revolving around common norms each individual made his own. Imagine Socrates recommending a canon to his pupils: "Read Parmenides and Pythagoras and you shall know all you ever need to know!" Imagine Aristotle instructing an Athenian youth that what he learned in the Lyceum was not meant to apply to life beyond the bleached stones where the two of them sat in the sun conversing. The German Enlightenment term Bildung possessed the same unifying cultural thrust; it brought together under the rubric of life-learning and self-reflective experience the ancient ideals of paidaeia encompassing the citizen who belongs at once to the actual polis and the cultural cosmopolis. The education of Émile (Rousseau) or the education of the young Werther (Goethe) was a lifetime task of which schooling represented only a phase. Émile's tutor did not imagine that his pupil could separate the cultivation of his civility from the reading of books; Goethe never conceived that Werther could or should wall off his life from his learning. These examples are from the European tradition of learning, but similar stories can be found in every culture and every civilization. To be civilized *is* to be educated, to be *gebildet*, to be trained by books filtered through life, life reexamined in classrooms. The young African-American will have her own books, her own poems and stories, her own treasured archives, but unless they connect to her experience they will lack the power to educate.

The trouble with the purist's canon is that it renders knowledge a product stripped of the process by which it is endowed with its quickening vitality and its moral legitimacy. Harvard requires all students to take a course in moral reasoning, but its well-intentioned faculty seem to have forgotten that, as John Dewey remembered,

> moral education in school is practically hopeless when we set up the development of character as a supreme end, and at the same time treat the acquiring of knowledge and the development of understanding, which of necessity occupy the chief part of school time, as having nothing to do with character. On such a basis, moral education is inevitably reduced to some kind of catechetical instruction ... lessons "about morals" [that] signify as a matter of course what other people think about virtues and duties.[30]

The canon does not produce the cultural education the Germans called Bildung; Bildung produces the canon, which consequently needs to be no less flexible and mutable than the life processes that make it. Similarly, it is not a free society that produces Bildung, but Bildung that produces a free society, keeping it from ossifying and perishing—helping it to overcome its most troubling contradiction, which is its tendency to institutionalize and petrify the spirt of freedom that animates it. The word is German, but Bildung is a universal feature of cultural learning.

We can draw both the purists and the vocationalists back to the central concerns of learning to be free by insisting on the centrality of community to both education and democracy, to both convention and freedom. Where in the quest to preserve the canon is a concern for the communal conditions of learning upon which its revival (and thus its preservation) depend? In the rush to serve the society that beckons from beyond the schoolyard, what has happened to the schoolyard's own precious community, whose delicate ties alone permit the young to learn the art of civility and to create a common language in the face of private differences so that they might conduct a conversation about common knowledge and shared belief?

It is not really a matter of making the liberal arts university into a community; for it already is a community, however corrupt and frangible it has become or however little it is seen as such by its privatized inhabitants, students, faculty, and administrators alike. It is a matter of recognizing the communal character of learning, and giving to community the attention and the resources it requires. Learning communities, like all free communities, function only when their members conceive of themselves as empowered to participate fully in the common activities that define the community—in this case, learning and the pursuit of knowledge in the name of common living. Learning entails communication, communication is a function of community. The equation is simple enough: no community, no communication; no communication, no learning; no learning, no education; no education, no citizens; no citizens, no freedom; no freedom—then no culture, no democracy, no schools, no civilization. Cultures rooted in freedom do not come in fragments and pieces. You get it all, or you get nothing.

The sociopathologies that currently afflict American universities (renewed racism, reemergent bigotry, substance and alcohol abuse, alienation, loneliness, suicide, cultural fragmentation and segregation in the name of hyperdifferentiation, and relativism and nihilism as a consequence of hyperskepticism) are then anything but contingent features of higher education, mere symptoms that can be isolated and treated one by one like so many cuts on an otherwise healthy body. They speak, rather, to a disease of the whole, a systemic affliction of education's integral body that is nothing less than the community of teachers and students in which education subsists.

When I consider the role of the real in teaching the abstract, the place of community in the world of learning, I am put in mind of the remarkable stanza that propels Walt Whitman's "A Song of Occupations" to its conclusion. Whitman writes:

When the psalm sings instead of the singer,
When the script preaches instead of the preacher,

When a university course convinces like a slumbering
    woman and child convince . . .
I intend to reach them my hand and make as much of
    them as I do of men and women.

Whitman always reminds us of the obvious, perhaps because it is the obvious that we always forget. Canons do not teach, teachers teach. Poems cannot enchant, only poets. History will not preserve us from the errors of the past or mark us with its stories, but historians just may—if they are teachers. Education is finally a matter of teachers teaching students; and where teachers teach and students learn there we will discover community. Or, to put it the other way around, only where there is a genuine community will there be genuine teachers and students, and anything resembling genuine learning.

Does the university have a civic mission? Of course, for it *is* a civic mission: the cultivation of free community; the creation of a democracy of words (knowledge) and a democracy of deeds (the democratic state). Perhaps it is time to stop complaining about the needs of society and worrying about the fate of the canon and despairing over the inadequacies of students, which, after all, only mirror our own. Perhaps it is time to start thinking about what it means to say that community is the beginning and the end of education—its indispensable condition, its ultimate object—and time, then, to do something about it in words and in deeds.

A place to start would be education-based community service: bringing community into the schools, and bringing schools into the community. Just how that might be done is the subject of the next and final chapter.

CHAPTER 7

TEACHING DEMOCRACY
THROUGH COMMUNITY
SERVICE

Like most books on education, this one is two-fifths analysis, two-fifths criticism, and one-tenth polemic. (Am I too kind to myself?) This leaves but a tenth or so of the manuscript for constructive proposals. Any proposal that claims to address the disheartening contradictions of modern education needs to be both realistic (specific, practicable, pertinent to actual educational challenges) and visionary (focused on democracy, citizenship, and learning to be free). In the previous chapter I argued that we might identify many of the contradictions of academe with its core deficiency: the corporal weakness of community in educational institutions. To focus on community is to address a series of concrete issues, including

• the quality and character of relationships inside the educational institution; mistrust, cynicism, disappointment, and bitterness currently weigh down our institutional relations, turning pedagogical allies into enemy camps of faculty, students, and administrators;

• the living arrangements of students, who need to experience an architecture of community and self-government in their dorms and classrooms if they are to take seriously the responsibilities of democratic living;

• experience itself as a significant teacher, which means finding ways to integrate academic teaching and experiential learning; this already occurs in such professional programs as social work, theater, and engineering, where the practicum and the internship play important roles, but it happens least where it is most needed, in the humanities, which seem especially prone to scholastic purism;

• civic education as an integral feature of liberal education, where autonomy, the capacity for public judgment, mutual responsibility, and some genuine empowerment are nourished in both an intellectual and a practical framework—such as that afforded by an academically rooted course with a practicum in community service;

• empowerment as a necessary condition of the free community, for both faculty and students; as the university has "progressed," faculty have had less rather than more power, and students seem more powerless than ever, being offered endless freedom to say no, to indulge their own opinions and needs and desires, but given little real responsibility and no genuine power at all; power is not a right at this stage—it is simply the necessary condition of teaching and learning;

• autonomy, as empowerment's concomitant and practical expression; students and teachers collaborating with parents are the heart of every school, from kindergarten to graduate seminars; administration has become far too large,[1] the space of autonomous classrooms far too small: the relationship between the two needs to be inverted;

• finally, teaching as the terminus of all research and the beginning of all learning for students and faculty alike; the validation of an epistemological arena where communication and consensus are crucial to knowledge and community, to truth as well as the democratic politics of living without truth.

These concerns converge toward a single strategy: the need to transform teaching liberty from a metaphor into a practical pedagogy. Up until now, I have spoken of citizenship, democracy, empowerment, autonomy, and liberty as if they were rhetorical ciphers for various old-fashioned liberal educational ideals. In this chapter, I want to treat them not as by-products but as a central aim of education. To teach liberty is to teach citizenship— to teach it concretely and practically in a land where its meanings have been watered down and compromised to a point that is approaching civic bankruptcy. I will presently propose a service-learning approach to civic education that I believe offers a promising springboard for broader reforms. But before doing so, I want to review the American conception of service and citizenship that must be the context for any program of education-based community service.

EDUCATION, SERVICE, AND THE BANKRUPTCY OF CITIZENSHIP[2]

In Chapter 2, I offered a story of America in which rights and obligations gradually became uncoupled. The America that has emerged from the story is a land in which government has to compete with industry and the private sector to attract servicemen to the military. It is a place where individuals regard themselves almost exclusively as private persons with responsibilities only to family and job, yet possessing endless rights against a distant and alien state in relationship to which they think of themselves, at best, as watchdogs and clients and, at worst, as adversaries and victims. The idea of service to country or an obligation to the institutions by which rights and liberty are maintained has nearly vanished. "We the People" have severed our connections with "It" the state or "They" the "bureaucrats" and "politicians" who run It. Problems of governance are always framed in the language of leadership—as if the preservation of democracy were merely a matter of assuring adequate leadership, electing surrogates to perform our civic duties. Our solution to problems in our democracy is to blame our representatives. Throw the rascals out—or place limits on the terms they can serve. Our own complicity in the health of our system becomes invisible. This is often a first step in the decline of a democratic state.

In the last decade, a certain healthy American distrust of out-sized or overbureaucratized government has become a zany antipathy toward all government, so that not even public schooling or progressive taxation are necessarily regarded as legitimate. Candidates for public office now sever themselves from parties and politicians and vie for the title of outsider. In the era of NOTA (none of the above) and Ross Perot, to be without political experience or political views is the sine qua non of running for office. As the reputation of government has declined, the reputation of markets—construed ahistorically as if they still existed in their most abstract and innocuous eighteenth-century form—has skyrocketed. There is apparently nothing government can do right, and nothing markets can do wrong. Even education must be suborned to their magic laws, the campaign for "choice" via vouchers actually constituting a radical privatization of pedagogy. As communism continues its worldwide collapse, nations in search of democracy increasingly seek to import market institutions, as if these alone could produce a free civil society and a democratic government. Governments, it is assumed, are as fallible as markets are infallible.

Yet modern attitudes toward government are symptoms rather than causes of deeper changes—changes visible, above all, in the altered meaning and importance of the idea of citizenship in Western democracy. The long-term effect of representative institutions, which have been crucial in the preservation of accountability and a minimal popular sovereignty in mass societies where more participatory forms of government seem untenable, has often been to undermine a vigorous participatory citizenship and to reinforce the distance between voters and their governors. We now view the democratic state as one more hostile exemplar of those bureaucratic Leviathans that encroach on our private lives and jeopardize our private freedoms. Freedom itself is associated with the absence of government, and national service is in turn construed by some as a species of tyranny or involuntary servitude: "Them" coercing "us" to serve "It" (the state), as if democracy were not precisely defined as the unity of the state and us! That service might be a condition of citizenship and citizenship the premise for the preservation of freedom is an argument that has little resonance in modern mass society where "voluntary" means private, private means market, and market means the presumption of a formal equality that rarely exists. Each dollar is in theory worth each other dollar, just as each vote is worth each other vote. But in fact actual markets are often skewed and monopolistic, and players in the private realm discover that they are anything but equals. Some outweigh others (who has more clout, Donald Trump or his driver?), and all are suborned to corporate entities in the private sector that compete as "free individuals." Markets promise equality but seldom yield it.

It is understandable that where the idea of citizenship has lost its vigor as a correlate of freedom, the idea of service may appear as coercive: not an entailment of rights, but an encroachment on them—an imperative imposed by others. It is also understandable that where markets are regarded so uncritically, coercion itself will appear as solely governmental, and all behavior that is nongovernmental will, by definition, be regarded as "voluntary" or free. Thus, the school dropout watching television all afternoon will be perceived as acting voluntarily: as if his reasoning was of the order "Let's see now, what should I do this afternoon? I can read Virgil in Latin; I can put on that new CD of *Parsifal*, or perhaps Herbie Hancock; or I can watch 'General Hospital.' " And the teenager working at McDonald's is likewise simply exercising his market freedom: "Should I be a bank president, a senator, a nuclear physicist, or a cook at McDonald's? Tough choice, but after watching the Clarence Thomas hearings (they preempted 'General Hospital'!) the Senate is definitely out, so, I guess I'll opt for being a fry slinger."

Yet while meaningful choice in the private sector bears no relationship to the ideal conditions assumed by advocates of the market, choice in the public sector has also been undermined by the erosion of citizenship. It is my argument here that service has lost much of its political potency precisely because citizenship has lost its currency. It has come to mean little more than voting, when it means anything at all. Democratic politics has become something we watch rather than something we do. As spectators to and clients of governments to which we otherwise feel no responsibility, it is hardly a wonder that service should appear as legitimate only as an alternative to government—a product of voluntarism or altruism or philanthropy.

The thousand points of light through which the lucky serve the needy may help illuminate our humanity, but they cannot warm or nurture our common soul, nor create a sense of *common* responsibility connected to our liberty, nor provide integral solutions to structural problems. Service retains its moral character, but only as an imperative of the private person. The model is compassion or charity, whose consequences are entirely supererogatory (not obligatory), and can never be the subject of political duties. Charity flourishes as an individualist counter to the private sector's individualist vices (greed, narcissism, and privatism, which from the point of view of competition and productivity may be virtues, but which, as conservative critics of libertarianism note, can undermine social mores). All those points of light warm the steely firmament of an overindividuated world, acting as a kind of antidote to black hole Reaganism. But what a cold and black firmament it is! I imagine New York real estate developer Arthur Zeckendorf spending Thursday evenings in a soup kitchen feeding the homeless his runaway development projects have helped to create; I conjure up white-collar criminals like

Leona Helmsley with a checkbook in one hand and a dustpan in the other paying her debt to society and, along the way, tainting the idea of service by associating it with punishment. To the extent, then, that service has been reduced to charity, and civic obligation and civic service have lost their place in our nation's political vocabulary, it is because we long ago bankrupted our practice of citizenship. Before introducing a proposal for community service as a part of the educational curriculum, I want to look more carefully at what has happened to citizenship, whose rehabilitation must become a chief objective of our reform pedagogy.

There are, of course, ample signs of a burgeoning interest in service in America today, but for the most part segregated from the discussion of citizenship. Some of the bills considered in Congress and the plan offered by Governor Bill Clinton in the recent presidential race tie service to the federal college loan program, and many others (along with most extant school and college service programs) embrace a spirit of private sector voluntarism that seems at odds with the obligations of citizenship.[3] The successful resuscitation of the idea of service will not proceed far without the refurbishing of the theory and practice of democratic citizenship, which must in turn become any successful service program's guiding spirit.

A vigorous conception of citizenship has not been bankrupted by choice or design. Rather, it has been an inevitable consequence of historical conditions that have combined with the characteristically old-fashioned "liberal" (in the sense here of laissez-faire) distrust of democracy to favor a less active understanding of the citizen than was current in the republican tradition from which modern democracy issued. Indeed, the entire history of citizenship in the West, from ancient Athens to the great democratic revolutions of the eighteenth and nineteenth centuries, has been one in which, as the compass of citizenship has expanded, its significance has contracted. More and more people have gained access to a civic status that has entailed less and less, a status that has grown ever more defensive and rights-oriented in character. A small handful of property-owning males once exercised a prodigious everyday franchise; now universal suffrage permits every man and woman to put a name on a ballot once a year in what many think of as an exercise in meaningless-ness. Or to conceive of themselves as rights bearers without any duties whatsoever.

Before considering modern remedies or advancing feasible programs for strengthening service in an appropriate educational setting, it may be of use to review briefly this ironic tradition in which, as the compass of the franchise grew, the value of the citizenship it conveyed was depreciated. This too is part of the American story; this too is why education for democracy must mean learning to be free.

THE GROWTH OF THE FRANCHISE AND THE DECLINE OF CITIZENSHIP

There seems little doubt that our richest conception of citizen-ship is derived from Athens in the fifth century B.C. when, par-adoxically, a slave society that excluded women, immigrants, resident foreigners, and of course slaves from the ranks of its citizens nonetheless afforded the remaining fifth of the population an extraordinarily powerful role in governance. Whatever special significance Athens has in our problematic canon is connected to the birth of democracy. The citizen participated (and was re-quired to do so) in legislative assemblies that met every ten days or so and acted as the sovereign authority of the polis, making policy on foreign and domestic issues from war and empire to tariffs and weights and measures. He also served regularly on juries with five hundred, a thousand, or sometimes more mem-bers, hearing cases concerning minor civil matters as well as cap-ital crimes and treason. He could be chosen by sortition (by lot) for roughly half of the civic magistracies by which Athens was governed on a day-to-day basis, and had to pay for and serve in the military campaigns that, as a citizen of the assembly, he had decided to pursue.

When Aristotle wrote in *The Politics* that man was a *zoon politikon* (a political animal), he meant that he was born to civic membership in a polity. Unlike the gods and the beasts who were capable of solitude, men were naturally sociable and found their identity in their membership in a community. Extrapolitical pursuits, both familial (regulated by women) and economic (undergirded by slave labor), were secondary: utilitarian activities aimed at procreation and sustenance, hardly more elevated than those of all animals, and less than representative of what it meant to be human.

Pericles is doing more than boasting when, in Thucydides' account of the funeral oration, he says: "We do not say that a man who takes no interest in politics is a man who minds his own business; we say that he has no business here at all." Even Socrates, no friend to Athenian democracy, in refusing to choose exile over death, reflected on how much he owed to Athens' laws, under which (he acknowledged) he was educated, provided for, and allowed to live. To a Greek, ostracism was a fate worse than death. To be outside the city, beyond the polis, was to forgo living as a human being. When Oedipus sought a punishment as horrific as his crimes, he chose not death but self-exile from Thebes.

Among the Greeks, citizenship was to most men as knowledge was to philosophers: a cherished object of veneration, even love. We might speak of a veritable *philopoliteia*: a love of the political so strong that it outweighed most other concerns. The quarrel Allan Bloom explores between philosophy and democracy acquires its force in part from the passion with which each side embraced its beliefs, the one side in the love of knowledge, the other in the love of political equality (what the Greeks understood as equality before the law, or *isonomia*).

This powerful sense of a community of equals, impassioned,

active, self-governing, although contradicted in many ways by its actual practices, has been a model of participatory politics ever since. It has been replicated only occasionally, most often in small homogenous civic polities such as the Italian republics of the late Renaissance and the Swiss confederation of the fifteenth and six-teenth centuries, and perhaps in New England village communities in our nation's earlier days. It has largely vanished in the modern world, where politics is the last refuge of scoundrels and things private are by far more venerable than things public (the old *res publica*). We have had our nostalgic yearners for the old philopoliteia: writers like Hannah Arendt, or disciples of Leo Strauss less concerned with the difference between aristocracy and democracy than with the demarcation between antiquity and mo-dernity understood as a demarcation between virtue and corrup-tion, justice and commerce, and public goods and private greed. But the ancient ideals of civic virtue and civic participation are gone, along with the belief that citizenship expresses the highest in human character, the most precious possession a man has to lose, a citizenship that—even as it facilitates common living—defines individual being.

By the time of the Romans, citizenship had already lost some of this high moral luster. The Romans took their lessons from the Athenians, who had tried futilely to extend an empire while jealously guarding the narrow boundaries of their citizenship and had ended up losing both empire and democracy. Roman citizen-ship was allowed to grow along with imperial ambition. From the very first legendary conquest over their neighbors (mytholo-gized as "The Rape of the Sabine Women"), the Romans gave to the survivors of that early slaughter the gift of Roman citizenship. As their empire grew, the conquered all became Romans, until by the second century A.D., when Rome's territory began to match its imperial imagination, peoples in distant Gaul and Ger-mania, whose language and customs were utterly alien to Rome's and whose peoples had knowledge of Romans only as efficient, irresistible warriors, nonetheless carried the name *cives* and shared minimal legal rights with their conquerors. In time, all of Europe and much of the Mediterranean was Roman; the idea of Roman citizenship, however, had lost the immediacy and vitality of its Athenian cousin. Active participation had been replaced by minimal legal rights. Many more men enjoyed far fewer powers. But Rome persisted when Athens had not, and the modern conception of citizenship as a form of thin legal personhood, rather than rich and textured human identity, appeared to take root. *Lex* flourished, participation eroded.

After the Renaissance and the rediscovery of Aristotle, antiquity enjoyed a renewed fashion, and early modern political theorists from Machiavelli to Harrington again took up classical conceptions of citizenship and civic virtue, developing a tradition of republican thought that influenced polities in the burgeoning nation-states of Europe. Nationalism inspired a new understanding of the citizen-subject with obligations to the crown that included military service; at the same time, the rise of national armies—how Machiavelli admired them!—reinforced the idea of a civic polity. But the focus was shifting.

The economic market, previously a locus for secondary private activity, increasingly evolved as the crucial arena of human productivity, and thus of potential human virtue. As the classical weighting of the public and political over the private and economic was inverted, liberty ceased to mean only license and individual ceased to mean only anarchist or idiot. Where once commerce had been associated with the insufficiency of individuals and virtue had been understood as a wholly public commodity, by the eighteenth century commerce had come to denote a system where virtue might acquire a private meaning (if only by the indirection of such devices as the invisible hand—today's supply-side economics). It was increasingly possible to associate freedom not only with dissent against illegitimate authority, but with private agency against even a legitimate state. Thus did the state, above all the democratic state, come gradually to be perceived as private liberty's primary nemesis. Thus did the ancient idea of public or positive liberty, perfectly compatible with democratic government, yield to negative liberty, seen as incompatible with any government at all.

The writings of Machiavelli and Montesquieu on the Continent, those of Harrington and his fellow republicans in England, struggled to restore vigorous citizenship and civic virtue to the political center. But the privileging of economic activity as the basis for social growth, and the concomitant stress on individual activity and private choice, both shaped and placed limits on the republican revival. The founding of new republics, particularly the United States, brought to the surface the deep controversy over whether public virtue or private economic activity was to be the basis for a productive and stable society. Calvinist doctrine tried to bridge the two conceptions, as John Patrick Diggins has shown in his remarkable book *The Lost Soul of American Politics*, but even where civic virtue held its own in theory, commerce seemed to prevail in practice.[4] The virtuous republic modeled on antiquity relied above all on the cultivation of citizenship and positive liberty and demanded civic education, civic participation, and sufficient civic activism to guarantee a responsible electorate. The new commercial republic, on the other hand, called for a limited state whose primary function was to protect the market and personal and private liberty, and for individuals whose primary motives were economic—the good citizen as the productive capitalist or the efficient worker—and who held the state and the democratic majority in suspicion. Why suspicion? Because they now saw their liberty as personal rather than public and vulnerable to the very communities from which public liberty was once thought to arise. Religion, it was hoped (by Tocqueville and others), might continue to tether men to the civic polity and ground responsibility, but the secularism it was meant to prop up was itself religion's chief adversary, and the public square had a naked aspect long before Richard John Neuhaus wrote *The Naked Public Square*.[5]

Ironically, the coming of capitalism gave a push to the franchise even as it presumed a limited and privatized conception of what the franchise entailed. The final victory of capitalism over feudalism in England arrived with the nearly simultaneous abolition of the corn laws (and thus trade barriers) and the radical extension of the franchise in the first half of the nineteenth century. Markets stood for a theoretical equality that workers hoped to turn into political practice; they offered a challenge to organizers and spurred the syndicalist and socialist movements; they motivated labor, and motivated labor demanded the vote. In challenging feudalism in the name of capitalism, Smith and Ricardo and Malthus assailed economic parasitism and privilege in a manner that invited an assault on political privilege and property and class limits on the franchise. If real property (land) could not bar capital from electoral representation, why should capital bar productive (though propertyless) labor from representation? The outline of Marx was already visible to a careful reader of Ricardo and Malthus.

Democracy was thus reborn in the modern world with capitalism as its midwife. Today capitalism is trying to return the favor, by affecting to play midwife to democracy in the countries emerging from communism and military dictatorship (although not with notable success). This capitalism, however, simultaneously transformed the classical values that constituted its own core. More and more people shared in a power that meant less and less. Property owners without noble titles, and then capitalists without real property and in time workers with neither capital nor property, won the rights of the citizen, only to discover that the rights of citizens they had won were reactive and cautionary rather than empowering and participatory—giving them protection against the state but little control over it. Hoping to win the right to self-government, men (and in time women) found themselves relegated to the passive role of watchdog: guardians of rights that no longer seemed to entail obligations, private persons whose liberty was now defined exclusively by the absence of state power. This story helps to explain why many of those who finally won the franchise in America continue to revile the nation from which it was won: their victory feels tainted by the loss of meaning in the prize they thought they had taken. Their citizenship neither made them the equals of the elites that had for so long stood in their way nor conveyed to them power of the kind they associated with those from whom it had been wrested.

The advocates of a stronger form of democratic participation acknowledged that self-government by a community was likely to be feasible only under very limited conditions: a homogenous population sharing a common history, a common religion, and common values; an uncomplicated economic frame characterized by modesty, relative austerity, and rough equality; and a limited territory ensuring both commonality and equality. Such conditions, theorists like Rousseau admitted, were fast disappearing in the modern West and seemed incompatible with almost everything associated with modernization.

Certainly the French Revolution seemed to provide ample evidence that the attempt to introduce radical democracy in the setting of an urban, industrializing mass metropolis was likely to result only in tyrannical collectivism and terror. Indeed, to the extent partisans of individualism, property, liberty, and the modern market felt threatened by the populist tradition, they argued not merely that democracy was atavistic, but that it was undesirable. Today, many Americans retain a distrust of participatory democracy, equating it with mob rule or the tyranny of opinion. They are still students and disciples of that powerful laissez-faire tradition of liberalism running from Godwin and Tocqueville and Constant to Walter Lippmann and Robert Nozick and Milton Friedman that places the fear of majoritarianism first among its many anxieties and thinks that we are born free and so do not need to learn it in schools or in our political communities. This fear may seem out of all proportion to the actual danger, above all in a republic as thoroughly hemmed in by constitutional constraints as ours. And if, as we have argued, liberty is secured *through* community, then community should not seem so threat-ening. Yet neo-Hamiltonian critics still insist that the public mind must be filtered and refined through the cortex of its betters. Give everyone the franchise, but don't let them do anything much with it. Protect them from the government with a sturdy barrier of rights, but protect government from them with a representa-tive system that guarantees they will not themselves be legislators. In short, let them vote the governors in and out, but don't let them govern themselves. Let them enjoy freedom from govern-ment, but don't let them govern themselves freely.

The hostility to citizenship and the contempt for *res publica* has by now taken a toll even on the constrained notion of citi-zenship permitted by limited government and by the dominion of market over public sector forces. We have noticed that only half of the eligible electorate participates in presidential elections, and the numbers fall off quickly in lesser elections, plummeting to 10 or 15 percent in local primaries—where, however, millions are spent by eager candidates trying to buy television time to win office. Where John Kennedy spent $13 million in 1960 winning the presidency, a candidate in a recent New York mayoralty pri-mary spent $13 million *losing* the Republican nomination! The "public airwaves" are licensed to private corporations, who sell them back to the public during elections at fees so exorbitant that a free electoral process can hardly be said to survive. Young Americans vote less often than old, Americans of color less often than whites, and poor Americans less often than the well off. And whether, as Frances Fox Piven and Richard Cloward argue, nonvoting is itself a political act of resistance or simply a sign of the morbidity of electoral politics, it is obvious that democracy even in its tenuous version is in some trouble.[6]

Yet despite the growth of unaccountable, elephantine corpo-rate bureaucracies, both conservative and libertarian critics con-tinue to single out the democratic state as liberty's most dangerous foe. No wonder, then, that the renewed call for national service uses the rhetoric of voluntarism, charity, and good works rather than the rhetoric of civility, responsibility, and good citizenship. This brings us back to the problem with which we began: the civic vacuum in which the issue of national service is discussed today even by its advocates.

A PROPOSAL FOR MANDATORY CITIZEN EDUCATION AND COMMUNITY SERVICE

For all of the welcome interest in the idea of service today in America, little can be expected unless it inspires a renewed interest in civic education and citizenship. Simply to enlist volunteers to serve "others less fortunate" or "those at risk" (we are *all* at risk!), or to conscript young people for some form of national service in the name of improving their moral character or forcing them to "repay the debt they owe their country" (the language of market contracts applied to politics and the public good) will do little to reconstruct citizenship or shore up democracy and do nothing at all to improve the caliber of our educational community. Moreover, it sells short the growing desire to do service, for that desire carries within it a longing for community, a need to honor what the sociologist Robert Bellah identifies as the "habits of the heart" nurtured by membership in communal associations.[7] When the need cannot be met by healthy democratic forms of community in a democracy, it is likely to breed unhealthy and antidemocratic forms: gangs, secret societies, conspiratorial political groups, and hierarchical clubs, for example. If we cannot bond as citizens, we will probably bond in the name of race or ethnic origin or gender, accentuating adversarial differences in the insidious ways that were expressed in the Clarence Thomas hearings in the autumn of 1991. For every failed campaign for a more democratic community, there are a dozen demagogues lying in wait. Participatory democratic communities permit an identification with others that is compatible with political liberty and that unites instead of dividing. That is their entire point.

Service to the neighborhood and to the nation are not the gift of altruists but a duty of free men and women whose freedom is itself wholly dependent on the assumption of political responsibilities. The severing of service from education and training in responsibility is in fact a relatively recent phenomenon. America's actual history suggests a nation devoted to civic education for citizenship and schools devoted to the nation's civic mission. The traditional American source of service was not the nineteenth-century poorhouse or its corollaries like noblesse oblige, but the older idea of the responsible citizen as a primary objective of liberal education. In this tradition, service is something we owe to ourselves or to that part of ourselves that is embedded in the civic community. It assumes that our rights and liberties are not acquired for free; that unless we assume the responsibilities of citizens, we will not be able to preserve the liberties they entail.

Historically, then, education in America cast training for citizenship as one of its primary purposes. American colleges and universities were first founded in the seventeenth and eighteenth centuries around the idea of service: service to church (many began as training seminars for the ministry), service to the local community, and service to the emerging nation. Because so many wealthy Americans sent their children to school in England, American schools boasted that they alone could serve Crève-coeur's new American man. This was true for all the schools founded before the Revolution (Harvard, William and Mary, Yale, and Princeton, to take the four oldest). And it was true for Queens College in New Brunswick (Rutgers University in its first incarnation), chartered in 1766 to promote "learning for the benefit of the community."[8]

By the nineteenth century Benjamin Rush's call for the nation's colleges to become "nurseries of wise and good men" who might ensure a wise and good country had become the motto of dozens of new church-related schools and land grant colleges. The Gilded Age took its toll on this spirit, however, and by the beginning of the twentieth century Woodrow Wilson was worrying that "as a nation we are becoming civically illiterate. Unless we find better ways to educate ourselves as citizens, we run the risk of drifting unwittingly into a new kind of Dark Age—a time when small cadres of specialists will control knowledge and thus control the decision-making process." Wilson urged—against the specializing spirit of the new German-based research universities, like Johns Hopkins—that the "air of affairs" be admitted into the classrooms of America and that "the spirit of service" be permitted once again to "give college a place in the public annals of the nation." Much of John Dewey's career was given over to the quest for bridging education and experience in the name of democracy as a way of life rather than just a political system.[9]

The call for a liberal education relevant to democracy gets renewed in each generation: In World War II, the fate of the war in Europe and the Pacific was seen as hinging in part on the capacity of America's schools and colleges to produce civic-minded, patriotic young Americans who understood the meaning of democracy and who (Paul Fussell notwithstanding) knew the difference between what they fought for and what their enemies fought for. In the 1960s, concern for democracy and the civic education of the young led many colleges to experiment with "relevance." Few reached as high or waxed as hyperbolic as Livingston College, a new school established at Rutgers University toward the end of the decade, whose first bulletin announced: "There will be freedom at Livingston College! For Livingston will have no ivory towers. It cannot; our cities are decaying, many of our fellow men are starving, social injustice and racism litter the earth. . . . We feel a strong conviction that the gap between the campus and the urban community must be narrowed." Although most other colleges aspired more modestly, many came to question the relationship of the ivory tower to the democratic nation. A number tried to develop programs of some value to the country's democratic agenda.

In recent years, the spirit that puts civic questions to the complacent professionalism and research orientation of the modern university has again sprung to life. In the early eighties, Ernest Boyer and Fred Hechinger asked that "a new generation of Americans ... be educated for life in an increasingly complex world ... through civic education [that] prepares students of all ages to participate more effectively in our social institutions."[10] Over the past few years, interest in civic education and community service has fairly exploded. At the beginning of the last decade, the Kettering Foundation issued a report calling for national youth service of at least a year for all young Americans.[11] Meanwhile, the Committee for the Study of National Service at the Potomac Institute issued a report on "Youth and the Needs of the Nation" asking for closer coordination and a genuine national policy for programs like the Peace Crops, Volunteers in Service to America, the Young Adults Conservation Corps, and the Job Corps. For nearly every cynical attack on relevance in education, there has been a thoughtful proposal for a closer link between education and experience, learning and community. Morris Janowitz, Charles Moskos, and Donald Eberly are among the serious commentators who have written deeply considered books on the link; they have offered a powerful impetus to legislative activity around national service.[12] The cause of service now has a plethora of sponsors on Capitol Hill, where nearly a dozen bills have been introduced in recent years in search of a viable program of national service. These legislative efforts, along with President Bush's Youth Engaged in Service program (YES) and the newly chartered National Commission on Service, suggest a salutatory interest reflected in the platforms of recent electoral contenders such as Senator Harris Woford in Pennsylvania and Governor Bill Clinton in the presidential primary. But few connect service directly either to citizenship in the larger community or to classroom learning. Many draw a misleading and dangerous (to democracy) picture of service as the rich helping the poor (charity) or the poor paying a debt to their country (service in exchange for college scholarships) as if "community" means only the dis-advantaged and needy and does not include those performing ser-vice. William Buckley's recent book *Gratitude* is typical in its celebration of generosity and altruism and its aversion to the ex-plicit language of citizenship.[13] Buckley does employ unfashion-able terms like "obligation" and "duty," but he stops short of the rhetoric of democracy.[14]

The language of charity drives a wedge between self-interest and altruism, leading students to believe that service is a matter of sacrificing private interests to moral virtue. The language of citizenship suggests that self-interests are always embedded in communities of action and that in serving neighbors one also serves oneself. When you live in a rooming house and help put out a fire in a neighbor's apartment, you are not just being altruistic. Barn raisings were more than exercises in kindness: every barn raised created new neighbors, extended the neigh-borhood, and enhanced the public community from which ev-eryone tangibly benefited in many ways. When sited in a learning environment, the service idea promotes an understand-ing of how self and community, private interest and public good, are necessarily linked. Legal right and civic responsibility—neither can stand alone—are only the final political expression of that linkage.

There are two complementary approaches to service learn-ing, to some degree mutually supportive but held also in a cer-tain tension with each other. On the campus, the first aims at attracting student volunteers into service projects as part of a strategy aimed at strengthening altruism, philanthropy, individ-ualism, and self-reliance. Service here is a vital extracurricular activity, necessitated by the demands of living rather than the demands of schooling. The second, rooted in the convergence of self-interest and public good in the setting of healthy com-munity, attempts to integrate service into the classroom and into academic curricula. It hopes to make civic education and social responsibility core subjects of high school and university education, and in so doing to help rehabilitate schools as successful learning communities.

Underlying these two approaches are conflicting—though not altogether incompatible—views of the real aim of student community service programs. The differences become clear around the issue of whether education-based service programs should be voluntary or mandatory. If the aim of service is the encouragement of voluntarism and a spirit of altruism—if service is seen as a supererogatory trait of otherwise self-regarding individuals—then clearly it cannot be mandated or required. Coercing voluntarism is an oxymoron and hardly makes pedagogical sense. But if service is understood as a dimension of citizenship education and civic responsibility in which individuals learn the meaning of social interdependence and become empowered through acquiring the democratic arts, then the requirement of service conforms to curricular requirements in other disciplines.

To coerce behavior is to impose beliefs externally on a resisting student: liberty thus runs the risk of being made over into the enemy of learning. But to require a pedagogy is to empower the person and thus to cultivate autonomy: liberty and learning become allies, although initially the first may be suspended in the name of securing the second. The practical issue is evident to anyone who works in service-learning programs: those most in need of training in the democratic arts of citizenship are in fact least likely to volunteer. Complacency, ignorance of interdependence, apathy, and an inability to see the relationship between self-interest and broader community interests are not only targets of civic education, they are obstacles to it, attitudes that dispose individuals against it. The problem to be remedied, apathy, here becomes the impediment to the remedy. Education is the exercise of authority (legitimate coercion) in the name of freedom: the empowerment and liberation of the pupil. To make people serve others may produce desirable behavior, but it does not create responsible and autonomous individuals. To make people participate in educational curricula that can empower them does create such individuals. The ultimate goal is not to serve others but to learn to be free, which entails being responsible to others.

In most purely volunteer service programs, those involved have already learned a good deal about the civic significance of service. Students who opt to take courses incorporating service have often done extensive volunteer service prior to enrollment. Such programs reach and help students who have already made the first and probably most significant step toward an understanding of the responsibilities of social membership. They provide useful outlets for the expression of a disposition that has already been formed. But the preponderant majority of young people who have no sense of the meaning of citizenship, no conception of civic responsibility, will remain entirely untouched by volunteer programs. Thinking that the national problem of civic apathy can be cured by encouraging voluntarism is like thinking that illiteracy can be remedied by distributing books on the importance of reading. What young people require to volunteer for education-based community service courses are the very skills and understandings that these courses are designed to provide.

There are, of course, problems with mandating education of any kind, but most educators agree that an effective education can be left entirely to the discretion of pupils, and schools and universities require a great many things of students—an old canon or a new multicultural perspective, basic English or basic science, 24 credits for a major or 120 credits to graduate. Are these requirements more closely tied to fundamental education or more vital to the preservation of American freedoms than civic learning? It is in the very nature of pedagogical authority that it exercises some coercion in the name of liberation. Civic empowerment and the exercise of liberty are simply too important to be treated as extracurricular electives.

Civic education rooted in service learning can be a powerful response to civic scapegoatism and the bad habits of representative democracy (deference to authority, blaming deputies for the vices of their electors). Where students use experience in the community as a basis for critical reflection in the classroom, and turn classroom reflection into a tool to examine the nature of democratic communities and the role of the citizen in them, there is an opportunity to teach liberty, to uncover the interdependence of self and other, to expose the intimate linkage between rights and responsibilities. Every one of the controversies introduced in earlier chapters is an appropriate subject for study in a well-conceived service-learning course. For students engaged in service, the nature of difference and its impact on community become crucial aspects of experience as well as abstract questions in an intellectual skirmish. For whites trying to work with other students in a multiracial community, racism is more than a hypothetical question. For young women faced with service establishment "clients" who refuse to take them seriously, the relationship of gender and power can no longer remain a textbook controversy. Hyperskepticism is brought up short by the necessity to take moral decisions leading to consequential action in the setting of a service placement. The canon will prove itself or fail to prove itself worthy in its capacity to inform experience and life activity in a way that cannot happen in the classroom. Whether Plato's "republic of speech" can be translated into a republic of deeds is of powerful consequence both to the academic world of speech and to the mundane world of deeds.

Education-based community service programs empower students even as they learn. They bring the lessons of service into the classroom, even as they bring the lessons of the classroom out into the community. A number of institutions around the country have been experimenting with programs, a few even envisioning mandatory curricula. Dinesh D'Souza pillories a number of leading universities for their inability to strike a balance in seeking new curricula and new rules for the novel multicultural world in which they find themselves. Yet many of these schools have demonstrated a boldness and clarity in exploring service learning. Stanford University, Spelman College, Baylor University, Notre Dame, the University of Minnesota, and Harvard University have all begun to explore the educational possibilities of service learning as a significant element in liberal education. Is it possible, then, that our schools and universities might regain their civic momentum through such service-learning programs? At least one institution has begun a practical experiment to find out: Rutgers, the State University of New Jersey.

A MODEL PROGRAM: EDUCATION-BASED COMMUNITY SERVICE AT RUTGERS UNIVERSITY

In the spring of 1988, President Edward Bloustein of Rutgers University gave a commencement address in the form of a meditation on the sad state into which America's large universities had fallen—the pathologies of community and the classroom that had created a sense of crisis in the nation at large. Remembering his own wartime experience in a proto-multicultural army, he proposed a mandatory program of citizen education and community service as a graduation requirement for all students at the State University of New Jersey. When President Bloustein asked me to chair the committee charged with exploring the idea of service in the academy, and trying to develop a program through which it could be realized, I had no idea how far service learning might take the university. In the course of the next three years, with the support of Bloustein's successor, Francis L. Lawrence, as well as many faculty and students, Rutgers pioneered an extended pilot program in which classroom civic education and practical community service were united in a number of bold new courses and a residence hall devoted to service learning. The Rutgers experience offers a model of how service learning can redefine what it means to teach liberty.[15]

The Rutgers program was premised on nine governing principles, which were hammered out in a year of discussion among faculty, students, and administrators. The principles, listed below, are remarkable in how they fold notions of community, democracy, and citizenship into pedagogy in an attempt to redress the pathologies of modern education.

1. That to teach the art of citizenship and responsibility is to practice it: so that teaching in this domain must be about acting and doing as well as about listening and learning, but must also afford an opportunity for reflecting on and discussing what is being done. In practical terms, this means that community service can only be an instrument of education when it is connected to an academic learning experience in a classroom setting. But the corollary is also true, that civic education can only be effective when it encompasses experiential learning of the kind offered by community service or other similar forms of group activity.

2. That the crucial democratic relationship between rights and responsibilities, which have too often been divorced in our society, can only be made visible in a setting of experiential learning where academic discussion is linked to practical activity. In other words, learning about the relationship between civic responsibility and civic rights means exercising the rights and duties of membership in an actual community, whether that community is a classroom, a group project or community service team, or the university/college community at large.

3. That antisocial, discriminatory and other forms of selfish and abusive or addictive behavior are often a symptom of the breakdown of civic community—both local and societal. This suggests that to remedy many of the problems of alienation and

disaffection of the young requires the reconstruction of the civic community, something that a program of civic education based on experiential learning and community service may therefore be better able to accomplish than problem-by-problem piecemeal solutions pursued in isolation from underlying causes.

4. That respect for the full diversity and plurality of American life is possible only when students have an opportunity to interact outside of the classroom in ways that are, however, the subject of scrutiny and open discussion in the classroom. An experiential learning process that includes both classroom learning and group work outside the classroom has the greatest likelihood of impacting on student ignorance, intolerance, and prejudice.

5. That membership in a community entails responsibilities and duties which are likely to be felt as binding only to the degree individuals feel empowered in the community. As a consequence, empowerment ought to be a significant dimension of education for civic responsibility—particularly in the planning process to establish civic education and community service programs.

6. That civic education as experiential learning and community service must not discriminate among economic or other classes of Americans. If equal respect and equal rights are two keys to citizenship in a democracy, then a civic education program must assure that no one is forced to participate merely because they are economically disadvantaged, and no one is exempted from service merely because they are economically privileged.

7. That civic education should be communal as well as community-based. If citizen education and experiential learning of the kind offered by community service are to be a lesson in community, the ideal learning unit is not the individual but the small team, where people work together and learn together, experiencing what it means to become a small community together. Civic education programs thus should be built around teams (of say 5 or 10 or 20) rather than around individuals.

8. That the point of any community service element of civic education must be to teach citizenship, not charity. If education is aimed at creating citizens, then it will be important to let the young see that service is not just about altruism or charity; or a matter of those who are well-off helping those who are not. It is serving the public interest, which is the same thing as serving enlightened self-interest. Young people serve themselves as members of the community by serving a public good that is also their own. The responsible citizen finally serves liberty.

9. That civic education needs to be regarded as an integral part of liberal education and thus should both be mandatory and should receive academic credit. Because citizenship is an acquired art, and because those least likely to be spirited citizens or volunteers in their local or national community are most in need of civic training, an adequate program of citizen training with an opportunity for service needs to be mandatory. There are certain things a democracy simply must teach, employing its full authority to do so: citizenship is first among them.

The program Rutgers developed on the foundation of these principles, endorsed by representatives of the student body and by the board of governors and currently being reviewed by duly constituted faculty bodies, calls for

A MANDATORY CIVIC EDUCATION COURSE organized around (though not limited to) a classroom course with an academic syllabus, but also including a strong and innovative experiential learning focus utilizing group projects. A primary vehicle for these projects will be community service, as one of a number of experiential learning options; while the course will be mandatory, students will be free to choose community service or nonservice projects as their experiential learning group project. The required course will be buttressed by a program of incentives encouraging students to continue to participate in community service throughout their academic careers at Rutgers.

COURSE CONTENT will be broad and varied, but should guarantee some coverage of vital civic issues and questions, including the following:

1. The nature of the social or civic bond; social contract, legitimacy, authority, freedom, constitutionalism—the key concepts of a political community;

2. The meaning of citizenship—representation versus participation, passive versus active forms of civic life; citizenship and service;

3. The university community; its structure and governance; the role of students, faculty, and administrators; questions of empowerment:

4. The place of ethnicity, religion, race, class, gender, and sexual orientation in a community: Does equality mean abolishing differences? Or learning to respect and celebrate diversity and inclusiveness? How does a community deal with differences of the kind represented by the disequalizing effects of power and wealth?

5. The nature of service: differences between charity and social responsibility; between rights and needs or desires. What is the relationship between community service and citizenship? Can service be mandatory? Does a state have the right to mandate the training of citizens or does this violate freedom?

6. The nature of leadership in a democracy: Are there special features to democratic leadership? Do strong leaders create weak followers? What is the relationship between leadership and equality?

7. Cooperation and competition, models of community interaction: How do private and public interests relate in a community?

8. The character of civic communities, educational, local, regional, and national. What is the difference between society and the state? Is America a "community"? Is Rutgers a community? Do its several campuses (Camden, Newark, New Brunswick) constitute a community? What is the relationship between them and the communities in which they are located? What are the real issues of these communities—issues such as sexual harassment, suicide, date rape, homophobia, racism, and distrust of authority?

VARIATIONS ON THE BASIC MODEL will be encouraged within the basic course design, with ample room for significant variations. Individual colleges, schools, and departments will be encouraged to develop their own versions of the course to suit the particular needs of their students and the civic issues particular to their disciplines or areas. Thus, the Engineering School might wish to develop a program around "the responsibilities of scientists," the Mason Gross School for the Performing Arts might wish to pioneer community service options focusing on students performing in and bringing arts education to schools and senior centers in the community, or Douglass College might want to capitalize on its longstanding commitment to encourage women to become active leaders by developing its own appropriate course variations.

EXPERIENTIAL LEARNING is crucial to the program, for the key difference between the program offered here and traditional civic education approaches is the focus on learning outside the classroom, integrated into the classroom. Students will utilize group projects in community service and in other extraseminar group activities as the basis for reading and reflecting on course material.

Experiential learning permits students to apply classroom learning to the real world, and to subject real world experience to classroom examination. To plan adequately for an experiential learning focus and to assure that projects are pedagogically sound and responsible to the communities they may engage, particular attention will be given to its design in the planning phase.

THE TEAM APPROACH is a special feature of the Rutgers proposal. All experiential learning projects will be group projects where individuals learn in concert with others; where they experience community in part by practicing community during the learning process. We urge special attention be given to the role of groups or teams in the design both of the classroom format and the experiential learning component of the basic course.

COMMUNITY SERVICE is only one among the several options for experiential learning, but it will clearly be the choice of a majority of students, and is in fact the centerpiece of the Rutgers program. We believe that community service, when related to citizenship and social responsibility in a disciplined pedagogical setting, is the most powerful form of experiential learning. As such, it is central to our conception of the civic education process.

AN INCENTIVE PROGRAM FOR CONTINUING SERVICE is built into the Rutgers project, because our objective is to instill in students a spirit of citizenship that is enduring. It is thus vital that the program, though it is centered on the freshman-year course, not be limited to that initial experience, and that there be opportunities for ongoing service and participation throughout the four years of college.

The Rutgers pilot program—at this stage it is still experimental and voluntary—is only one among many new efforts at a number of different schools and universities aimed at incorporating service learning into academic curricula. Service learning, in turn, is only one example of a number of approaches that, without abandoning the intellectual integrity of autonomous educational institutions, attempt to give practical meaning to the philosophy which places teaching liberty at the center of liberal education.

In a vigorous democracy capable of withstanding the challenges of a complex, often undemocratic, interdependent world, creating new generations of citizens is not a discretionary activity. Freedom is a hothouse plant that flourishes only when it is carefully tended. Without active citizens who see in service not the altruism of charity but the responsibility of citizenship on which liberty ultimately depends, no democracy can function properly or, in the long run, even survive. Without education that treats women and men as whole, as beings who belong to communities of knowledge, there may be no stopping place on the slippery road from dogmatism to nihilism. Without schools that take responsibility for what goes on beyond as well as in the classroom, and work to remove the walls that separate the two worlds, students will continue to bracket off all that they learn from life and keep their lives at arm's length from what they learn. Without teachers who are left alone to teach, students will fall prey to the suasion of an illiterate society all too willing to make its dollars their tutors.

National service is not merely a good idea; or, as William Buckley has suggested, a way to repay the debt owed our "patrimony." It is an indispensable prerequisite of citizenship and thus a condition for democracy's preservation. Democracy does not just "deserve" our gratitude; it demands our participation as a price of survival. The Rutgers program and others like it offer a model that integrates liberal teaching, experiential learning, community service, and citizen education. It also suggests a legislative strategy for establishing a national service requirement without raising up still one more elephantine national bureaucracy. Require service of all Americans through federal guidelines; but permit the requirement to be implemented through service-learning programs housed in schools, universities, and, for those not in the school system, other local institutions, such as the YMCA or the Chamber of Commerce. Employing the nation's schools and colleges as laboratories of citizenship and service might at once offer an attractive way to develop civic service opportunities for all Americans and help educate the young to the obligations of the democratic citizen. This would not only serve democracy, it could restore to our educational institutions a sense of mission they have long lacked.

EPILOGUE

What is the mission of education in a democracy? In the first instance, democracy itself, just as a primary mission of democracy is public education. The spirit of inquiry (asking tough questions) coupled with the capacity to judge (offering provisional answers) defines both liberal education and education for liberty, both critical learning and deliberative democracy.

If we are to restore our schools to democracy and return democracy to our schools, we need to reconsider the meaning of liberty in our own lives. We are unlikely to teach the young to embrace liberty if we have laid our own aside in pursuit of safety or prosperity or national competitiveness; or if we have confounded liberty with the unbridling of consumer appetites and the unleashing of selfishness. If excellence and democracy are to be reconciled, they must first be reconciled within us. Many Americans have been persuaded that in trying to educate everyone, they will only manage to nurture mediocrity. But mediocrity is an evasion of freedom, not its product. If our schools are mediocre, it is because we have failed as educators to raise our children to commonly high standards, not because we have succeeded as democrats in offering them standards that are too common.

Education is a society's passport for travel through time. Perhaps we have marginalized the solemn questions raised by education because we have lost our confidence, our interest, our hope in the future. Schools are the public nurseries of our future, and their wanton neglect entails a kind of silent social suicide. What happens today in a third-grade classroom or a college seminar determines whether tomorrow the great American community flourishes or falls. Whether schools produce merely literate private individuals and competent workers or truly democratic citizens will condition our global destiny. Brooding isolationists are advising America to withdraw from the world, while traditional internationalists are advocating engagement at all costs. Truth is, we cannot be successful cosmopolitans until we become successful parochials. For America to speak in the voice of liberty abroad, all Americans must speak the language of liberty at home. Neither foreign aid nor public relations nor all the Pentagon's might can speak as eloquently for democracy abroad as flourishing democratic institutions at home. Like our skeptical students, the people of the world have noses for hypocrisy. What we do here will be the measure of their trust and admiration.

As with parochialism and cosmopolitanism, we fall too easily into casting our choices in terms of incompatible opposites: liberty or equality, freedom or participation, democracy or excellence, rights or obligations, the individual or the community. We are aroused by the supposed closing of the American mind but remain inert at the prospect of the closing of American schools. Cultural literacy is a voguish subject, but just plain illiteracy fails to get our attention. For many of us, liberty means only freedom *from*, a wall we raise around private selves to fence out others: the government, competitors, sometimes even neighbors or families. A grandfather's freedom to visit his grandchildren may thus now seem to require that he bring suit against his son or daughter. A citizen's freedom—"Get the government off my back!"—

may seem to demand that she dismantle the collective institutions by which she acquires power over her common life, as if government were some Kafkaesque "They" that had nothing to do with her. Insisting on my private rights may mean the community can have no public rights. Thus liberty comes to feel like another word for selfishness, for solitude, and for being left alone. Such feelings and habits are hard to unteach. If we are in their grip, how can we educate our children to get beyond them? To teach our children liberty, we may first have to teach ourselves. A good place to start is with the meaning of liberty itself.

In its most accessible and sensible form, liberty is a bridge between individuals and their communities rather than a wall separating them. This is perhaps what the philosopher Rousseau meant when he described freedom as obedience to a law we prescribe to ourselves, thus reminding us of the intimacy of rights and responsibilities, of freedom and limits, of liberation and self-government. To obey laws we give to ourselves is in fact a very persuasive definition of democracy. It sets freedom in its civic context: we are free *through* laws we make for ourselves rather than free *from* the laws. The latter is merely anarchy, what old-fashioned moral philosophers once called licentiousness.

One of America's most perspicacious observers, Alexis de Tocqueville, put liberty in its proper civic setting. Contemplating what he called "ancient liberty" in his own prerevolutionary France before the Bourbon kings had destroyed the local Parlements and their liberties and privileges, Tocqueville concluded that, far from securing individuals against one another, freedom actually "can deliver the members of a community from that isolation that is the lot of the individual left to his own devices, compelling them to get in touch with one another, promote an active sense of fellowship."[1] More recent writers have echoed Tocqueville. To Hannah Arendt, the public nature of liberty suggested that only the citizen could be free. "Freedom generally speaking," she wrote, "means the right 'to be a participator in government,' or it means nothing at all."[2] Hannah Arendt was correct, but for many Americans this seems only to prove that freedom means, if not quite "nothing at all," very little indeed.

Freedom means more than being left alone. Democracy and excellence *are* compatible. Education is their broker. Democracy is the rule of citizens, and citizens alone are free. For citizens are self-conscious, critical participants in communities of common speech, common value, and common work that bridge both space and time. As freedom yields community, so the forms of community and commonality alone yield freedom. Education makes citizens; only citizens can forge freedom. Democracy allows people to govern themselves; indeed, it insists that they do so. Education teaches them the liberty that makes self-government possible.

Although many educational conservatives will try to persuade us otherwise, the question is not whether we prefer excellence or democracy. It is whether the excellence we naturally wish for can be democratic, whether our democracy, which is about a life in common, must mean a common life of mediocrity. To its critics, democracy has traditionally meant mob rule: the rule of the rabble, of base prejudice and ignorant opinion. In this view, popular sovereignty becomes the sovereignty of mediocrity and the celebrated commonwealth becomes a euphemism for the lowest common denominator. The faith in democracy must refuse the antinomy. It cannot and does not argue for the virtue of mob rule; rather, it insists that democracy means raising the common denominator, transforming the individual through education into a deliberative citizen. Citizens are aristocrats of the polity and in a democracy everyone is a citizen. Once upon a time, kings might jest that they truly were democrats: it was just that in their democracy, there was only a single citizen—the king himself. Commoners and democrats can claim more accurately today that they truly are aristocrats, practitioners of the government of excellence. It is just that their aristocracy, having emerged from democracy's schools, is an aristocracy of everyone.

The ardent believer in democracy may even share with Plato

(and with his modern spokesman, Allan Bloom) the quest for a government of reason. But where Plato hoped to bring the rule of reason to the passive multitude through a handful of philosopher kings, the advocate of democratic education hopes to bring the multitude to reason through public education. Reason *can* rule in a democratic society, but only when common men and women are educated to reasonableness. Plato did not think common people capable of higher education or of reasonableness, and as we have noted, many of his cynical disciples today share his gloom. Public education is democracy's answer to Plato. It enables individuals to become citizens capable of discovering common ground and rendering sound political judgments. The point of democracy is not to empower the ignorant and the unreasonable but to educate them so that, when empowered, they can govern reasonably and live well. Americans like to think of democracy as rule for, of, and by the people. More accurately, it is rule for, of, and by *citizens*, who are as different from ordinary "people" as a competent jury is from the allegedly vicious defendant it refuses—because it retains a "reasonable doubt" about his guilt—to convict; as different as the honest voter who spurns a bribe is from the party hack who tries to bribe him.

Conservative skeptics will hurry to point out that there is in all talk about education and self-government a foolish optimism, a weak echo of nostalgic utopianism. Cynics on the left will add that a too-cheerful disposition will aid and comfort those who abuse democracy and exploit the good name of education for purposes of manipulation and repression. And both skeptics and cynics will be right, for the aspiration to democratic education requires an often utopian, sometimes foolish, always risky faith in the human capacity for change. Yet the language of hope is the natural language of our multicultural Western civilization, the idiom that has drawn so many immigrants to American shores. It is the language of the early Christian search for redemption; of the Renaissance daring that opened nature and the world to probing exploration; of Protestantism's quest for an intimacy between individuals and their God brokered by the Word rather than by priests; of the Enlightenment pursuit of reason; of the American pioneer's restless push westward; and, perhaps most importantly, of the revolutionary quest for suffrage, justice, and emancipation that often had to struggle against Christianity and the Enlightenment and pioneer imperialism—in short, of each and every movement for human liberty that defines our precarious modernity. Redemption depends on this language; science assumes it; the idea of progress embodies it; education demands it. Democracy is hope incarnated as political realism.

To pessimists and determinists and nihilists—there are plenty around as we approach the next millennium—hope is the fatal flaw in modernity's project of liberation. To democratic educators it is that project's necessary condition. To the degree America chooses to retain its faith and hold fast to the aspirations yielded by its story, liberty may still have a future. The choice, however, is anything but foreordained. The story's magic is that its ending depends on those who tell the tale. The American story created the American people, but part of its magic was that it created a story about women and men who would in time choose their own story's outcome. Will they? And what story—whose story—will it be?

NOTES

1. Since 1972, teachers' salaries have increased sixty-eight postinflation dollars a year. Average salary in 1990 was $31,000; under $23,000 in North and South Dakota, Arkansas, and West Virginia; between $35,000 and $40,000 in Connecticut, Washington, D.C., New York, California, Maryland, and New Jersey. Lawyers' salaries averaged $60,000, chemists $47,000, and accountants $36,000. (*The Berkshire Eagle*, July 1990).

2. Immanuel Wallerstein and Paul Starr, *The University Crisis Reader* (New York: Vintage Books, 1971). Readers anxious to learn how the views of some key players have changed (or not) over the years are urged to consult this anthology. Clues to chapter 3 in this text appear in a letter reprinted in the anthology that I sent to the *New York Times* in 1970.

3. In *A Nation at Risk: The Imperative of Educational Reform* (Washington, D.C.: Carnegie Foundation, 1983), the National Commission on Excellence wrote with more than a little melodrama of a nation threatened by "a rising tide of mediocrity" that imperiled "our very future as a Nation and a people." It made an ominous comparison between what is happening to American education and "an act of war."

4. A few examples: Nabisco has spent tens of millions of dollars on a "Next Century's Schools" program. Aside from donations to schools (e.g., Coca-Cola promised $50 million over the course of the nineties), many corporations are being forced to open their own educational centers for remedial work with poorly educated employees. Boston University took over Boston's

Chelsea school district, but despite an infusion of cash, has achieved mixed results. See chapter 6 for a further discussion.

5. Allan Bloom, *The Closing of the American Mind* (New York: Simon & Schuster, 1987); Roger Kimball, *Tenured Radicals: How Politics Has Corrupted Higher Education* (New York: Harper & Row, 1990); John Silber, *Shooting Straight: What's Wrong with America* (New York: Harper & Row, 1990); Charles Sykes, *Profscam: Professors and the Demise of Higher Education* (New York: St. Martin's, 1990); Dinesh D'Souza, *Illiberal Education* (New York: Free Press, 1991).

For a discussion from the other side, see the stream of excellent publications from the Carnegie Foundation for the Advancement of Education, as well as Bruce Wilshire's *The Moral Collapse of the University* (Albany: State University of New York Press, 1990) and Page Smith's *Killing the Spirit: Higher Education in America* (New York: Viking, 1990). For a summary of both points of view, see the collection of articles in "The Changing of the University," *Partisan Review 58*, no. 2 (Spring 1991) On "P.C.," See Paul Berman, ed. *Debating P.C.: The Controversy Over Political Correctness on College Campuses* (New York: Laurel/Dell, 1992).

6. This district, comprising a forty-seven-campus, 31,000-student area, is the fifteenth largest in California. The district filed for bankruptcy on April 19, 1991, and is currently being reorganized.

7. Conservatives and progressives alike agree that American education is top-heavy with layers of expensive administration smothering the classrooms where learning goes on. See the collection of articles in *Academe* (November–December 1991) for a sampling of the debate about bloated administration in higher education. Per capita spending on public education in America is high compared to some other advanced societies, but the status and comparative wages of teachers, and the money set aside for actual educational programs, remain low.

8. In New Orleans, two months have been added to the school year, but "experts" seeking instant results (the American disease) are already calling the experiment a failure.

9. The Carnegie Foundation for the Advancement of Teaching, *Report Card on School Reform: The Teachers Speak* (Washington, D.C.: Carnegie Foundation, 1988), 11. For accounts from the perspective of teachers, in marked contrast to all the lugubrious conservative tomes, see Tracy Kidder's *Among Schoolchildren* (Boston: Houghton Mifflin, 1989) and Samuel G. Freedman's *Small Victories: The Real World of a Teacher, Her Students and Their High School* (New York: Harper & Row, 1990), as well as Jonathan Kozol's striking school portrait, *Savage Inequalities* (New York: Crown, 1991).

10. Inequalities in school district financing are stunning: In New Jersey, the fifty-four richest districts spend over $4,000 per pupil in their schools, while the twenty-eight poorest spend less than $2,900. Princeton schools (which spent a whopping $8,344 per pupil in 1990) offer a computer for every eight children; Camden has one for every fifty-eight children. Montclair's kids can learn foreign languages in preschool; Patterson's have to wait until they reach tenth grade. (Figures are the 1984–1985 school year. *New York Times*, June 1990, sec. E). A similar story can be told in Maryland where Montgomery County's wealthy districts take in $6,000 per elementary school pupil, while rural Caroline County's districts take in $4,000. For twenty-nine students in

Caroline's Preston School, this amounts to $57,000 their class doesn't have. (*Washington Post*, national weekly edition, 21–27 January 1991).

11. John E. Chubb and Terry M. Moe, *Politics, Markets and America's Schools* (Washington, D.C.: Brookings Institution, 1990). Chubb and Moe go on to argue that "school organization" (related to teacher "morale") is the other critical factor.

CHAPTER 1: TEACHING TEMPORALITY

1. There are many tellings of the same tale in Athenian tragedy; each age of Athens had its own interpretations dictated by the needs of the times as well as the attitudes of the playwrights. In other tellings, Orestes does not find peace nor Athens justice; rather Orestes wanders the world, a tormented and lost soul. This less optimistic story found its way into later tragedy, when Athens no longer hoped for redemption as a city. The connections between women and vengeance and men and impartiality are the beginning of a long tradition of gendered storytelling in which the storytellers (men) created tales that rationalized their hegemony over women (see chapter 3).

2. See also Richard N. Current, Alexander de Conde, and Harris L. Dante, *United States History: Search for Freedom* and June R. Chapin, Raymond J. McHugh, and Richard E. Gross, *Quest for Freedom: Investigating United States History*. Similarly, many texts incorporate the story (myth?) of progress into their titles (e. g., George Earl Freeland, *America's Progress as a Civilization* and Irwin Unger and H. Mark Johnson, *Land of Progress*).

3. Frances Fitzgerald, *America Revised* (New York: Vintage Books, 1980). Her work is nicely updated and supplemented by Paul Gagnon in *Democracy's Untold Story: What American History Textbooks Should Add* (Washington, D.C.: American Federation of Teachers, 1989).

4. Dennis F. Thompson published a fascinating account of James Madison's library in "The Education of a Founding Father: The Reading List for John Witherspoon's Course in Political Theory, as taken by James Madison," *Political Theory*, vol. 4, no. 4 (November 1976).

CHAPTER 2: TO BE AN AMERICAN

1. Sanford Levinson, *Constitutional Faith* (Princeton, N.J.: Princeton University Press, 1988).

2. According to a two-year study conducted by the College Board and the Western Interstate Commission for Higher Education, a 35 percent minority public school population is anticipated by 1995 (Karen De Witt, "Large Increase Is Predicted in Minorities in U.S. Schools," *New York Times*, 13 September 1991). By 1995, California, New York, Texas, New Jersey, and Illinois school populations are projected to become over 50 percent nonwhite.

3. Werner Sallors, *Beyond Ethnicity: Consent and Descent in American Culture* (New York: Oxford University Press, 1986), 152.

4. Justice Felix Frankfurter, as cited in Levinson, 3.

5. Jack Beatty, "The Patriotism of Values," *The New Republic*, 4–11 July 1981, 18–20.

6. Cited in "Talk of the Town," *The New Yorker*, 22 April, 1991, 27–31.

7. Louis Hartz, *The Liberal Tradition in America* (Boston: Beacon Press, 1952).

8. Edmund S. Morgan, *Inventing the People: The Rise of Popular Sovereignty in England and America* (New York: Norton, 1988). Morgan is more concerned with the invention of the concept of popular sovereignty, which he claims began in the mid-seventeenth century, than with the invention of nationality. But as we shall see, in America the two are directly related.

9. Michael Walzer, "To Be an American," *Social Research* 57, no. 3 (Fall 1990).

10. Garry Wills, *Under God: Religion and American Politics* (New York: Simon & Schuster, 1990).

11. Few German Jews wished to be regarded as "Jewish-Germans" before the Nazis. Once they were thus designated, they became Jews without German identity or rights.

12. See Scott Berg's account in *Goldwyn* (New York: Knopf, 1989). Also see Neal Gabler's *An Empire of Their Own: How the Jews Invented Hollywood* (New York: Crown Publishers, 1988).

13. Cited in Michael Kammen's *People of Paradox: An Inquiry Concerning the Origins of American Civilization* (New York: Knopf, 1972), 31.

14. Cited in Frances Fitzgerald's *America Revised* (New York: Vintage Books, 1980), 49. With America and innocence coupled, it was easy for nativists and Protestants to associate European corruption with popery and migration from Mediterranean Europe.

15. The best account of this is perhaps Henry Steele Commager's *The Empire of Reason: How Europe Imagined and America Realized The Enlightenment* (Garden City: Anchor Press/Doubleday, 1977). Bernard Bailyn gives a full account of the power of Enlightenment ideas in prerevolutionary America in *Ideological Origins of the American Revolution* (Cambridge, Mass.: Harvard University Press, 1967).

16. Hartz, *Liberal Tradition*. Daniel Boorstin makes a similar argument in *The Genius of American Politics* (Chicago: University of Chicago Press, 1953).

17. 2 Sam. 7:10. See Conor Cruise O'Brien, *Godland* (Cambridge, Mass.: Harvard University Press, 1988), 6–7.

18. Hector St. John Crèvecoeur, *Letters from an American Farmer* (New York: Penguin American Library, 1981), 68–69.

19. Thomas Paine, *The Rights of Man*, in *Paine: Complete Works*, vol. 1, ed Eric Foner (New York: Citadel Press, 1945), 376.

20. See Kammen, *People of Paradox*, where the Pulitzer Prize–winning historian argues that the hybrid claims of Americans are belied by their inexorably hyphenated character. This is also Michael Walzer's view. See note 9.

21. Generally sensitive to spheres of difference, Michael Walzer overlooks the differences between a unitary public culture of citizenship and the plural-

istic private culture of ethnic identity in his discussion of liberal pluralism. See note 9.

22. See Rogers M. Smith, "One United People: Second-Class Female Citizenship and the American Quest for Community," *Yale Journal of Law and the Humanities*, vol. 1, no. 2 (May 1989), 229–293.

23. John Cornwell, *The Free and the Brave* (New York: Rand McNally, 1967), 140.

24. *Stereotypes, Distortions and Omissions in U. S. History Textbooks* (New York: Council on Interracial Books for Children, and the Racism and Sexism Resource Centers for Educators, 1977), 18.

25. Herbert Aptheker, *American Negro Slave Revolts* (New York: International Publishers, 1952). This work was a doctoral dissertation at Columbia University. Aptheker's agenda was not necessarily identical to that of the American Communist party. Nonetheless, in trying to tell another side of the story (one rarely aired in the 1940s and 1950s), Aptheker represents a caricature of the relationship between a political vision and a historical story with which all historians must come to terms.

26. *American History for Today* (New York: Ginn and Co., 1970), 193.

27. "Even the best men err," Melville concludes, "in judging the conduct of one with the recesses of whose condition he is not acquainted." Henry James depicts the same American innocence in his character Daisy Miller, who embarks on a voyage of innocence through old, decaying Europe.

28. James Madison, "Note to Speech on the Right to Suffrage," in *The Complete Madison*, ed. Saul K. Padover (Milwood, N. Y.: Kraus Reprint, 1953), 40.

29. Judith N. Shklar, *American Citizenship: The Quest for Inclusion* (Cambridge, Mass.: Harvard University Press, 1991), 1, 12. For a source on which Shklar and many others (including this author) rely, see Rogers M. Smith, "The 'American Creed' and American Identity: The Limits of Liberal Citizenship in the United States," *Western Political Quarterly* vol. 41, no. 2 (June, 1988) 225–251. Also see Kenneth L. Karst, *Belonging to America: Equal Citizenship and the Constitution* (New Haven: Yale University Press, 1989).

30. Shklar, *American Citizenship*, 23.

31. See "The Declaration of Sentiments and Resolutions of the First Women's Rights Conference" in *History of Woman Suffrage*, ed. E. Stanton, S. Anthony, and M. Gage (New York: Fowler & Wells, 1881), 170–173.

32. W. Garrison and F. Garrison, *William Lloyd Garrison: 1805–1879* (New York: Arno Press, 1969), 408.

33. L. Buchanan, *John Brown: The Making of a Revolutionary* (New York: Grosset & Dunlap, 1969), 119–120.

34. *Dred Scott* v. *Sandford*, 19 How. 393 (1857).

35. James Madison, *The Federalist Papers* no. 54.

36. James Madison to Frances Wright, September 1825, *Letters and Other Writings*, vol. 3 (Philadelphia: Lippincott, 1867), 495.

CHAPTER 3: LOOSE CANONS

1. Perhaps that is why critics of the sixties focus on campus rebels and ignore the civil rights revolution, which fits none of their preconceptions about liberals.

2. See James Miller's riveting account of the period, *Democracy Is in the Streets* (New York: Simon & Schuster, 1987).

3. Roger Kimball, *Tenured Radicals: How Politics Has Corrupted Higher Education* (New York: Harper & Row, 1990), 1.

4. See John Dewey's scathing critique of science in search of certitude in *The Quest for Certainty* (New York: Capricorn Books, 1960).

5. See Thomas Kuhn's *The Structure of Scientific Revolutions* (Chicago: University of Chicago Press, 1962, 1970), and Jurgen Habermas, *Knowledge and Interests* (Boston: Beacon Press, 1971). Their arguments were not radically reductionist; they did not propose that knowledge was merely a function of interests, only that interests were implicated in knowledge.

6. Gabriel Abraham Almond and Sidney Verba, *Civic Culture* (Princeton, N. J.: Princeton University Press, 1963).

7. Samuel Huntington, "One Soul At a Time: Political Science and Political Reform" (Presidential Address delivered at the 1987 Annual Meeting of the American Political Science Association, Chicago).

8. Samuel Huntington, "Democratic Distemper," *The Public Interest* (Fall 1975), 9–38.

9. Leo Strauss, "Epilogue," in *Essays in the Scientific Study of Politics*. ed. Herbert J. Storing (New York: Holt, Rinehart and Winston, 1962), 326. Storing's controversial volume included essays by Walter Berns, Leo Weinstein, Robert Horwitz, as well as Strauss and Storing, all of which savaged the new positivistic social science. Its demolition of the new sciences of voting studies, administration, pluralist/group politics, and "scientific propaganda" studies generated a furor no less political than was to greet later leftists who made some of the same claims for "relevance" and "politics."

10. Ibid., 327.

11. Isabel Wilkerson, "Race Hatred Shatters 'Tolerant' College," *International Herald Tribune*, 14 April 1992.

12. Recently, Leonard Jeffries, Jr., a City College of New York professor who likes to talk about the "sun" people and the "ice" people, used the occasion of a New York State–sponsored summer festival to lash out at "rich Jews." New York Governor Mario Cuomo, City University chancellor Ann Reynolds, and many others immediately called for "action," including possible dismissal of the professor from his departmental chairmanship (carried out in the spring of 1992). Around the same time, Amiri Baraka protested Spike Lee's making a film about the life of Malcolm X (Lee had earlier argued that white directors like Norman Jewison had no business directing films about blacks.)

What is interesting about these cases is how the normal polarities concerning "political correctness" are reversed. Public officials who normally condemn the silencing of speech because it "offends" someone are now themselves offended and anxious to both silence and punish the offender. An African-American angry at whites for distorting or censoring African-American history is busy trying to stop another African-American from making a film about an African-American hero. Once again, the question seems to be who is offending whom, and how much power they have. In the academy, these questions need to be settled internally.

13. The best account was offered by PBS's "Frontline" episode "A Class Divided," rebroadcast on 26 March 1985.

14. David Steiner, "Beyond Pure Process: The Search For a Theory of Democratic Education" (Paper delivered at the 1990 Annual Meeting of the American Political Science Association, San Francisco). He concludes "The Stanford canon" was filled with figures who wrote in the vernacular of popular tongues (Dante, Chaucer, Rabelais, Cervantes, Luther); with figures who turned their worlds inside out or upside down (Goethe, Hegel, Shakespeare, Galileo, Machiavelli, Darwin); with rebels, malcontents, and disaffected types (Pico, Luther, More, Rousseau, Locke, Descartes, Flaubert, Dostoyevski); with tragedians (Homer, Sophocles, Aeschylus, Euripedes, Virgil, Goethe, Shakespeare); with out-and-out cultural revolutionaries and blasphemers (Marx, Nietzsche, Freud)." Seery's quote is from a paper delivered at the same meeting. After the reform of the curriculum (before it was later abolished totally), "some feared tokenism, but actually it was an easy move to include the works of Sappho, Marie de France, Christine de Pizan, Mary Wollstonecraft, Mary Shelley, Virginia Woolf, Frederick Douglass and Richard Wright; for these writers fit right in the Western tradition and quite nicely." (John Evan Seery, "My Turn: A Great-Bookish Tell All" [Paper delivered at the 1990 Annual Meeting of the American Political Science Association, San Francisco], 5.)

CHAPTER 4: RADICAL EXCESSES AND POST-MODERNISM

1. American leftists have been puzzled by the interest of the French left in Leo Strauss, the spiritual father of the traditional defenders of the canon (see chapter 5). But in fact, conservatives and radicals have shared a distrust of liberal establishmentarianism with its pretense of universalism and neutrality.

2. Molefi Kete Asante, the author of *Afrocentricity: The Theory of Social Change* (Buffalo, N.Y.: Amulefi, 1980) offers a perfect example of this straying logic when he says: "Afrocentricity resonates with the African-American community because it is fundamental to sanity" ("Putting Africa at the Center," *Newsweek*, 23 September 1991). The same could be said of religion, divorce, alcohol, and any number of other things; that something helps keep us sane is important, but it cannot by itself constitute an argument.

3. Michael Wood used this phrase while reviewing Derrida for *New York Review of Books*, "Deconstructing Derrida," 3 March 1977, 27.

4. Cited by David Lehman, *Signs of the Times: Deconstruction and Fall of Paul de Man* (New York: Poseidon Press, 1991), 251.

5. Michel Foucault, "What Is an Author?" In *Textual Strategies: Perspec-*

tives in Post Structuralist Criticism, ed. Josue V. Harar (Ithaca, N.Y.: Cornell University Press, 1979), 149.

6. Derrida offered these strictures as part of an attempt to exonerate Paul de Man, the deconstructionist who in the 1980s was not only discovered to have written articles for the fascist Belgian weekly *Le Soir* in 1941 and 1942, but to have engaged in elaborate cover-ups in the intervening years after coming to America to pursue an illustrious academic career.

7. I say "Marxism" and "Freudianism" because I have in mind certain simplistic versions of reductionism more typical of disciples than of the masters upon whom they draw. This is not to say that there are not reductionist features—some would say less persuasive than others—in Marx and Freud themselves.

8. Perhaps the best example of this conundrum is Proudhon's famous attack on capitalism under the slogan "Property is theft." If property is theft, we lose the standard by which theft is measured and the slogan is deprived of its force.

9. Cited in Jean Ferguson Carr, "Cultural Studies and Curricular Change," *Academe* (November–December 1990), 25–28.

10. This is no metaphor: Major universities offer courses on the "texts of MTV," and increasingly—even where multiculturalism is not involved—literary theory insists on the equivalence of, say, Milton and Louis L'Amour.

11. Compare Martin Bernal, *Black Athena: The Afroasiatic Roots of Classical Civilization*, 2 vols. (New Brunswick, N.J.: Rutgers University Press, 1987, 1991), and Asante, *Afrocentricity*.

12. Derrida, cited in Lehman, *Signs of the Times*, 99.

13. Ibid.

14. On Heidegger, especially in the context of Allan Bloom's discussion, see chapter 5, as well as Tom Rockmore, *On Heidegger's Nazism and Philosophy* (London: Havester/Wheatsheaf, 1992), and the pioneering work by Viktor Farras.

15. William F. Buckley, Jr., *God and Man at Yale* (Chicago: Regnery Gateway, 1951). Nothing has changed. In 1990, Ari L. Goldman discovered an astounding lack of faith at the Harvard Divinity School; see *The Search for God at Harvard* (New York: Times Books, 1991). The divinity school may have lost its spiritual bearings, but it is supersensitive to the new worldly controversies. When some wag changed a sign on paper recycling bins labeled "colored" and "white" to "paper of color," the joke elicited a very serious response and led to the changing of the signs to "bleached paper" and "dyed paper." Jokes can play a role in discrimination, but they also signal our humanity and our humility. Learning that the National Association of Student Personnel Directors published "An Anti-Harassment Checklist for Campuses" which demanded that professors scold their colleagues when they learned of "inappropriate jokes and examples in the classroom," we can assume the association lacks both a sense of humor and the slightest regard for academic freedom or the First Amendment.

16. Buckley, *God and Man*, 145–146.

17. Tocqueville introduces this passage by saying: "Despotism may gov-

ern without faith, but liberty cannot. Religion is much more necessary in the republic which they set forth in glowing colors than in the monarchy which they attack; it is more needed in democratic republics than in any other." *Democracy in America*, vol. 2 (New York: Vintage Books, 1960), 318.

18. "It cannot be denied that democratic institutions strongly tend to promote the feeling of envy in the human heart," Tocqueville said. Democratic institutions "awaken and foster a passion for quality they can never satisfy." Ibid., 208.

19. This is from Tocqueville's introduction. Ibid., vol. 1, 7.

20. As paraphrased by Henry Louis Gates, Jr., in "I Am Other," *The Responsive Community*, vol, 1, no. 2 (Summer 1991), 85. Gates argues in his essay that the problem remains (citing Richard Rorty) how to "combine reproduction and reform" (p. 87).

21. Arthur Schlesinger, Jr., cited in Robert Reinhold, "Class Struggle," *New York Times Magazine*, September 1991. See also Schlesinger, *The Disuniting of America: Reflections on a Multicultural Society* (New York: Whittle Communications, 1991). Schlesinger served on and was sharply critical of the New York State Commission of Education's report on multiculturalism, which was published in the spring of 1991 to a cacophony of critical response. It is hard keeping track of the correct ideological identity of players in this game: Allan Bloom charges Schlesinger, this defender of the American canon against multicultural excess, with "fabricating myths" justifying, among other things, "the tyranny of the majority"! Allan Bloom, *Giants and Dwarfs* (New York: Simon & Schuster, 1990), 17–19.

Nathan Glazer, another member of the commission, supported the report, arguing that "many of us are simply not aware how far advanced our schools are on the road to a black-oriented multiculturalism," and suggesting that the total failure of traditional schooling for inner-city youth warrants bold if not controversial steps. "In Defense of Multiculturalism," *The New Republic*, September 1991.

22. Catherine R. Stimpson, "Multiculturalism: A Big Word at the Presses," *New York Times Book Review*, September 1991.

23. As noted earlier, African-American film director Spike Lee, himself under assault by Amiri Baraka and others for being too "middle-class" and white-thinking to properly film the life of Malcolm X, had argued that Norman Jewison was not fit to direct the film in an earlier version. Similarly, Asian-American groups briefly persuaded Actors' Equity that the superb British actor Jonathan Pryce (who had played the role in London) should not be permitted to portray the half-Asian character "The Engineer" in the New York run of *Miss Saigon*, because no white actor could understand an Asian character. Pryce was finally allowed to play the role in New York, not because good sense prevailed but because producer Cameron MacIntosh threatened to cancel the production, reminding us that whatever else P.C. is, it is an ideology without power. Pryce eventually won a Tony.

24. For excessive differentiation and excessive political correctness, there is nothing to compare to the National Council of Churches' statement that the events following Columbus's discovery of America in 1492 were "an in-

vasion and colonization with legalized occupation, genocide, economic exploitation and a deep level of institutional racism and moral decadence." (*New York Times*, 27 June 1991.) Clause by clause, the statement is not untrue, but as a whole it adds up to a good deal more than the truth.

25. Evan Carton, "The Self Besieged: American Identity on Camus and in the Gulf," *Tikkun* 6, no. 4 (July/August 1991), 40–47. On the P.C. issue, in addition to the Paul Berman anthology cited above (Prologue, note 5) see Frederick Siegel's "The Cult of Multiculturalism," *The New Republic*, February 1991, 34–36.; M. Novak, "Thought Police," *Forbes* (October 1, 1990), 212. J. Taylor, "Thought Police on Campus," *Reader's Digest* (May 1991), 99–104; "Taking Offense" [cover story, special section] *Newsweek* (Dec. 24, 1990), 48–55; B. Ehrenreich, "Teach Diversity—With a Smile." *Time* (April 8, 1991), 84; the collected articles in "The Multicultural Campus," in a special issue of *Academe* (November–December 1990) and the new, hysterical anti-P.C. monthly *Heterodoxy*, edited by those far-right apostates Peter Collier and David Horowitz. For a comparative perspective, see the British Commission for Racial Equality, *Britain: A Plural Society* (London, 1989): and the discussion by François Foret. P. Renault, M. F. Toinet, and F. Weil in "Renouveau de l'Utopie democratique," *Le débat* (March–April 1992).

26. For an account, see Susan Chira, "Teaching History So That Cultures Are More Than Footnotes," *New York Times*, 10 July 1991, 17, and Robert Reinhold, "Class Struggle," *New York Times Magazine*, 26 September 1991.

27. Cited in Reinhold, "Class Struggle," 47.

28. Henry Louis Gates, Jr., "Whose Culture Is it Anyway?" *New York Times*, May 1991.

29. Reading Bernal is not exactly child's play, nor is it an exercise in polemics. A typical passage: "The important Phoenician divinity, Melqart or Mlk qrt, who was the patron deity of the Phoenician city of Tyre, could provide a bridge between Gilgamesh and Heracles. Both a detailed passage from Herodotus and inscriptional evidence make the identification of Melqart and Heracles absolutely clear." *Black Athena*, vol. 2, 107. No doubt the connection is "absolutely clear" to anyone who, like Bernal, is fluent in a dozen or more modern and antique languages and is a master of six or eight social science and comparative linguistic fields.

30. Chinua Achebe, "An Image of Africa: Racism in Conrad's Heart of Darkness," in *Hopes and Impediments* (New York: Doubleday, 1989).

31. I have described this common fate in "Jihad versus McWorld," *Atlantic Monthly*, March 1992.

32. This issue is nicely captured by Phillip G. Vargas, who writes: "Do we truly wish to make American society our society, or do we prefer to remain the shadow people? Do we really intend to participate fully and make our individual contributions to America's experiment in self-realization and self-government? Or will we remain in the back of the auditoriums, quiet and passive, because of misplaced fear that moving to center stage will cost us our language and culture?" Vargas does not doubt the answer: "In order to succeed, Hispanic Americans and their children must give first priority to learning to function in American society and the world in general; and this means being

able to speak and write English well. The alternative is to retreat into our personal, warm and accepting communities, there to hide from the dynamics of the world around us." "Speaking Spanish in the Shadows," *Washington Post* national weekly edition, 8–14 April 1991.

33. Katha Pollitt, "Canon to the Right of Me," *The Nation*, September 1991. In a "country of real readers," Pollitt observes, "a debate like the current one would not be taking place." Pollitt argues that it is only because no one reads anything outside the classroom that the content of books taught in the classroom becomes so important and contentious.

34. Diane Ravitch and Chester R. Finn, *What Do Our Seventeen-Year-Olds Know? The First National Assessment of What American Students Know About History and Literature* (New York: Harper & Row, 1987). Diane Ravitch is herself the author of a multicultural framework from which publishers developed texts for the California school system. For Schlesinger, see note 21.

35. As noted earlier, there is a considerable controversy over Bernal's argument that classical civilization showed the imprint of Egypt and the Middle East as clearly as Dorian tribes and Judeo-Christianity, at least up until a nineteenth-century European (primarily German) academic conspiracy did away with the evidence. The debate has moved from esoteric journals to the popular press. "Was Cleopatra Black?" screams the headline of a recent *Newsweek* cover story on Afrocentrism (September 1991).

There is also some question as to whether the object of those citing Bernal is to discredit Western civilization or to take the credit for its virtues. Cheikh Anta Diop's *Civilization or Barbarism: An Authentic Anthropology* (New York: Lawrence Hill Books, 1991), as well as *The African Origin of Civilization* (New York: Lawrence Hill Books, 1974), seems to want to do the first but avoid the second by proving that all civilization worth talking about is African—thus replicating, in reverse, European arrogance. Either way, the issues are worthy of discussion and criticism in the classroom, where they themselves become exercises in exposing the power interests of putatively neutral "knowledge."

36. As Meg Greenfield has noted, "It is no accident that so many people who resist social remedies on a national level are at the same time willing and eager to help when it comes to their neighbors." People will not help others without "some genuine feelings of connection and mutual interest and shared purpose"; yet those most in need of common remedies are embarked on strategies that emphasize their differences and that deny the possibility of empathy among peoples—seemingly a suicidal political strategy! "Nationalizing Their Pitch," *Newsweek*, 6 August 1991.

CHAPTER 5: CONSERVATIVE EXCESSES AND ALLAN BLOOM

1. Allan Bloom, "Western Civilization" in *Giants and Dwarfs* (New York: Simon & Schuster, 1991), 17. Among his critics, Bloom is certain, "the first and loudest voices in the chorus came from the Ivy League, particularly those with some connection to Harvard." Or was it just that Bloom only

noticed the critics from Harvard? In any case, in the same talk he confessed, "Compared to the Ivy League, I would have at worst to be called a moderate elitist."

2. *New York Times Book Review*, 5 April 1987. The reviewer was Roger Kimball, the author of *Tenured Radicals*, discussed in previous chapters, and a regular contributor to Hilton Kramer's conspicuously conservative *New Criterion*.

3. Reviewed for the *Los Angeles Times* by Albert Haywood, 17 May 1987.

4. *Insight*, 11 May 1987.

5. There are endless arguments about the empirical basis for the claims that American education is in decline. SAT scores are down, but the greatest decline is among whites, the greatest improvement among nonwhites. American schools are deemed inferior, but American universities are thought to be the best in the world and continue to draw graduates from all over the world, including Germany, Japan, and other countries usually regarded as pedagogically superior. Europe's universities enroll a far smaller percentage of the population yet are little better (some say far worse) than ours.

The latest figures from the Department of Education's major 1991 study "Trends in Academic Progress" suggest that American schools will not be able to meet many of the educational goals set by the Bush administration for the year 2000. On the other hand, the study reports some modest progress, particularly in closing the gap between whites and minorities, and it concludes that students in math and science today are no worse off than those in 1970.

6. Allan Bloom, *The Closing of the American Mind* (New York: Simon & Schuster, 1987), 279.

7. Ibid.

8. E. D. Hirsch, Jr., *Cultural Literacy: What Every American Needs To Know* (Boston: Houghton Mifflin, 1988).

9. "The Democratization of the University," in *Giants and Dwarfs*, 367.

10. Jurgen Habermas, "Work and Weltanschauung: The Heidegger Controversy from a German Perspective," *Critical Inquiry* 15, no. 2 (Winter 1989), 456. Despite Bloom's eloquent critique of Heidegger and his roots in Nietzsche, Bloom shares with them a certain celebration of "spirit" and the noble soul that, as Bloom has shown, can be extremely dangerous when translated into politics.

11. A thoughtful and telling essay on the life of Socrates as a philosopher who must live in a democracy is included in Bloom's collection *Giants and Dwarfs* under the title "The Political Philosopher in a Democratic Society: A Socratic View."

12. Bloom, 245.

13. See Alison Lurie, *The War Between the Tates* (New York: Random House, 1974) for a thinly fictionalized account. See also Cushing Strout, Jr., ed., *Divided We Stand: Reflections on the Crisis at Cornell* (Garden City: Doubleday, 1970).

14. Bloom, *Closing*, 137.

15. Ibid., 134–135.

16. Ibid., 122.

17. Ibid., 89.

18. Ibid., 124.

19. Ibid., 126.

20. Ibid., 65.

21. Ibid., 121.

22. Ibid., 233.

23. Ibid., 249.

24. Frederick Starr, "The Closing of the American Mind," *Washington Post Book World*, 19 April 1987, 87.

25. Bloom, *Closing*, 89.

26. It is a tribute to the resonance of Bloom's style of conservatism that the two-hundredth anniversary of the French Revolution was celebrated in the West, especially in America and France, by a surge of doubt among its foremost beneficiaries about the meaning and fruits of that revolution. Bloom, at least, does not regard himself as a beneficiary.

27. Like Nietzsche and Heidegger, about whom they are both sharply critical, both Strauss and Bloom worship the Greeks. Some moderns have argued that the attachment to the Greek tradition or aristocratic spirit and the noble soul engenders an elitism that sits uncomfortably with modern democracy. In Heidegger the philosopher it nurtured a discontent which perhaps helped open Heidegger the man to Hitler.

28. Leo Strauss, *Natural Right and History* (Ithaca, N.Y.: Cornell University Press, 1953), 1–2.

29. Ibid., 3.

30. Ibid.

31. Not incidentally, it is the logic connecting natural law thinking and Straussianism that accounts for the alarm over Justice Clarence Thomas's naturalism in his otherwise opaque testimony before the Senate prior to his confirmation to the Supreme Court.

32. Strauss, *Natural Right*, 5.

33. Bloom, *Closing*, 178.

34. It is in this ambivalence that we see the dual role of the ancients in Bloom; their idealism and their understanding of reason inure him to the postmodern critique arising out of Nietzsche's and Heidegger's work, but their celebration of spirit and the fine-souled philosopher-king attract him to Nietzsche's and Heidegger's striving for higher forms of spirit in a mediocre, all-too-egalitarian modern world.

35. Bloom, *Closing*, 145.

36. Ibid., 231.

37. Two great pre-war texts adumbrate Bloom's concerns: Julien Benda's *The Betrayal of the Intellectuals*, trans. Richard Aldington (New York: Norton, 1969) and Jose Ortega y Gasset's *The Revolt of the Masses*, trans. Anthony Kerrigan (South Bend, Ind.: University of Notre Dame Press, 1985).

38. See, for example, May Horkheimer and Theodore Adorno, *Dialectic of Enlightenment* (New York: Herder & Herder, 1972), and Michel Foucault, *Discipline and Punish* (New York: Vintage Books, 1979).

39. Bloom, *Closing*, 381.

40. See Allan Bloom's introduction to his excellent edition of *Plato's Republic* (New York: Basic Books, 1968), as well as his response to Dale Hall's critique, reprinted as "Aristophanes and Socrates: A Response to Hall," in *Giants and Dwarfs*.

41. Bloom, *Closing*, 130.

42. Richard Hofstadter, *Anti-Intellectualism in American Life* (New York: Knopf, 1963).

43. Bloom, *Closing*, 303. Bloom is discussing Kant's contribution to the destruction of classical philosophy's reflectiveness.

44. Bloom, *Closing*, 229.

45. Bloom, *Closing*, 35.

46. Ibid., 283.

47. This is a question Bloom cannot answer without putting aside his gentle deceptions. A Reagan-era *Newsweek* essay was titled "The Cult of Leo Strauss" and featured "an obscure philosopher's Washington disciples." (*Newsweek*, August 1987.) What it failed to ask was how a cult organized around political innocence and a benign contempt for worldly power could have "Washington disciples."

48. For this account, see I. F. Stone, *The Trial of Socrates* (Boston: Little, Brown, 1988), which is supported by the earlier and more scholarly work of M. I. Finley. Stone's is a provocative work meant to defend modern democracy, although it is probably too one-sidedly harsh toward Socrates the philosopher.

CHAPTER 6: WHAT OUR FORTY-SEVEN-YEAR-OLDS KNOW

1. John Dewey, *Democracy and Education* (New York: Macmillan, 1916), 415–416.

2. Children's Defense Fund, *The State of Our Children—1991* (Washington, D.C.: Children's Defense Fund, 1991), 5. *Newsweek* reports that 27 percent of all American chldren are born out of wedlock—nearly two-thirds of black children are. Steve Waldman, "Deadbeat Dads," *Newsweek*, May 4, 1992.

3. Dinesh D'Souza, *Illiberal Education* (New York: Free Press, 1991).

4. Charles J. Sykes, *Profscam* (New York: St. Martin's, 1990), 54.

5. See Claudia H. Deutsche, "The Corporate Role in the Classroom," *New York Times* education supplement, 24 March 1991, 21.

6. William E. Kirwan, quoted in "Corporate Lessons in Campus Quality," *New York Times* education supplement, August 1991.

7. James B. Rule, "Biotechnology: Big Money Comes to the University," *Dissent*, Fall 1988.

8. Jaron Bourke and Robert Weissman, "Academics at Risk: The Temptations of Profit," *Academe* (September–October 1990) in a special issue on "The Entrepreneurial University."

9. IBM ad, *The New York Times Magazine*, April 1991.

10. Chester E. Finn, Jr. (coauthor with Diane Ravitch of *What Do Our Seventeen-Year-Olds Know*), quoted in Karen de Witt's article on Finn, "Education Pundit Heard as Voice of Revolution," *New York Times*, 2 August 1991. Also see Finn's *We Must Take Charge: Our Schools and Our Future* (New York: Free Press, 1991).

11. See Russell Jacoby, "The Greening of the University: From Ivory Tower to Industrial Park," *Dissent* (Spring 1991).

12. Arthur Schlesinger, Jr., *The Disuniting of America: Reflections on a Multicultural Society* (New York: Whittle Communications 1991).

13. C. P. Snow, *The Two Cultures and the Scientific Revolution* (Cambridge, England: Cambridge University Press, 1959), 4. See the polemic reply by F. R. Leavis, *Two Cultures: The Significance of C. P. Snow* (New York: Pantheon, 1962).

14. Alan C. Kors. Speech delivered at the conference "Reclaiming the Academy: Responses to the Radicalization of the University" sponsored by The National Association of Scholars, November 12–13, 1988, New York, New York.

15. Stephen H. Balch. Speech delivered at the conference "Reclaiming the Academy: Reponses to the Radicalization of the University" sponsored at The National Association of Sholars, November 12–13, 1988, New York, New York. The multicultural left is organizing in turn, having established its own organization, the Union for Democratic Intellectuals.

16. In this sense, prohibiting students from drinking enhances their ultimate freedom of choice by preventing them from being subjugated by addiction.

17. Dewey, *Democracy and Education*, 164–165.

18. See Ivan Illich, *Medical Nemesis: The Expropriation of Health* (London: Calder & Boyars, 1976).

19. E. D. Hirsch, Jr., *Cultural Literacy: What Every American Needs To Know* (Boston: Houghton Mifflin, 1987), and *The Dictionary of Cultural Literacy* (Boston: Houghton Mifflin, 1988).

20. See *Closing of the American Mind*, part 1, "Students."

21. Unfortunately, the quiz is not a joke: All the "correct" answers are based on fact.

22. Scholastic, in league with CBS records, apparently believed that songwriter Joel's random accumulation of famous names from the fifties through the eighties would "turn kids on" to history.

23. *Los Angeles Times* commented: "The bank routinely rejected students who listed majors in the humanities, such as English, history, and art. The bank's rationale is that these students are less likely to repay debts because they will not land the high-paying jobs that go to business or engineering graduates." Cited in Russell Jacoby's excellent piece on "The Greening of the University," *Dissent* (Spring 1991).

24. During the Depression, libraries in Brooklyn stayed open twenty-four hours a day.

25. Figures from PEN American Center Newsletter 75 (Summer 1991).

26. Mary Wollstonecroft, *Vindication of the Rights of Woman* in *The Works*

of *Mary Wollstonecroft*, Vol. 5, Janet Todd and Marilyn Butler, eds. (New York: New York University Press, 1989), 229.

27. Dewey, *Democracy*, 101.

28. Walt Whitman, "Democratic Vistas," in *The Portable Walt Whitman* (New York: Penguin Books, 1945), 344.

29. Dewey, *Democracy*, 416.

30. Ibid., 411.

CHAPTER 7: TEACHING DEMOCRACY THROUGH COMMUNITY SERVICE

1. Roughly half of New York City's public school teachers do not conduct classes regularly—which means that the effective teacher-pupil ratio is only 1:32, although the actual figures should provide a 1:15 ratio. (American Federation of Teachers.)

2. A portion of this section was delivered as a paper to a conference on national service at the Hoover Institution, and subsequently published in William M. Evers, ed., *National Service: Pro and Con* (Stanford, Calif.: Hoover Press, 1990).

3. The Nunn-McCurdy Bill introduced into the 1990 Congress proposed tying federal student financial aid (primarily loans) to a service requirement.

4. John Patrick Diggins, *The Lost Soul of American Politics* (New York: Basic Books, 1985), 352.

5. Richard J. Neuhaus, *The Naked Public Square: Religion and Democracy in America* (Grand Rapids, Mich: Eerdmans, 1986).

6. Frances Fox Piven and Richard H. Cloward, *Why Americans Don't Vote* (New York: Pantheon, 1988).

7. Both in their earlier *Habits of the Heart* (Berkeley: University of California Press, 1985) and their more recent *The Good Society* (New York: Knopf, 1991), Robert Bellah and his colleagues argue that in response to radical individualism and markets, Americans are manifesting and expressing a powerful need for a sense of community.

8. The Charter of Queen's College read: "That a College be erected for that purpose within our Providence of New Jersey to promote learning for the benefit of the community."

9. John Dewey, *Democracy and Education* (New York: Macmillan, 1916). The larger context for his discussion of democratic education is provided in *The Public and Its Problems* (New York: Henry Holt, 1927). The pragmatist origins of service as education in democracy can be found in William James's famous essay "The Moral Equivalent of War," in *The Writings of William James: A Comprehensive Edition* (Chicago: University of Chicago Press, 1977).

10. Ernest Boyer and Fred Hechinger, *Higher Learning in the Nation's Service* (Washington, D.C.: Carnegie Foundation for the Advancement of Teaching, 1981). By the time this was written, a number of studies had already appeared on service education, including the Carnegie Council on Policy Stud-

ies in Higher Education's *Giving Youth a Better Chance: Options for Education, Work and Service* (San Francisco: Jossey-Bass, 1979), the National Commission on Resources for Youth's *New Roles for Youth in the School and Community* (New York: Citation Press, 1974), and Ralph W. Tyler, ed., *From Youth to Constructive Adult Life: The Role of the Public School* (Berkeley, Calif.: McCutchan, 1978).

11. National Commission on Youth, *The Transition of Youth to Adulthood* (Boulder: Westview Press, 1980)

12. A generic discussion of service, education, and patriotism can be found in Morris Janowitz's important study *The Reconstruction of Patriotism: Education for Civic Consciousness* (Chicago: University of Chicago Press, 1983). The most recent advocacy text is Charles C. Moskos, *A Call to Civic Service: National Service for Country and Community* (New York: Free Press, 1988). Donald J. Eberly has written widely on service, most recently recounting his early experience with service in the Peace Corps in his *National Service: A Promise to Keep* (Rochester, N.Y.: John Alden Books, 1989).

13. William Buckley, Jr., *Gratitude: Reflections on What We Owe to Our Country* (New York: Random House, 1990)

14. Just how unfashionable this language is can be seen from the *Harper's* forum on "Who Owes What to Whom: A Constitutional Bill of Duties," *Harper's* (February 1991), in which I participated along with Christopher Lasch, Mary Ann Glendon, Christopher Stone, and Mayor Daniel Kemmis of Missoula, Montana.

15. "Final Report of the Committee on Education for Civic Leadership on a Program of Citizen Education and Community Service for Rutgers University" (New Brunswick, N. J.: Rutgers University, 1989).

EPILOGUE

1. Alexis de Tocqueville, *The Ancien Regime and the French Revolution*, trans. S. Gilbert (New York: Doubleday, 1955), xiv.

2. Hannah Arendt, *On Revolution* (New York: Viking Press, 1965), 221.

BIBLIOGRAPHY

Achebe, Chinua. *Hopes and Impediments*. New York: Doubleday, 1989.

Almond, Gabriel Abraham, and Sidney Verba. *Civic Culture*. Princeton, N.J.: Princeton University Press, 1963.

Aptheker, Herbert. *American Negro Slave Revolts*. New York: International Publishers, 1952.

Arendt, Hannah. *On Revolution*. New York: Viking Press, 1965.

Assante, Molefi Kete. *Afrocentricity: The Theory of Social Change*. Buffalo, N.Y.: Amulefi, 1980.

Bailyn, Bernard. *Ideological Origins of the American Revolution*. Cambridge, Mass.: Harvard University Press, 1967.

Bellah, Robert, et al. *The Good Society*. New York: Knopf, 1991.

——. *Habits of the Heart*. Berkeley: University of California Press, 1938.

Benda, Julien. *The Betrayal of the Intellectuals*. Trans. Richard Aldington. New York: Norton, 1969.

Berg, A. Scott. *Goldwyn*. New York: Knopf, 1989.

Berman, Paul, ed. *Debating P.C.*: The Controversy Over Political Correctness on College Campuses. New York: Laurel/Dell, 1992.

Bernal, Martin. *Black Athena: The Afroasiatic Roots of Classical Civilization*, 2 vols. New Brunswick, N.J.: Rutgers University Press, 1987, 1991.

Black, Hugo. *A Constitutional Faith*. New York: Knopf, 1967.

Bloom, Allan. *The Closing of the American Mind*. New York: Simon & Schuster, 1987.

——. *Giants and Dwarfs*. New York: Simon & Schuster, 1990.

Boorstin, Daniel. *The Genius of American Politics*. Chicago: University of Chicago Press, 1953.

Boyer, Ernest, and Fred Hechinger. *Higher Learning in the Nation's Service*. Washington, D.C.: Carnegie Foundation for the Advancement of Teaching, 1981.

Buchanan, L. *John Brown: The Making of a Revolutionary*. New York: Grosset & Dunlap, 1969.

Buckley, William F., Jr. *God and Man at Yale*. Chicago: Regnery Gateway, 1951.

——. *Gratitude: Reflections on What We Owe to Our Country*. New York: Random House, 1990.

Carnegie Council on Policy Studies in Higher Education. *Giving Youth a Better Chance: Options for Education, Work and Service*. San Francisco: Jossey-Bass, 1979.

Carnegie Foundation for the Advancement of Teaching. *A Nation at Risk: The Imperative of Educational Reform*. Washington, D.C.: Carnegie Foundation, 1983.

——. *Report Card on School Reform: The Teachers Speak*. Washington, D.C.: The Carnegie Foundation, 1988.

Children's Defense Fund. *The State of Our Children—1991*. Washington D.C.: Children's Defense Fund, 1991.

Chubb, John E., and Terry M. Moe. *Politics, Markets and America's Schools*. Washington, D.C.: Brookings Institution, 1990.

Commager, Henry Steele. *The Empire of Reason: How Europe Imagined and America Realized the Enlightenment*. Garden City, New York: Anchor Press/Doubleday, 1977.

Commission for Racial Equality, Britain. *A Plural Society*. London, 1989.

Cornwell, John. *The Free and the Brave*. New York: Rand McNally, 1967.

Council on Interracial Books for Children and the Racism and Sexism Resource Center for Educators. *Stereotypes, Distortions and Omissions in U.S. History Textbooks*. New York: Council on Interracial Books for Children and the Racism and Sexism Resource Center for Educators, 1977.

Dewey, John. *Democracy and Education*. New York: Macmillan, 1916.

——. *The Public and Its Problems*. New York: Henry Holt, 1927.

——. *The Quest for Certainty*. New York: Capricorn Books, 1960.

Diggins, John Patrick. *The Lost Soul of American Politics*. New York: Basic Books, 1985.

Diop, Chiekh Anta. *The African Origin of Civilization*. New York: Lawrence Hill Books, 1974.

——. *Civilization or Barbarism: An Authentic Anthropology*. New York: Lawrence Hill Books, 1991.

D'Souza, Dinesh. *Illiberal Education*. New York: Free Press, 1991.

Eberly, Donald. *National Service: A Promise to Keep*. Rochester, N.Y.: John Alden Books, 1989.

Evers, William M., ed. *National Service: Pro and Con*. Stanford, Calif.: Hoover Press, 1990.

Finn, Chester E., Jr. *We Must Take Charge: Our Schools and Our Future.* New York: Free Press, 1991.

Fitzgerald, Frances. *American Revised.* New York: Vintage Books, 1980.

Foner, Eric, ed. *Paine: Complete Works.* New York: Citadel Press, 1979.

Foucault, Michel. *Discipline and Punish.* New York: Vintage Books, 1979.

Freedman, Samuel G. *Small Victories: The Real World of a Teacher, Her Students and Their High School.* New York: Harper & Row, 1990.

Gabler, Neal. *An Empire of Their Own: How the Jews Invented Hollywood.* New York: Crown Publishers, 1988.

Gagnon, Paul. *Democracy's Untold Story: What American History Textbooks Should Add.* Washington, D.C.: American Federation of Teachers, 1989.

Garrison, W., and F. Garrison. *William Lloyd Garrison: 1805–1879.* New York: Arno Press, 1969.

Goldman, Ari L. *The Search for God at Harvard.* New York: Times Books, 1991.

Habermas, Jurgen. *Knowledge and Interests.* Boston: Beacon Press, 1971.

Hacker, Andrew. *Two Nations: Black and White, Separate, Hostile, Unequal.* New York: Charles Scribner's Sons, 1992.

Harar, Josue V., ed. *Textual Strategies: Perspectives in Post Structural Criticism.* Ithaca, N.Y.: Cornell University Press, 1979.

Hartz, Louis. *The Liberal Tradition in America.* Boston: Beacon Press, 1952.

Hegel, George Friedrich Wilhelm. *The Philosophy of History.* New York: Dover Publications, 1956.

Hirsch, E. D., Jr. *Cultural Literacy: What Every American Needs to Know.* Boston: Houghton Mifflin, 1988.

Hofstadter, Richard. *Anti-Intellectualism in American Life.* New York: Knopf, 1963.

Horkheimer Max, and Theodore Adorno. *Dialectic of Enlightenment.* New York: Herder & Herder, 1972.

Illich, Ivan. *Medical Nemesis: The Expropriation of Health.* London: Calder & Boyars, 1976.

James, William. *The Writings of William James: A Comprehensive Edition.* Chicago: University of Chicago Press, 1977.

Janowitz, Morris. *The Reconstruction of Patriotism: Education for Civic Consciousness.* Chicago: University of Chicago Press, 1983.

Kammen, Michael. *People of Paradox: An Inquiry Concerning the Origins of American Civilization.* New York: Knopf, 1972.

Karst, Kenneth L. *Belonging to America: Equal Citizenship and the Constitution.* New Haven: Yale University Press, 1989.

Kidder, Tracy. *Among Schoolchildren.* Boston: Houghton Mifflin, 1989.

Kimball, Roger. *Tenured Radicals: How Politics Has Corrupted Higher Education.* New York: Harper & Row, 1990.

Kozol, Jonathan. *Savage Inequalities.* New York: Crown, 1991.

Kuhn, Thomas. *The Structure of Scientific Revolutions.* Chicago: University of Chicago Press, 1962.

Leavis, F. R. *Two Cultures: The Significance of C. P. Snow.* New York: Pantheon, 1962.

Lehman, David. *Signs of the Times: Deconstruction and the Fall of Paul de Man.* New York: Poseidon Press, 1991.

Levinson, Sanford. *Constitutional Faith.* Princeton, N.J.: Princeton University Press, 1988.

Lurie, Alison. *The War Between the Tates.* New York: Random House, 1974.

Madison, James. *Letters and Other Writings.* Philadelphia: Lippincott, 1867.

Melville, Hermann. *Benito Cereno.* New York: Modern Library, 1952.

Miller, James. *Democracy Is in the Streets.* New York: Simon & Schuster, 1987.

Morgan, Edmund S. *Inventing the People: The Rise of Popular Sovereignty in England and America.* New York: Norton, 1988.

Moskos, Charles C. *A Call to Civic Service: National Service for Country and Community.* New York: Free Press, 1988.

National Commission on Resources for Youth. *New Roles for Youth in the School and the Community.* New York: Citation Press, 1974.

National Commission on Youth. *The Transition of Youth to Adulthood.* Boulder, Colo.: Westview Press, 1980.

Neuhaus, Richard J. *The Naked Public Square: Religion and Democracy in America.* Grand Rapids, Mich.: Eerdmans, 1986.

O'Brien, Conor Cruise. *Godland.* Cambridge, Mass.: Harvard University Press, 1988.

Ortega y Gasset, Jose. *The Revolt of the Masses.* trans. Anthony Kerrigan. South Bend, Ind.: University of Notre Dame Press, 1985.

Padover, Saul K., ed. *The Complete Madison.* Milwood, New York: Kraus Reprint, 1953.

Piven, Frances Fox, and Richard H. Cloward, *Why Americans Don't Vote.* New York: Pantheon, 1988.

Ravitch, Diane, and Chester E. Finn, Jr. *What Do Our Seventeen-Year-Olds Know? The First National Assessment of What American Students Know About History and Literature.* New York: Harper & Row, 1987.

Rockmore, Tom. *On Heidegger's Nazism and Philosophy.* London: Harvester/ Wheatsheaf, 1992.

Sallors, Werner. *Beyond Ethnicity: Consent and Descent in American Culture.* New York: Oxford University Press, 1986.

Schlesinger, Arthur, Jr. *The Disuniting of America: Reflections on a Multicultural Society.* New York: Whittle Communications, 1991.

Shklar, Judith N. *American Citizenship: The Quest for Inclusion.* Cambridge, Mass.: Harvard University Press, 1991.

Silber, John. *Shooting Straight: What's Wrong with America.* New York: Harper & Row, 1990.

Smith, Page. *Killing the Spirit: Higher Education in America.* New York: Viking, 1990.

Snow, C. P. *The Two Cultures and the Scientific Revolution.* Cambridge, England: Cambridge University Press, 1959.

Stanton, E., S. Anthony, and M. Gage, eds. *History of Woman Suffrage.* New York: Fowler & Wells, 1881.

Stone, I. F. *The Trial of Socrates.* Boston: Little Brown, 1988.

Storing, Herbert J., ed. *Essays in the Scientific Study of Politics*. New York: Holt, Rinehart and Winston, 1962.

Strauss, Leo. *Natural Right and History*. Ithaca, N.Y.: Cornell University Press, 1953.

Strout, Cushing, Jr. *Divided We Stand: Reflections on the Crisis at Cornell*. Garden City: Doubleday, 1970.

Sykes, Charles. *Profscam: Professors and the Demise of Higher Education*. New York: St. Martin's, 1990.

Tocqueville, Alexis. *The Ancien Regime and the French Revolution*. New York: Doubleday/Anchor, 1955.

——. *Democracy in America*. New York: Vintage, 1960.

Tyler, Ralph W., ed. *From Youth to Constructive Adult Life: The Role of the Public School*. Berkeley, Calif.: McCutchan, 1978.

Wallerstein, Immanuel, and Paul Starr. *The University Crisis Reader*. New York: Vintage Books, 1971.

Whitman, Walt. *The Portable Walt Whitman*. New York: Penguin Books, 1945.

Wills, Garry. *Under God: Religion and American Politics*. New York: Simon & Schuster, 1990.

Wilshire, Bruce. *The Moral Collapse of the University*. Albany: State University of New York Press, 1990.

Wollstonecroft, Mary. *The Works of Mary Wollstonecroft*. Janet Todd and Marilyn Butler, eds. New York: New York University Press, 1989.

INDEX

ABOUT THE AUTHOR

Benjamin R. Barber is the Whitman Professor of Political Science at Rutgers University and the director of the Walt Whitman Center at Rutgers. He is the author of *Strong Democracy* and *The Struggle for Democracy*, and writes regularly for *Harper's, The New York Times, The New Republic, The Atlantic*, and many other publications.

Until now, the current crisis in education has been defined by controversy over what should be taught, who should be taught, and, increasingly, who should pay for it. What is less discussed is what these questions mean for the future of our country, our society, and our very value system, the basis of which is democracy. In this brilliant, controversial, and profoundly original book, Benjamin R. Barber fundamentally alters the terms of the current debate over the value of opportunity in American education, politics, and culture.

In *An Aristocracy of Everyone,* Barber argues that the fashionable rallying cries of cultural literacy and political correctness completely miss the point of what is wrong with our society. While we fret about "the closing of the American mind" we utterly ignore the closing of American schools. While we worry about being edged out by Japanese technology, we fail to tap the more fundamental ideological resources on which our country was founded. As Barber argues, the future of America lies not in competition but in education. Education in America can and must embrace both democracy and excellence.

But how can this goal be achieved? Barber explodes the notion that the so-called canon of accepted history and literary texts is a monolithic structure and demonstrates persuasively that our national story has always comprised an intermingling of diverse, contradictory, often subversive voices. Multiculturalism has, from the very start, defined America. From his gripping portrait of America poised on the brink of unprecedented change, Barber offers a daringly original program for effecting change: for teaching democracy depends not only on the preeminence of education but on a resurgence of true community service.

A ringing challenge to the complacency, cynicism, and muddled thinking of our time, *An Aristocracy of Everyone* will stand as a watershed volume in American intellectual history. It will change the way you feel about being an American citizen.